CLOCKWORK
RHETORIC

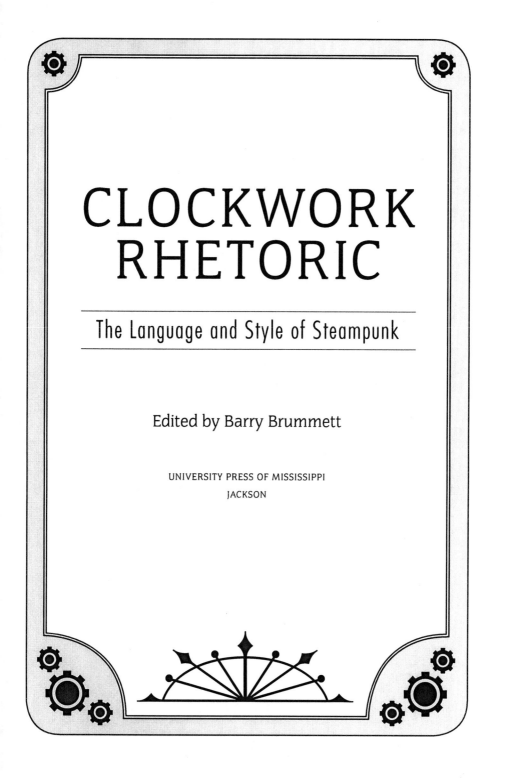

CLOCKWORK RHETORIC

The Language and Style of Steampunk

Edited by Barry Brummett

UNIVERSITY PRESS OF MISSISSIPPI

JACKSON

www.upress.state.ms.us

Designed by Peter D. Halverson

The University Press of Mississippi is a member of the Association of
American University Presses.

First printing 2014

∞

Library of Congress Cataloging-in-Publication Data

Clockwork rhetoric : the language and style of steampunk / edited by
Barry Brummett.
pages cm
Includes bibliographical references and index.
ISBN 978-1-62846-091-9 (cloth) — ISBN 978-1-62846-092-6 (ebook)
1. Steampunk fiction—History and criticism. 2. Narration (Rhetoric)
3. Style, Literary. 4. Steampunk culture. I. Brummett, Barry, 1951–
editor of compilation.
PN3448.S73C58 2014
700'.411—dc23   2014001979

British Library Cataloging-in-Publication Data available

CONTENTS

○

ACKNOWLEDGMENTS

Any press takes a chance in bringing out a new book, especially when the book is the first of its kind. The editor and contributors wish to thank the University Press of Mississippi for their wise guidance and efficient development of this manuscript.

Editor's Introduction

The Rhetoric of Steampunk

BARRY BRUMMETT

⚙

THE NINETEENTH AND EARLY TWENTIETH CENTURIES CONTAIN A VAST REP-
ertoire of images and themes taken from industrialization in the Age of
Steam. Factories contribute images of boilers, pipes, gears, cogs, pistons, the
helmets and goggles of workers in the factories, the belts and chains driving
gears and wheels. Firearms of the period show their mechanisms with cylin-
ders, blued metal, pawls, hammers, tubes. The locomotives of the American
West provide their own boilers, heavy metal moving at dangerous speeds,
pistons, and gears. This time period also contains the imaginary mechanical
images of H. G. Wells and Jules Verne, fantastic machines made to explore
time, the depths of the sea, or outer space. The clothing of the period does
not share the same machine aesthetic but has its own aesthetic of exploration
and empire, inextricably linked to the mechanical sensibilities of the indus-
tries of the time.

This fertile trove of images and themes has since roughly the early 1990s
been mined for the emergence of a new movement, largely aesthetic, called
Steampunk. Steampunk is growing in popularity in popular culture and may
be found in film, television, clubs, music, and comics conventions among
other venues.

Steampunk resituates aesthetic elements from the Age of Steam into our
world. It imagines an aesthetic that would occur had steam and electricity
remained the primary industrial sources of power. Suppose watches ran on
tiny steam engines, suppose dirigibles instead of airplanes ruled the skies,
suppose people wore the clothing of the era still—what would our society be
like with those suppositions? Sometimes Steampunk imagines what would
happen if later technological innovations had emerged during the Age of
Steam, a premise often found in *The Wild Wild West* or *Briscoe County* television and film iterations. Sometimes Steampunk imagines the course of social

and scientific development of Age of Steam technologies and aesthetics in parallel universes, as in Philip Pullman's *His Dark Materials*. Sometimes in conjunction with comics or science fiction conventions, Steampunk is found in the costume play of participants. Steampunk, then, is an aesthetic and performative movement that in our time has moved in on many other genres and aesthetics. It is an aesthetic on the make, becoming more popular every year.

In this volume, we want to address this question: *When these images and themes of the nineteenth and early twentieth centuries are used today aesthetically, what social and political messages are urged upon audiences, readers, and participants of that aesthetic?* Or, in other words, what is the *rhetoric* of Steampunk in use today? If someone shows up at a comics convention wearing a long linen duster, a watch that looks like a little steam engine, a top hat, industrial goggles, and a fabulous weapon of some sort constructed around a small boiler and smokestack, what does this apparition do to those who see it? To those who perform it? If Steampunk images are borrowed by film or television today, what social or political influence does that usage have the power to create in its audience?

We do not propose the study of the historical or literary sources of Steampunk themes and images per se. It is important to be aware of that vast closet of Steampunk references, for today's usages retain some of their meanings. But this volume is not a historical study of Victorian and Edwardian literature and icons. Instead, we want to know what happens to those images and themes when used today, and that usage is what is called Steampunk.

The essays in this volume use a wide variety of theories and methods, but central to them is a shared understanding that texts in popular culture have a rhetorical impact on audiences, the potential for which may be discovered through textual analysis. This theoretical grounding, developed in several works,[1] sees the text as primary in the rhetorical transaction and as able to generate meanings, based on the discursive, semantic possibilities within their constituent signs, that affect how people think about and perceive the world. Our texts run from embodied performances to films to jewelry to novels, but we approach texts as primary in creating the possibilities for rhetorical effects, possibilities that are then inflected by audience and context.

Behind the questions we ask is the idea that the images and themes of Steampunk cohere in some way, that they form a symbolic economy that will influence the social-political economy of those who create and consume Steampunk texts. In this volume we are after the logic of that economy; we want to know how Steampunk reliably coheres around an aesthetic logic that generates rhetorical effects. Given the unavoidable politics of our era, this means asking questions having to do with the distribution of power in society, often along lines of race, gender, class, sexual orientation, and so forth. How is Steampunk gendered, and what does its presence in a text or performance do to affect gendered attitudes? Because Steampunk arose from a context of European imperial domination of Asian, African, and other non-white peoples, do Steampunk images and themes have racial implications? Age of Steam images are of mechanical power and industrial might; how do those images bear meanings of power and force into today's texts? Because rhetoric always emerges into specific historical and cultural contexts, a subsidiary question we will be considering is how Steampunk works today in our peculiar historical moment: why over the past few decades has Steampunk emerged, and how does it engage this particular historical moment?

Although the essays in this volume span a wide range of specific topics, they cohere around the question of how a contemporary text creates rhetorical effects using the Steampunk repertoire. This anthology opens with a general theoretical introduction from David Beard of the University of Minnesota Duluth. Beard presents a comprehensive conceptual map of Steampunk. In doing so, he explains the possibilities and dimensions for the rhetorical impact of Steampunk texts.

The remaining chapters are divided into three groupings suggested by Beard's introduction: A Rhetoric of Steampunk Ideology, A Rhetoric of Steampunk Semiotics, and A Rhetoric of Steampunk Narrative. In the first group, Mirko Hall of Converse College and Joshua Gunn of the University of Texas at Austin hold that Steampunk tries to reclaim a nineteenth-century utopian ideology from the dystopian industrial realities that often resulted. Steampunk appropriates and alters memory, in their view. The vision was first articulated in Victorian literature, especially, they argue, that of Verne. This utopian vision is based on the trope of the technician hero, which they argue is a site of fluid male subjectivities, with rhetorical effects on the audience's understanding of masculinities. Kristin Stimpson of the University of Texas at Austin notes the lack of obvious aesthetic connection between the costumes often associated with Steampunk and the machine aesthetic of gears, pistons, shafts, and so forth. Nostalgia, a politics of memory, makes use of materials of visual culture across these usages to reinscribe empire. Also, the American West is a theme that seems not aesthetically unified. Stimpson argues that an ideology of empire unifies the style, specifically to support a racial politics in a context of colonialism. Mary Anne Taylor of the University of Texas at Austin explores several texts to argue that there are feminist possibilities in the fan culture surrounding Steampunk. These possibilities are created by Steampunk's breakdown of the binary between bodies and machines. She explores the implications for gendered politics today and the ideology of feminism.

In discussing Steampunk semiotics, we focus on the ways in which particular signs used in Steampunk are appropriated from their original Industrial Age context and applied in different ways. Elizabeth Birmingham of North Dakota State University argues that the Victorian Age is a resource of signs that are applicable in many times and places, and that Steampunk is one strategy of application. Although its subject would appear to be medieval, the Japanese television series *Fullmetal Alchemist* uses Steampunk signs for rhetorical purposes. The series portrays the state through the figure of "alchemy," a failed way of thinking. Birmingham examines ways in which a neo-Victorian aesthetic centered on Victorian signs can have rhetorical effect today. In my contribution, I study texts in which Steampunk "jumps scale" up or down, becoming very small or very large. The scale of signs, large or small, is of importance in Steampunk. The aesthetic simulations of empowerment or of being controlled by the state are two rhetorical effects of these shifts in scale. Jaime Wright of Saint John's University argues that Steampunk reflects cultural anxiety over the escape of objects from the usual conventions of shared memory. Steampunk shows objects as strangely caught up in systems of meaning instead, and she studies Guy Ritchie's 2009 film *Sherlock Holmes* to show this. A specific effect studied is the classism of Holmes as presented in the film.

Our third group of essays is composed of studies of narrative texts that make heavy use of Steampunk, with rhetorical consequences. John Thompson of Saint Edward's University argues that the radical visual anachronisms of the television polyseries *Dr. Who* render scenic motivations impossible. In doing so, it problematizes collective memory. Into this motivational vacuum steps the Doctor, who foregrounds the agent as the only unifying center of the texts. The class position of the Doctor influences the ways in which audiences read the texts and form their own judgments of class. John McKenzie of Lakeland College sees the Steampunk text as an example of allohistory, which imagines alternative paths of historical development and thus problematizes collective memory. Our current received ideas of the historical are challenged, as history is seen as malleable and changeable. This changeability may then be used to challenge ideas of class, gender, race, and so forth. He examines several literary texts to show this. Andrew Mara of North Dakota State University claims that the tension between backward-looking memory (steam) and forward-looking chaos (punk) is creatively productive. He uses the idea of *electracy* to examine memory juxtaposed to visions of chaos. This juxtaposition is studied in texts of embodied performances of Steampunk at a conference. Mara identifies ways in which nostalgia defines race and gender with rhetorical effect. Lisa Horton of the University of Minnesota Duluth examines different narrative iterations of the Sherlock Holmes story, showing how different uses of Steampunk in each can have rhetorical effects. She especially focuses on fan culture's appropriations of these narratives.

Note

1. Kenneth Burke, *A Grammar of Motives* (Berkeley: University of California Press, 1962); Kenneth Burke, *The Philosophy of Literary Form*, 3rd ed. (Berkeley: University of California Press, 1973); and Barry Brummett, *Rhetorical Dimensions of Popular Culture* (Tuscaloosa: University of Alabama Press, 1991).

Introduction

A Rhetoric of Steam

DAVID BEARD

> Steampunk has become popular now because it is no longer just fiction. It is an
> international design and technology effort. Steampunk is a counterculture arts and
> crafts movement in a 21st century guise.
>
> —BRUCE STERLING, "User's Guide to Steampunk"

BRUCE STERLING, COAUTHOR OF ONE OF THE MORE INFLUENTIAL NOVELS IN-
voking steampunk ideas,[1] spoke those words at an early steampunk convention—a meeting of individuals who are committed to expressing themselves
through steampunk. Steampunk conventions are distinct from other kinds
of popular culture conventions (comic book conventions, science fiction
conventions, historical reenactment get-togethers) in significant ways, although it is a steampunk presence in those other pop culture gatherings that
introduces a wider array of people to what steampunk is.

I first encountered steampunk in comic books, when *The League of Extraordinary Gentlemen* reintroduced nineteenth-century adventure heroes
into high-tech adventure comics. In the second *Hellboy* movie, the character
Johann Krauss (a man of ectoplasm sealed into a suit built from a madman's
array of gears, levers, and valves) struck me as cool precisely because his suit
wasn't virtual reality. Krauss's suit was old-school science fiction, of the kind
I watched with my grandfather on Saturday afternoon TV in the syndicated
television of the 1970s. I had no idea it was "steampunk."

I became more conscious of steampunk as a coherent intellectual and
creative project as I learned about re-creations of popular icons in a steampunk style. For example, movie and theater prop designer Gordon Smuder
designed a steampunk light saber, the tool that Luke Skywalker used to duel
Darth Vader in the original *Star Wars* trilogy.[2]

Instantly, I could recognize why the young boy still in my heart would love any light saber. Nearly every boy raised during the 1970s dreamed of being the boy from Tatooine who has a secret destiny as a Jedi. I wanted that light saber and I wanted to be a Jedi. At the same time, I recognized the spin that derived from the steampunk style. No boy from Tatooine could carry the light saber, which seemed suited more to an Edwardian adventurer. It was ornate and deeply textured, with components of wood and brass. And I also recognized the do-it-yourself, thrift-store aesthetic—I recognized that the switches and buttons were parts from antique lamps, reworked into something new. To be a steampunk light saber was to be all of these things at once—playing with my childhood imagination, allowing me to reimagine my favorites in a new context, all within a DIY, thrift-store, craft aesthetic.

At that moment, I recognized that to understand the central questions of steampunk culture is to understand the central questions of rhetorical studies in the twenty-first century.

On the one hand, the fact that we can "steampunk" a light saber means that steampunk can be imagined, as rhetoric often is, as "just" a style, a system of ornament to be applied to ideas. We can apply wooden handles and wind-up keys to a light saber the way we can apply metaphors and elegant language to ideas.

On the other hand, to its practitioners, steampunk is a different kind of rhetoric. It is not reducible to the application of gears and clockwork to preexisting objects. Participants in steampunk culture believe that they are steampunk from the ground up—the core of their ideas, the core of their creations, the core of at least some of their values, can be understood in terms of steampunk.

This deeper self-understanding of steampunk is analogous to the preferred understanding of rhetorical studies as an area of inquiry in the twenty-first century: rhetoric is part of thought and part of communication from the ground up, as well. We do not dress our ideas in rhetoric to share them with the world. Rather, rhetoric is the means by which we formulate and communicate our ideas, values, and beliefs.

This collection holds that deeper understanding both of steampunk and of rhetoric at the core of our vision. When we speak of a rhetoric of steampunk, as we will, over and over again in this book, we don't mean that we dress our ideas in dirigibles and locomotives. Rather, we mean that there is a core set of ideas, values, and beliefs that are formulated and communicated through steampunk literature, film, art, costume, and design. Our exploration of steampunk rhetoric, then, is an explanation of those ideas, values, and beliefs as we can see them in steampunk discourse.

To introduce steampunk, this essay outlines both the historical antecedents of steampunk media and the historical moment in which the contemporary steampunk movement arises. Then, it differentiates steampunk as a field of media consumption from steampunk as a field of human subcultural creativity and expression. Fans of steampunk media read novels and comics, they watch movies and TV, they purchase doodads and whatchamacallits. But, on another level, they also write, they draw, paint, and design; they cut, craft, and sew. To understand steampunk, we will need to understand both halves of this activity system: the acts of consumption and production.

Then, this chapter outlines the ways that steampunk operates as a rhetoric and an ideological system. At the same time that steampunk promises the possibility to reimagine relationships between gender, race, and technology, it inculcates values that bind steampunks together. As a rhetoric, it generates a utopian *nostalgia* or *memory*, rather than a utopian *vision*, and so cannot guide new sociopolitical relationships. Steampunk defines how we wish things might have been, instead of how we can work for change in the future.

The chapter will conclude with a set of conjectures about the uses and gratifications that come from engaging in steampunk culture. Participating in this utopian memory has meaning to the participants, even as it has clear and identifiable limitations.

Historical Roots of Steampunk

Steampunk derives from at least three root systems: the nineteenth century's own fantastic representations of the changes that transformed its social and cultural fabric, some key science fiction works of the mid- and late twentieth century, and the DIY aesthetic of the punk and postpunk eras. We will discuss each in turn, attempting to draw these root systems into the tangle of practices that constitute contemporary steampunk culture.

Nineteenth-Century Antecedents

Steampunk claims antecedents in the nineteenth century's own popular self-representations of the encounter between technology and the human. Technology, understood as an optimistic engine that responds to the will and creativity of the tinkerer and the adventurer, was a powerful theme in the serialized and fantastic fiction of the period.

Serialized fiction like Edward S. Ellis's *Steam Man of the Prairies*[3] appeared in the 1860s and provided an abundant set of images that would be picked up as part of a larger steampunk aesthetic. The "Steam Man" of Ellis's novel represents the explosion of the locomotive onto the American landscape—the plume of smoke ripping across the horizon. At the same time, envisioned on a very human scale, the Steam Man is domesticable—the Steam Man, unlike the locomotive, operates on a level that the tinkerer-adventurer can understand and engage. (Questions of the scale of technology are at the core of steampunk aesthetics, as Barry Brummett will outline in a subsequent chapter. Steampunk is in part a response to the sense that science and technology have become too massive for human intervention.)

More popular sources for steampunk include the works of Jules Verne and H. G. Wells. Wells's time traveler, for example, is the consummate steampunk tinkerer; his invention is not the gleaming chrome of the starship *Enterprise* of later science fiction but a patchwork of gears and levers that, in the aggregate, somehow take the traveler far into the future. As for Verne, the image of the *Nautilus* defines the ornate science fiction technology of the nineteenth century.[4] Even Edgar Allan Poe wrote a short story in this vein ("The Balloon Hoax").[5] The visual style of steampunk develops organically from the fantasy and science fiction works of the Victorian period in both the United States and United Kingdom.

Mid- and Late Twentieth-Century Neo-Victorian Innovations

Steampunk is the grandchild of these genuinely Victorian-era texts. The movement is also a result of innovation in literature in the twentieth and twenty-first centuries: neo-Victorian science fiction and novels outlining alternative history (*allohistory*, as described by John McKenzie later in this volume).

Among fans of steampunk, Michael Moorcock's *Warlord of the Air* is identified as "proto-steampunk" or "neo-Victorian" science fiction. The steampunk fascination with dirigibles as air transit can be traced to Moorcock's work. Harry Harrison's *A Transatlantic Tunnel, Hurrah!* (also published as *A Tunnel through the Deeps*) is similarly neo-Victorian. This neo-Victorian fiction is an umbrella genre under which steampunk fiction resides.[6] Academic reflection on steampunk and related genres can be found in *Neo-Victorian*

Studies, a peer-reviewed electronic journal "dedicated to the exploration of the contemporary fascination with re-imagining the nineteenth century and its varied literary, artistic, socio-political and historical contexts in both British and international frameworks."[7]

Late Twentieth-Century "Punk" Culture

Finally, tracing a third line of influence, steampunk derives the "punk" portion of its name from two prior usages: the "punk" music culture and the "cyberpunk" literary and media culture.

The steampunk literary tradition was jump-started by the cyberpunk tradition. A key early steampunk work (*The Difference Engine*) was written by William Gibson and Bruce Sterling, science fiction authors and cyberpunk pioneers. In *The Difference Engine*, Gibson and Sterling retell history as it might have been if Charles Babbage, inventor, had built his "difference" and "analytical" engines—early computers. What attracted readers in the cyberpunk community is the depiction of "clackers," the punch-card computer programmers who are analogous to "hackers." But, among the steampunk community, the recovery of the nineteenth century as a site for fantastic fiction has made this work a touchpoint.[8]

In both cyberpunk and steampunk, there is a countercultural, counterinstitutional, countercorporate impulse. There is a rejection of the black boxes that mask technology and turn us into passive consumers. As Jacqueline Christi put it, "we are surrounded by technology. Our world is filled with machines that are comprised of wire, chipboards and circuits. Electricity flows through our lives and people desire to comprehend why it works, not only that it does. All of the answers have been hidden by smooth panels"[9] The "punk" in steampunk (and in cyberpunk) wants to rip off the panels and play with the guts of the technology.

In that sense, steampunk is rooted in a "do-it-yourself" aesthetic, like all punk cultures. In punk music, the emphasis on DIY meant the sense that anyone could pick up a guitar and make some noise. In cyberpunk, anyone could become a hacker. In steampunk, the celebration of the tinkerer and the inventor continues that spirit. As Mirko Hall and Joshua Gunn will discuss later in this anthology, the steampunk tinkerer is modeled on the genius-adventurer of popular Victorian romantic fiction. He is a person of particular Victorian sensibilities: culturally refined, eternally optimistic, and imaginatively engaged. But he also is a product of the postindustrial age, versed in the DIY ethos. In this anthology, John R. Thompson will explain the ways that one particular media icon, the twenty-first-century reintroduction of *Doctor Who*, exemplifies the steampunk hero as well. Whether Wells's time traveler or the BBC's Time Lord, the steampunk hero patches together his time machine and slips into the unknown for adventure.

The DIY culture of steampunk is central to separating it from a purely fan culture (like *Star Trek* fandom or baseball fandom). Bruce Sterling described this difference at an address to a steampunk convention:

> the heaviest guys in the steampunk scene are not really all that into "steam." Instead, they are into punk. Specifically, punk's do-it-yourself aspects and its determination to take the means of production away from big, mind-deadening companies who want to package and sell shrink-wrapped cultural product.[10]

As the Catastrophone Orchestra and Arts Collective put it: "Ours is not the culture of Neo-Victorianism and stupefying etiquette, not remotely an escape to gentleman's clubs and classist rhetoric."[11] Anyone with grits, determination, and an innovative spirit can imagine themselves as such a steampunk hero or heroine.

There are two general forms or practices that participation in steampunk culture can take: imagination fueled by the consumption of steampunk literary culture (novels, graphic novels, film, and more), and imagination fueled by the steampunk maker culture (costuming and crafting of many types). We'll discuss each of these in turn in the next two sections.

Steampunk and Media Consumption

Steampunk has become an arena of media consumption. We can map that media landscape and so offer the reader a sense of what is available to consume.

As a subgenre of science fiction, steampunk has been subdivided into dozens of subgenres and connected into a web. In the third issue of *SteamPunk Magazine*, fans argue that when an outsider inquires, "What is steampunk?," "it is the insider's duty to the nature of steampunk to speak in terms that are descriptive rather than definitive. Steampunk can blur into clockpunk can blur into sandalpunk can blur into biopunk can blur into goth can blur into

punk can blur into metal, and nobody needs to get hurt in the process!"[12]
Some of the genres are described below.

> *Boilerpunk*: While a great deal of steampunk is focused on the neo-
> Victorian gentleman, the boilerpunk variety of steampunk focuses
> on the lives of the lower classes who literally "work the boilers" that
> generate the steam.
>
> *Clockpunk*: Clockpunk is steampunk that deemphasizes steam tech-
> nology in favor of clockwork technologies—a gear-based aesthetic
> and a wind-up key are typical visual motifs.
>
> *Dieselpunk*: Dieselpunk is steampunk in which diesel or nuclear tech-
> nologies replace steam technologies; this subgenre is typically set
> later than the Victorian era (say, in the interwar period, the Great
> Depression in the United States). Dieselpunk swaps the iconogra-
> phy of Jules Verne for the 1939 New York World's Fair and Rosie
> the Riveter.
>
> *Mannerspunk*: Steampunk that emphasizes elaborate social hierarchies
> as plot points in the narrative tends to be labeled mannerspunk.
>
> *Weird West*: A substantial amount of reimagining of the nineteenth
> century in the United States passes under the name Weird West.

The more deeply one reads, the more subgenres become clear: raygun gothic,
gaslight romance, stitchpunk, and many more.[13] Additionally, steampunks
can follow their passions into other genres: young adult fiction (Scott Westerfeld's *Leviathan* and *Behemoth*),[14] romance (Kady Cross's *The Girl in the
Steel Corset*), and graphic novels (Phil and Kaja Foglio's *Girl Genius*[15] and
Mike Mignola's *Amazing Screw-On Head*). Steampunk has arrived as a literary form, even recognized by the Library of Congress as PN3448.S73 (History and criticism) and PN6120.95.S69 (Collections).

Beyond print literature, steampunk is a transmedia phenomenon. While
we have yet to see a central, defining steampunk motion picture, several
movies participate in the steampunk aesthetic (e.g., the Weird West motion picture *Cowboys & Aliens* and the *Sherlock Holmes* movies of 2009 and
2011, as analyzed in this anthology by Lisa Horton). Also in this anthology,
Elizabeth Birmingham analyzes an anime (Japanese animation) that participates in the steampunk aesthetic. Steampunk music is trickier to identify; some bands deploy a steampunk aesthetic in their album design and
stage performance, while some claim that aesthetic by virtue of instruments
played or lyrics sung. If we speak with the broadest possible set of definitions,

steampunk bands like The Cog Is Dead, Clockwork Dolls, and Dr. Steel and the Clockwork Quarter lay claim to being Steampunk musicians.[16] Finally, video games like *Space: 1889* carry steampunk onto one's gaming screen.[17]

In short, *one* way to participate in steampunk culture is to consume some selection of these media products. In much the way that *Star Trek* fandom and sports fandom are sustained by regular consumption of those texts, steampunk is sustained in the same way. But if participation in steampunk culture were limited to consuming media, it would be difficult to distinguish steampunk from other forms of fandom; at best, it might merit a footnote in the history of fan cultures. Steampunk is also a participatory, transformative culture, and so is worthy of additional attention.

Steampunk as a Participatory, Transformative Culture

Steampunk is a subculture separate from or at least complementary to the consumption of media and literary texts. Steampunk also exists as a field of art and a site of creativity. In this section, I outline the nature of that creative activity, which has been recognized by the arts community (the first museum exhibit of original steampunk objects was held at the Museum of the History of Science at Oxford;[18] the author of this chapter has given a lecture on steampunk as an art movement at the Duluth Art Institute as part of that organization's annual exhibition[19]). First, I will discuss the narrative act of steampunk creation. The steampunk artist creates from the inside out, generating a character and a context, and only then begins to develop the trappings: a costume, a hairdo, weapons, gadgets, and other accessories. Then, from that act of storytelling, we can move to discuss the material culture of steampunk.

Steampunk fans tend to agree: the beginning of creative work starts with the creation of a story. According to Libby Bulloff, there are four broad categories of steampunk characters, modeled on idealized roles that can be taken up in steampunk narratives:

- the street urchin (an archetype borrowed from Charles Dickens)
- the tinker (an archetype borrowed from H. G. Wells)
- the explorer (an archetype borrowed from H. Rider Haggard or Edgar Rice Burroughs)
- and the aesthete (an archetype something like Oscar Wilde).[20]

When one selects a steampunk identity, one can begin to craft the texture of a life. What has your tinker invented? A time machine? A mining machine to burrow to the center of the earth? What adventures has she had because of this invention? A trip to the future, where she has seen the postapocalyptic radiation nightmare? A trip to the moon, where she has met creatures who live in the dark recesses of the craters? A trip to Africa, where she has encountered a land of beasts long thought extinct?

Steampunk fiction, then, becomes part of steampunk as a form of life: "steampunks strive to build whatever they can with their own hands."[21] This is why *SteamPunk Magazine*, in addition to printing fiction and art, also runs articles on constructing charcoal filters for water and on papier-mâché as a medium for creating steampunk artifacts (in no. 3), electrolytic etching (in no. 1), sewing work aprons and welding modified bicycles (in no. 2), and even building a Jacob's ladder (an arcing current across two antennae, commonly found in a mad scientist's lab) (in no. 4). The goal, wherever possible, is not to purchase one's costume and accessories, which would be akin to purchasing an identity from a prefabricated set. It is to create and construct that identity. Most acts of steampunk creation, from costuming to designing complicated gadgets, begin with storytelling.

Gordon Smuder demonstrates this narrative complexity in his designs for Vulcan's Hammer, a ray-gun design that comes with several accessories. The ray gun is built from pieces from a travel chess set, more lamp switches, and finials; its ammo cartridges are built from mint tins. These bits and pieces are brought together by imaginative design as well as by story. Smuder embeds his props in a narrative (with an inventor, Professor Wetherbee). On his website, Smuder alternates between telling his story, as a designer, and Wetherbee's story, as an inventor (for example, developing the "phlogiston sieve").

From the plate designed to press the logo onto metal, to the graphic design on the box of cartridges, to the design of the cartridges themselves—the steampunk aesthetic is multimodal. Smuder infuses that narrative into every aspect of his work. Steampunk goes further because it works from the inside out—it requires a narrative logic that goes beyond stamping clockwork symbols on objects.

The visual features of steampunk apparel, steampunk machinery, steampunk art, and steampunk photography/illustration are found to be more or less genuine based on the narrative constructed to justify it. Visuals are evaluated against a narrative logic. Accessories (like the ubiquitous goggles) are judged based on whether the character would require goggles (as a tinker might when welding). Hues and tones that reflect the steampunk aesthetic must also, specifically, reflect the lived experience of the character (dulled greens and grays for a character in a boilerpunk storyline, for example). The backdrop symbols (the dirigible, the submarine, the ubiquitous clockwork ornamentation) aren't simply ornamentation; they are ways to shorthand the narrative logic by which the character lives. The strategic deployment of those symbols allows the maker to declare membership in a community of steampunk.

Bruce Sterling declared that character formulation in steampunk is part of a broader social and personal exploration:

> If you like to play dress-up, good for you. You're probably young, and, being young, you have some identity issues. So while pretending to be a fireman, or a doctor, or a lawyer, or whatever your parents want you to be, you should be sure to try on a few identities that are totally impossible. Steampunk will help you, because you cannot, ever, be an authentic denizen of the 19th century. You will meet interesting people your own age who share your vague discontent with today's status quo. Clutch them to your velvet-frilled bosom.[22]

Sterling is cynical in his tone, but he's correct: steampunk is an opportunity to build a character, to build an identity, and, in so doing, to explore community. In the constitution of a community, we can find the reinforcement of values, ideas, and beliefs.

Steampunk as a Rhetorical System

We are here to make the past look better. Simply kill a king here and invent a technology some years earlier and there you go, history fixed! The Victorian era, though all filled with smog and tuberculosis, suddenly seems like a time worth living in, for the brass is shining and the stars are within reach!

—NICK OTTENS[23]

To function as a rhetorical system in the richest sense of the term, steampunk must connect its surface system of style (its dirigibles, goggles, and clockwork aesthetic) to values, ideas, and beliefs. Rhetoric, after all, is not only surface adornment but integral to the formation and propagation of ideas, values, and beliefs. We can trace the ideological constructions that follow from the culture, the creative practice, and the narratives of steampunk.

Steampunk conventions both challenge and reify certain social relationships: (a) technological relations, (b) gender relations, and (c) race relations. In all three cases, steampunk promises to imagine some alternative to the tradition and history we have inherited—even as steampunk narratives confine us in other ways. Steampunk is a project to create a utopian past. Steampunk promises a past (and therefore a present and future) that revalues technology and makes choices that sustain, rather than destroy, our environment and our relationships. It promises gender relations that allow the individual woman to achieve heroic roles. At the same time, it reifies gender norms that inadvertently perpetuate the domination of women. While steampunk promises to rethink race relations, it does so by creating a past dependent upon reductive media stereotypes. The result, in all three areas, is that many steampunks trade positive sociopolitical action today for idealized fictions of yesterday.

Science, Technology, and Society

Steampunk makes definite statements on the relationship between science, technology, and human social relations. Steampunk's historical point of divergence is the period immediately prior to the adoption of internal combustion engines and before the experiments in atomic physics. These inventions changed our relationship to technology forever. As McKenzie says, "Steampunk preserves a moment in technological history in which the destructive potential of science was still largely unrealized, when inventors were imagined to be journeyman tinkerers like Edison or Da Vinci rather than scientists like Oppenheimer." Steampunk culture attempts to reclaim that earlier, less complicated relationship to technology.

Steampunk articulates this critique of technology and society by creating imaginary alternative histories in its fiction and by arguing, in its nonfiction (for example, in *SteamPunk Magazine*), for critiques of the Whiggish, progress-presuming narrative of technological progress. As Carolyn Dougherty writes: "We tend to describe it as an almost predetermined progress, a fairly straightforward evolution from less complex to more complex and from less efficient to more efficient. If we look more carefully at how technologies are chosen, however, we discover anomalous narratives that refute this model."[24] Her anomalous example is the airship; she believes that the airship is the technologically most elegant technology—more fuel efficient, more technologically efficient, and so on. In her mind, we rejected the preferable technology. Dougherty asks what kind of culture would prefer the airship to the jet: one that values the environment, that values sustainable resources, that

values safety. These are the values she exhorts us to enact through participation in steampunk culture. Such relationships are similarly advocated by
Hilde Heyvaert:

> Now let's be realistic, ours is a movement that inherently embraces
> several things that are good for the environment. The vast majority of
> 'punks that are artisans and crafters are masters at upcycling bits and
> pieces that many would think of as useless only to turn them into fine
> works of art. Discarded bits and bobs like old watch pieces become
> beautiful brooches, old bits of leather a lovely harness, old bedding or
> curtains become wonderful garments, and so on and on.[25]

An understanding of the rhetoric of technology in steampunk must synthe-
size both the representations of technology in its fictional worlds (worlds of
airships instead of jet planes) and accounts of practice—of anticorporate,
anti-mass-production ethos among steampunk crafters and makers. Such a
synthesis makes clear that steampunk is dreaming of an alternative way to
envision people's relationships both to technology and to each other as mediated by technology. What may be harder to parse is the rhetorical effective-
ness of these dreams. We cannot return to the dirigible as a transportation
technology as a matter of policy. What, then, is the rhetorical function of
airship dreams?

Gender Relations

Gender is a vibrant dimension of steampunk dreams of the future. Carol Mc-
Cleary, in the *Gatehouse Gazette*, tells us that the steampunk era was

> an exciting epoch, a time of brave hearts and warm souls, of poetry and
> great art and inquiring minds, of duels fought for honor and affairs
> of the heart. A time when women were treated like chattels and their
> names were only supposed to appear in newspapers thrice—when she
> was born, when she got married, and when she died.[26]

If steampunk is to be set against a neo-Victorian backdrop, its practitioners
must address these issues. To dream of airships while failing to dream of alternatives to patriarchal values is at least a possible point of contention.

Steampunk is often celebrated as gender-equalizing genre, in which
heroines stand toe-to-toe with heroes. Jaymee Goh, writing in *SteamPunk*

Magazine, gives us the standard answer to questions about gender in steampunk: "Gender is also easily subverted, as many women re-imagine the steampunk world to be a more gentle time for their gender, unfettered and unlimited. There are many women who play sky captain, or other roles that would, in more realistic play, be denied to them."[27] As rhetorical critics sensitive to the implications of rhetoric for both challenging and reifying social values, we can recognize the importance of these moves.

But even within the steampunk community, there is concern that this is not enough. Amanda Stock celebrates the strong roles women have played in steampunk fiction, media, and fan culture:

> Strong women abound in steampunk: lead characters as Briar Wilkes from Cherie Priest's *Boneshaker* (2009), editors and contributors to publications such as C. Allegra Hawksmoor of *Steampunk Magazine*, podcasters including Emmett and Claude Davenport of *The Clockwork Cabaret*, and community leaders such as Lee Ann Farruga of Steampunk Canada and Steampunk Ottawa. Unlike some areas of geek culture which have historically been male dominated, the steampunk scene has fostered a whole host of talented, creative women.[28]

Despite this progress, Stock sees inadvertent misogyny through the perpetuation of aspects of Victorian culture in steampunk. As plot device, "having women specifically come down with 'the vapors' or faint at the first sign of danger (or anything else for that matter) doesn't break down Victorian sensibilities; it maintains them."[29] More troubling is the infusion of antifeminist or misogynist principles into steampunk behavior. Stock lays it out without pulling any punches: "One cannot rule out the ever present danger of geek misogyny."[30] Stock warns that steampunk may be at the core of a "retrosexual" movement (in which television shows like *Mad Men* participate), in which men yearn, nostalgically, for a time when gender differentiation was clearer.

It remains an open question whether steampunk recrafts gender politics the way it recrafts the politics of science and technology. When Allie Kerr, writing in *SteamPunk Magazine*,[31] tells us that female characters in Victorian penny dreadfuls were pointed critiques of social mores, she is recuperating an important political gesture. At the same time, there is little effort to recover authentic gender roles. The pointed critique of social mores of the dominant, masculinist culture does little to express and revalue the culture and practices of women. Similarly, when a lady steampunk decides that she, too, can be an airship captain, she does more to critique the social system that oppressed women in the nineteenth century than, perhaps, she does to recover and re-value a genuine women's identity of the nineteenth century or to create a new women's identity for a steampunk twenty-first century.

Race Relations and the Politics of Empire

Any fiction set in the nineteenth century begins against a backdrop of imperialism, manifest destiny, and slavery. When the genres of steampunk reinvent the technological history of the nineteenth century, they have an opportunity to re-create the history of social, economic, and race relations that darkened that century. Steampunk sometimes does, sometimes does not, take that opportunity. As Jaymee Goh tells us succinctly: "The presence of race in steampunk, for many, is often theoretical, and not a messy reality that the average steampunk has to deal with."[32] Race may not be grappled with directly by steampunks—but that does not mean that it is not an issue for the subculture. By failing to address race, other tensions become visible in the steampunk community.

If steampunk creators do not expressly challenge racial oppression inherent in the nineteenth-century culture that serves as imaginative resources, then perhaps that oppression can be presumed to stand, unquestioned, in the steampunk imagination. Not to address race in a fictional re-creation of Victorian culture is to reify Victorian conceptions of race and empire. This has the effect, articulated by Goh, of continuing "the marginalization of specific groups, which in turn limits the genre and playing ground, alienating the very people we claim to welcome."[33]

The consequence of failing to challenge issues of race, class, and imperialism enters into other subgenres of steampunk, such as dieselpunk creations that draw upon early twentieth-century technologies. At the same time that dieselpunk costume, art, and literature celebrates the work ethic of scrappy Americans, surviving the Depression on their own (often technological) ingenuity, we can reasonably ask whether dieselpunk should also address the totalitarian politics of the 1930s.

Steampunk can even draw from ostensibly inaccurate representations of race to produce creative reimaginings. The issue of racial difference in the context of empire becomes a site of play. As Nick Ottens noted,

> steampunk allows us to reject the chains of reality and all the racism and guilt associated with it, to explore anew this imagined world of

sultans and saber-rattling Islamic conquerors; harems and white slavery; samurai, dragons and dark, bustling bazaars frequented by the strangest sort of folk. Isn't this, after all, steampunk's very premise? To delve into a past that never really was.[34]

Such a perspective would welcome, for example, efforts to incorporate belly dance into steampunk practices,[35] to explore "victoriental" themes in steampunk,[36] also called "ricepunk." The call here is to recover the romance of the nineteenth-century popular imagination without the connections to the systems of slavery, colonialism, and empire.

The end result is not entirely positive. These creative reimaginings call us to rethink the past in a way that does nothing to recover a genuine experience of people of color. By reclaiming the romanticized other, victoriental or ricepunk steampunk does little to reconfigure contemporary race and ethnic relations. Much of steampunk art and literature stalls out at the opportunity to effect positive social change in encounters with race.

Looking Forward: A Rhetoric for the Future of Steampunk

There are voices in steampunk that are moving forward productively, pushing new avenues of creativity. The annual immersion convention held in Madison, Wisconsin, called TeslaCon, has set new standards for a steampunk experience as well as made possible some new conversations among the diverse populations who participate in steampunk culture.

The convention participates in a fictional narrative, which, like the staging, decorations, lighting, audio, and video enhancements to the hotel environment, is designed by one man: Eric Larson, or Lord Bobbins. Participants are not issued badges, as in typical fan conventions, but "passports," which give them entrance to the convention and the convention's storyline. Admission is capped (between six hundred and a thousand people for past events) to make sure that the immersion experience can be maintained. For TeslaCon 3, the narrative was a voyage to the moon. The storyline includes a cartoonesque villain (the evil Dr. Proctocus, who sabotaged the spaceship in which the convention was being held). While the narrative of good versus evil is relatively flat, the immersion experience allows a richer dimension of conversation and cultural work to occur.

TeslaCon, as an immersion convention, attracts those members of the steampunk community who are most committed. Participants have a variety of perspectives and adapt their own particular interests to steam culture. For example, some are interested in historical reenactment (perhaps formerly working at Civil War events) and want to bring a new creative energy to their work. Others are fiction fans who have come to love the characters in Scott Westerfeld's novels. Some participants are music fans hoping to connect with others who love Abney Park. And still others are entrepreneurs, from steampunk chocolatiers to steampunk button sellers to full-blown craftspeople working with leather and blowtorches or operating nineteenth-century letterpresses for custom printing. And some are lovers of cosplay, for instance a couple cosplaying *Star Trek: The Next Generation* (as Data and companion, holodeck-steampunk style).

TeslaCon also includes dissenting voices who, in the crucible of an immersion convention, raise issues that can be glossed over in fanzines, blogs, and websites. Panels addressing multiculturalism at TeslaCon 2 carry more weight than casual online postings on the topic because of the commitment and passion of the participants. Reenactments of suffragette struggles at TeslaCon 3 are more than theater; they become a catalyst for more conversations about gender in steampunk. And, amid the sellers of games and chocolates, a young woman sits, knitting, in front of a display of "Occupy Wall Street"–style photocopied posters calling for reconsiderations of race, empire, class, and gender in steampunk. (The display is even more powerful when you consider the role that knitting has in protest work, or "craftivism"—her presence is an act of rhetoric.) TeslaCon's seventy-two hours of immersion are an opportunity for conflicting motives and conflicting values to work their differences out together.[37]

Lord Bobbins himself has recognized this work and has integrated it into his own exhortations about the nature of steampunk. At the end of TeslaCon 3, he announced that anyone attending TeslaCon 4 from outside the United States would be given a free ticket—to encourage international dialogue missing from discussions of steampunk. At TeslaCon 4, the "Congress of Steam" will serve a role in mediating discussions about the future of steampunk. Bobbins discussed conflicts on the horizon: the values of historical reenactors (who maintain that the best steampunk outfits must be made only from materials available in the nineteenth century) are in tension with the values of cosplayers (who seek creativity before authenticity). Bobbins exhorted members of the community to work together to resolve these issues at the congress.

Notably, and significant in pointing to possibilities for steampunk's future work, Bobbins's address (traditional, persuasive rhetoric delivered in forty-five minutes at the end of the show) made clear that the future of steampunk lay in the hands of the attendees at TeslaCon. Other fandoms, from *Star Trek* to baseball to soap operas, depend on corporations to shape the scope and form of their fandom. Steampunk is self-generating and limited only by the will of its creators. No one, not Disney Studios nor Warner Brothers, owns steampunk, and in that sense, if steampunk fans take their work seriously, they can begin to remake their fandom and eventually remake the world.

Conclusion: The Uses and Gratifications of Steampunk

Steampunk, like all media rhetorics, serves its practitioners both socially and psychologically. Steampunk fans and steampunk creators use this media rhetoric to express their values and, sometimes, to seek gratification through escape. Nick Ottens, writing in the *Gatehouse Gazette*, claims that the subgenres of steampunk serve their fans differently:

> We live in tough times. Some of us are having trouble finding a job. Others have had to give up their homes. Others still worry whether their savings might actually be worth something by the time they retire.
>
> Steampunk can be an escapist genre. It can make the past seem all perfect even if it's a huge deception. Few of us would probably be better off living in the nineteenth century. But it's nice reminiscing about the beauties of a past that wasn't, especially if the present is so depressing.
>
> Dieselpunk, on the other hand, confronts the [Great] Depression and all the miseries of its era head on, whether it's totalitarianism, mysticism or the brutal technologies of war that are deployed against the forces of the Free World. There's no time to sit around and dream of a better past. There's also no excuse to wait for a better tomorrow. Dieselpunks roll up their sleeves and start building.[38]

The narratives from different genres of steampunk carry an ideological load, just like any other rhetoric. Insofar as steampunk is a participatory rhetoric, it encourages fans to create identities and constitute social relationships through common love of steampunk aesthetics. In the end, disappointingly, participation in steampunk culture provides an escape from the complexities and challenges of contemporary social life without much of a plan for working through those challenges. At events like TeslaCon, we are only beginning to arrive at ways to use steampunk rhetoric as a staging ground for positive social action.

Notes

David Beard can be reached at the Department of Writing Studies, Humanities 420, University of Minnesota Duluth, Duluth, MN, 55812, or via email at dbeard@d.umn.edu.

1. William Gibson and Bruce Sterling, *The Difference Engine* (London: Victor Gollancz, 2011).

2. Smuder's work can be found at the website for the Gentleman's Gadgeteer Society, at https://www.facebook.com/pages/The-Gentlemens-Gadgeteer-Society-of-London/116853635074859.

3. Edward S. Ellis's "The Huge Hunter, or Steam Man of the Prairies" was originally published in 1868 as part of the series Irwin P. Beadle's American Novels and is discussed in Jeff VanderMeer and S. J. Chambers, *The Steampunk Bible* (New York: Harry N. Abrams, 2011).

4. The influence of Wells and Verne is discussed in VanderMeer and Chambers, *The Steampunk Bible*, and in Major Thaddeus Tinker [John Naylor], *The Steampunk Gazette* (Hauppage, N.Y.: Barrons, 2012).

5. Poe's work is discussed in VanderMeer and Chambers, *The Steampunk Bible*, 20–27.

6. VanderMeer and Chambers cast an even wider net in identifying influences. In addition to discussing (for example) *Warlord of the Air*, they draw lines of influence from Moorcock's larger body of work; see *The Steampunk Bible*, 59–60.

7. See the special issue in 2010, "Steampunk, Science, and (Neo)Victorian Technologies" (edited by Rachel A. Bowser and Brian Croxall), examining many of the works we've discussed and more. Rachel A. Bowser and Brian Croxall, "Introduction: Industrial Revolution," *Neo-Victorian Studies* 3, no. 1 (2010): 1–45. At http://www.neovictorianstudies.com/past_issues/3-1%202010/NVS%203-1-1%20R-Bowser%20&%20B-Croxall.pdf.

8. James H. Carrott and Brian David Johnson interview Sterling about his relationship to steampunk in *Vintage Tomorrows: A Historian and a Futurist Journey through Steampunk into the Future of Technology* (Sebastopol, Calif.: Maker Media, 2013), 362-364.

9. Jacqueline Christi, "Explorations into Steampunk Lifestyle," *Gatehouse Gazette* 18 (May 2011): 7. At http://www.ottens.co.uk/gatehouse/gazette-18/.

10. Bruce Sterling, "User's Guide to Steampunk," *SteamPunk Magazine* 5 (n.d.): 32. At http://www.combustionbooks.org/downloads/spm5-imposed.pdf.

11. Catastrophone Orchestra and Arts Collective, "What Then, Is Steampunk? Colonizing the Past So That We Can Dream the Future," *SteamPunk Magazine* 1 (n.d.): 4. At http://www.combustionbooks.org/downloads/SPM1-web.pdf

12. Collection of People, "What Is Steampunk? Steampunk Is Awesome," *SteamPunk Magazine* 3 (n.d.): 6. At http://www.combustionbooks.org/downloads/spm3-web.pdf.

13. VanderMeer and Chambers offer an alternate list of genres in *The Steampunk Bible*, 54–55.

14. Westerfeld is interviewed in Carrott and Johnson, *Vintage Tomorrows*, 149–157.

15. Phil and Kaja Foglio are interviewed in Carrott and Johnson, *Vintage Tomorrows*, 92–115.

16. A discussion of steampunk music and handcrafted steampunk instruments can be found in Tinker, *The Steampunk Gazette*, 162–171.

17. Ibid., 231.

18. VanderMeer and Chambers, *The Steampunk Bible*, 120–123.

19. Duluth Art Institute, Steampunk Spectacular (event), Duluth, Minn., May 2013. At http://www.duluthartinstitute.org/component/content/article/10-exhibitions/133-steampunk-spectacular-event-schedule.

20. Libby Bulloff, "Steam Gear: A Fashionable Approach to the Lifestyle," *SteamPunk Magazine* 2 (n.d.): 8–13.

21. Christi, "Explorations into Steampunk Lifestyle," 6.

22. Sterling, "User's Guide to Steampunk," 30.

23. Nick Ottens, "How'd You Like Your Past, Sir?," *Gatehouse Gazette* 6 (May 2009): 3. At http://www.ottens.co.uk/gatehouse/Gazette%20-%206.pdf.

24. Carolyn Dougherty, "On Progress, On Airships," *SteamPunk Magazine* 5 (n.d.): 25. At http://www.combustionbooks.org/downloads/spm5-web.pdf.

25. Hilde Heyvaert, "The Steampunk Wardrobe," *Gatehouse Gazette* 12 (May 2010): 19. At http://www.ottens.co.uk/gatehouse/gazette-12/.

26. Carol McCleary, "The Life and Times of Nellie Bly," *Gatehouse Gazette* 15 (November 2010): 13. At http://www.ottens.co.uk/gatehouse/gazette-15/.

27. Jaymee Goh, "On Race and Steampunk," *SteamPunk Magazine* 7 (n.d.): 18. At http://www.steampunkmagazine.com/pdfs/spm7-web.pdf.

28. Amanda Stock, "Battle of the Sexes? How Steampunk Should Be Informed by Feminism," *Gatehouse Gazette* 15 (November 2010): 4. At http://www.ottens.co.uk/gatehouse/gazette-15/.

29. Ibid.

30. Ibid.

31. Allie Kerr, "All Fashions of Loveliness: Women in Victorian Penny Dreadfuls," *SteamPunk Magazine* 7 (n.d.): 58–61. At http://www.steampunkmagazine.com/pdfs/spm7-web.pdf.

32. Jaymee Goh, "On Race and Steampunk," *SteamPunk Magazine* 7 (n.d.): 19. At http://www.steampunkmagazine.com/pdfs/spm7-web.pdf.

33. Ibid., 20.

34. Nick Ottens, "Editorial," *Gatehouse Gazette* 11 (March 2010): 3. At http://www.ottens.co.uk/gatehouse/Gazette%20-%2011.pdf

35. Ay-leen the Peacemaker, "Shimmies and Sprockets," *SteamPunk Magazine* 7 (n.d): 48–53. At http://www.steampunkmagazine.com/pdfs/spm7-web.pdf.

36. *Gatehouse Gazette*, special issue on Victorientalism, vol. 11 (March 2010). At http://www.ottens.co.uk/gatehouse/Gazette%20-%2011.pdf.

37. Coverage of TeslaCon 2 is available in the February 2013 issue of *Cloud Orchid Magazine*. At http://cloudorchidmagazine.com/2013/02/03/the-steampunk-special-issue-vol-2-released/.

38. Nick Ottens, "Depressing Times," *Gatehouse Gazette* 20 (September 2011): 3 At http://www.ottens.co.uk/gatehouse/Gazette%20-%2020.pdf.

A RHETORIC OF
STEAMPUNK
IDEOLOGY

"There Is Hope for the Future"

The (Dis)Enchantment of the Technician-Hero in Steampunk

MIRKO M. HALL AND JOSHUA GUNN

WAVE-GOTHIC-TREFFEN (WGT) IS ONE OF THE WORLD'S PREMIERE DARK MU-sic and arts festivals.[1] Held annually in Leipzig, Germany, the event attracts more than twenty thousand enthusiasts for four days of concerts, films, readings, and workshops. Fans of Steampunk have joined the gathering in surprisingly large numbers over the past several years. In addition to the long-standing Victorian picnic at Clara-Zetkin-Park, WGT now has its very own Steampunk picnic at Schillerpark, located near the city's landmark cultural center, the Moritzbastei. A steady stream of online photojournalism from 2013—distributed by such international news agencies as the Associated Press, Reuters, and Agence France-Presse—show most of these Steampunk fans to be dressed as some kind of male Victorian "technician-hero:"[2] cybernetic versions of airship pilots, industrial engineers, private detectives, and professors of the natural sciences.[3] As established critics of the genre have argued, a large majority of these aficionados belong to a "distinct demographic" of Anglo-European, middle-class males, who perpetuate a classic understanding of Victorian masculinity and public propriety, but one now imbued with strong techno-utopian impulses.[4] In this chapter, we examine this phenomenon by exploring how a certain fantasy of the technician-hero not only is modeled on the aura of the genius-adventurer of popular Victorian romantic fiction but also incorporates a move toward the disenchantment with the supernatural or "magic." This fantasy is an explicit attempt to redeem a thoroughly administered world through the use of anachronistic, revolutionary technology that, in the end, continues to court a similar sense of wonder. In order to articulate this thesis, we draw upon several resources: classic novels, blockbuster films, and online pictures of contemporary Steampunk subculture aficionados.

Steampunk as a Techno-Utopian Fantasy

TechnoTopics

Steampunk originated in the late 1980s as a multifaceted aesthetic-technical movement with global reach, and it has been gaining in popularity and visibility ever since.[5] Spanning art forms as diverse as literature, cinema, fashion, and music, Steampunk is a unique amalgamation of nineteenth-century Victorian romance fiction (the novels of H. G. Wells and Jules Verne), mid-twentieth-century science fiction (Walt Disney's filmic adaptations of Verne's works), and premillennium cyberpunk (the novels of William Gibson and Bruce Sterling). Besides the pleasures afforded by imaginative role playing and the creation of new fictive worlds, the culture of Steampunk—as evidenced by online declarations and manifestos, including those of such astute practitioner-critics as Dru Pagliassotti and Professor Calamity[6]—is engaged in a distinctly ideological project. Even though Steampunk has never had a monolithic superstructure in terms of cultural-political philosophies, its foundation in a kind of nostalgic Victorian masculinity can neither be overlooked nor simply ignored: it continues to exert considerable influence today. In an important suggestion by Steampunk historian Jeff VanderMeer, many enthusiasts are not necessarily experts in the arts and culture of the era but are rather appropriating a variety of popular constructs of Victoriana that are already circulating in wider society.[7]

There are several key historical reasons for locating the origins of Steampunk—and its persistent conditions of intelligibility—in the Victorian Era of Great Britain (ca. 1830–1900) and, to a lesser extent, the Gilded Age (ca. 1870–1900) in America. Arguably the most powerful nation in the world at that time, Great Britain witnessed a period of amazing achievements in science, technology, and medicine that ushered in with remarkable speed our modern age of convenience and splendor. But it was also a country obsessed with imperial conquests in Africa and Asia and riddled by oppressive social hierarchies and ghastly urban disparities between the bourgeoisie and the proletariat that were brought about by the Industrial Revolution. It is this condition—the dystopian world of sweaty soot, blood, and tears, which is depicted in Friedrich Engels's *The Condition of the Working Class in England* and in novels of Charles Dickens such as *Hard Times* and *Oliver Twist*—that always remains the vexing problematic in Steampunk culture. As an ideological project, then, Steampunk attempts to *reclaim* and, ultimately, *redeem* the nineteenth century—revolving around the construct of "Victorian

England"—in a manner similar to German critic Walter Benjamin's particu-lar version of historical materialism.[8] As Pagliassotti writes, by *"recycling and rethinking history's lost dreams and obsolete technologies . . . steampunk is poised to offer the world, with an ironic wink and a shiny brass-and-wood carrying case, a vision of the future that offers cautious hope instead of dystopian despair"* (emphasis in original).[9] In other words, this movement strives to rescue histo-ry's lost dreams (the final eradication of poverty, pollution, and inequality[10]) through the use of anachronistic technologies (steam-powered machines and analog difference engines). In lieu of a dirty, dehumanized past, Steampunk attempts to create an entirely new vision of the future-in-the-past: a techno-utopian world free of human/human and human/machine alienation. It is a project specifically designed to reclaim machine technologies as "icons of a new utopian landscape"[11]—as tools that "repurpose the best of that time while correcting for the worst," in a kind of adolescent "do-over" fantasy.[12]

TechGenre

The technological paradigm surrounding Steampunk takes its origins from a historical continuum of scientific breakthroughs that spans most of the nine-teenth and part of the early twentieth century. This period was marked by unprecedented advances in technological ingenuity surrounding machines and mechanical (re)production.[13] Although Americans like Thomas Edison and Alexander Graham Bell participated in these breakthroughs (as well as Guglielmo Marconi, the Italian pioneer of radio), British inventors like Sir Charles Babbage and computer scientists like Alan Turing tend to be cel-ebrated in the imaginary of Steampunk. (Within a specifically American context, however, it is Edison, whose prolific discoveries in the field of mass communications have made him the inventor par excellence in U.S. Steam-punk.) Because of its vast global trade connections, Britain had a complex network of international markets to provide the necessary material condi-tions for fostering technological and scientific advances. Additionally, Vic-torian England had a cultural-political climate of societal betterment that was supported by the need for scientific invention and progress. The era witnessed the advent of amazing new devices and machines in the area of communication technology (the electric telegraph, cinema, and telephones) and transportation modes (aircraft, automobiles, railroads, and steamships). These advances were made possible by industrial processes that were under-pinned by the development and application of steam technology. It is these types of originating inventions that continue to be mapped onto the visual imagery of Steampunk in a manner that is either anachronistic (like ironclad vintage typewriters) or retro-futuristic (like steam locomotives powered by analog computers). But perhaps the most visible of these technological wonders are those literary-fictive machines or "vehicular utopias" that have served as the blueprint for every subsequent Steampunk techno-creation: Wells's mechanical time machine or Verne's hyperbolic submarine, the *Nautilus*.[14]

Steampunk as a Victorian Masculine Fantasy

Stereotypes of Victorian Masculinity

The increased functional differentiation of European (and Victorian) society—caused by the progressive industrialization and administration of civil society—precipitated the creation of two distinct spheres of cultural-political influence. This differentiation had a profound effect on middle-class gender dynamics: it enacted a public sphere of agonistic, competitive males in the world of politics and employment, and a private sphere of sensuous, nurturing females in family and home.[15] The centrality of a masculine ideology in Victoriana, as well as persuasive feminist challenges to this discursive construction, have been extensively researched, and we draw our readers' attention to several key texts of this literature.[16] Although contemporary Steampunk fantasy offers a direct challenge to this centrality (such as the graphic novels of Alan Moore or *Girl Genius* by Phil and Kaja Foglio), most of the discourses influencing this genre lead back—rather ironically—to a Frenchman, Jules Verne. For this reason, we believe that the Victorian gentleman in such a scenario is the default fantasy figure of Steampunk.

In this chapter, we concentrate on those qualities that imbued the Victorian gentlemen with certain idealized characteristics. These qualities can be conveniently summed up in one word: *power*. This gentleman adhered to a strong moral code—in the service of God and Empire—that was saturated with the virtues of courage, industry, ingenuity, sobriety, resolution, and virility. He no longer received his status from aristocratic origins or positions of patronage, but rather from his own self-discipline and pursuit of moral and intellectual excellence. Of course, constructions of masculinity are always historically specific and operative across often volatile fields of normativity, and much scholarship continues to be conducted on rethinking (simplistic) notions of a unified Victorian masculinity.[17] One experience, however, is constant: masculinity is "always a spectacle exposed to a public gaze."[18] The Victorian gentleman of Steampunk is no different and, owing to his conspicuousness, is especially a subject of public visibility. Although gender constructions may indeed be disruptive in Steampunk,[19] it remains surprising (and rather curious) that those figurations of male identity in the popular imaginary of Steampunk still tend to emulate normative Victorian masculinity—in particular, a masculinity poised on the autonomy so blatantly represented by the machine-as-surrogate phallus.

Illustration: The Technician-Hero as (Dis)enchanter

Returning to our friends at Wave-Gothic-Treffen, online galleries of Steampunk fans invariably depict what literary scholar James Maertens might label as the "technician-hero" (male figurations of engineers, explorers, detectives, physicians, and scientists) in his study of the myths of "*mechanized* and *mechanizing* masculinity" in nineteenth-century European literature.[20] Their Steampunk personae are directly modeled on the white, male, and socially mobile genius-adventurer of popular Victorian romantic fiction, particularly in the works of Wells and Verne. As embodiments of typical male Victorian sensibilities—filtered through a techno-utopian Steampunk aesthetic—they create an auratic presence that suggests to onlookers such idealized qualities as cultural refinement, imaginative engagement, and eternal optimism. Furthermore, they are dutifully outfitted with technological accoutrements ranging from analog computers, aviator goggles, mechanical prostheses, hydraulic pocket watches, and sleek ray guns to utilitarian military gear.[21] These accoutrements are suggestive of the anachronistic mechanical gadgetry seen, most notably, in director Barry Sonnenfeld's 1999 reworking of a television classic, *Wild Wild West*. This nexus of adventurism, ingenuity, and technology is embedded within a larger discursive network that valorizes Steampunk's utopian impulse to secure the great dreams and hopes of humankind—through modes of technology that have previously gone awry. In this way, the technician-hero becomes a product of the postindustrial age: a global citizen intimately versed in the political activism that is today more readily perceived by consumers of popular culture as the province of cyberpunks, hackers, and WikiLeaks freedom (data)fighters.

In his effort to secure the great dreams and hopes of humankind, the Steampunk technician-hero manipulates—in the words of Walter Benjamin—technology "not [as] a fetish of doom but a key to happiness."[22] Such techno-utopianism is analogous to Benjamin's figure of the "experimental, polytechnical aesthetic 'engineer.'"[23] This figure is the historical materialist par excellence, who utilizes the past experiences of bygone eras (here, the nineteenth century) to actualize their hidden revolutionary energy (their unrealized wants, hopes, and aspirations) in order to effectuate social-emancipatory change. To accomplish this, the technician-hero uses the capacities and potentialities of technology to functionally transform society.

Of course, as Benjamin and his colleague Theodor W. Adorno often emphasized, technology can be deployed for both progressive and regressive political means. To guarantee its progressive use, the unique dialectical character—that is, the specific logic—of each technological device must be understood and its potential for technical innovation maximized. These potentialities must be actualized in the "service of emancipatory intentions."[24] That is to say, the technician-hero must use such technological potentiation—together with progressive political intentions—in order to positively transform the world. Quoting Pagliassotti, the technician-hero "(re)creates a future that writers and artists once dreamed humanity would be living now—a future of dazzling airships and interplanetary travel, of time travel and trade with alien species. It's a future created through the benign miracles of science and technology, absent poverty, pollution, inequality, and ignorance."[25]

As a principally aesthetic vehicle for an ideology of Victorian masculinity—inclusive of moral and physical power, whiteness, technological fetishism in the service of country or community, and so on—Steampunk fantasy abounds with variations of the technician-hero. Owing to its origins in popular literature, perhaps the best-known representative characters are Wells's nameless protagonist, the "Time Traveller," or Verne's infamous "no man," Captain Nemo. The many ways in which the technician-hero has been updated and modified over the past century, however, highlight the contours of a Victorian sensibility long after the death of Queen Victoria. Insofar as the public image or *appearance* of the Steampunk hero is central to this discursive construction, popular film also provides a series of stark examples.

Owing to its Victorian moorings, the films frequently and most readily identified as "Steampunk" are characteristically helmed by the British, such as Stephen Norrington's poorly received (and rightly so) adaptation of Alan Moore's celebrated comic series *The League of Extraordinary Gentlemen* (2003); Guy Ritchie's 2009 reboot of Sherlock Holmes into a multifilm, technocentric franchise; and Christopher Nolan's 2006 stage magician mystery, *The Prestige*.[26] The wildly creative director Terry Gilliam (*Brazil, Time Bandits, The Adventures of Baron Munchausen*) is sometimes discussed as advancing a British Steampunk aesthetic in his fantastic films—if only for repeated recourse to the majesty of the hot air balloon. However, his frequently critical, dystopic visions often lack the unbridled optimism, omnipotence, or moral righteousness so typical of the technician-hero.[27] Nevertheless, most of these widely seen films feature white protagonists whose power is enhanced—or who are made "complete"—by technological innovation and gadgeteering.[28] For a film to feature Steampunk as a central vehicle for Victorian masculinity, the gadget and machine are almost always figured as prosthetic enhancements of the technician-hero that seem to be, at least initially, the consequence of *magic*.[29]

We mention "magic" here to underscore a plot device in Steampunk films that depends heavily on how the technician-hero appears to others: his seeming omnipotence is *perceived* as a consequence of magic (or deals made with devils). The unknowing masses—in our time, seemingly outspoken fundamentalist Christians—tend to mistake technological achievement as a variant of preternatural power. This perceived power, however, is actually a result of "scientific" ingenuity, a point Verne accused Wells of failing to underscore in his competing "romances" that would later become "science fiction."[30] At least for Verne, the wonder typically afforded to the supernatural should be appropriately displaced by the scientific genius of the technician-hero, based on a "groundwork of actual fact" and "contemporary engineering skill and knowledge."[31]

This stress on the secular, material basis of technological achievements—fueled by human genius—is usefully homologous to Benjamin's observation that the "exhibition" or "cult value" of an artwork (its "aura") is gradually eroded in its age of technological reproducibility.[32] Writing in 1936, Benjamin's primary concern with the decay of "aura"—despite explicit protests to the contrary—was the possibility that the increasingly ubiquitous technologies of the moving picture could be harnessed toward progressive, antifascist ends and that the cinema had the potential to inspire a critical revolutionary consciousness among its spectators. Interestingly enough, by comparing the magician and surgeon to the painter and cameraman, Benjamin's hope was similar to Verne's conviction in the nonfiction of fiction, mirroring the mistrust of illusion that can be traced throughout many Steampunk fantasies.[33]

In keeping with Benjamin's mistrust of enchantment, we suggest that there is a tacit code to the Steampunk genre that we term the "rule of disenchantment": whatever technological wonders are central to a Steampunk story, they are decidedly neither magical nor produced by supernatural means. This rule is (mostly, not always) adhered to in these films as the unmasking of a devious genius—a kind of technician antihero—who is "unveiled" by a more proper scientific righteousness. For example, in Ritchie's refashioning of Sherlock Holmes in the 2009 film, the villain Lord Henry Blackwood presents himself as a powerful occultist who, although hanged as punishment for a series of murders, uses magic to resurrect himself from the grave and take over the world by initially bombing Parliament. Holmes foils Blackwood's plans and—through a technological ingenuity of his own—disarms Blackwood's bomb "machine" and reveals that his death and resurrection are not the products of supernatural prowess, but rather an ingenious and elaborate hoax.³⁴ Blackwood appears to be an omnipotent wielder of the supernatural because his powers *seem* technically implausible. However, Holmes's unvarnished, working-class street cred unmasks him as a creative, technically savvy fraud.

The mistaking of technical ingenuity for magic is also a frequent thematic in Hollywood Steampunk fantasies that replicate—despite obvious revolutionary differences—the ideology of Victorian masculinity. Kerry Conran's visually stunning "dieselpunk" film *Sky Captain and the World of Tomorrow* (2004) features, for example, a technical antihero and the mysterious Dr. Totenkopf, whose efforts to create a "World of Tomorrow" through technological innovation—initially for preserving a self-destructive humankind through the creation of a gigantic ark-like rocket—are perverted into destructive machines after his demise (when robots and flying vehicles are mistaken as otherworldly). With the help of the technological hero Dex Dearborn, Sky Captain reveals the scientific know-how behind Dr. Totenkopf's organization and restores a proper, moral consciousness missing from the automatons fashioned to outlive Totenkopf's death, thereby saving the world.

A climatic scene in *Sky Captain* represents the Steampunk rule of disenchantment most conspicuously: after the protagonists penetrate Dr. Totenkopf's compound, they are greeted by a chatty, menacing hologram of the evil genius's head (created with "remixed" film footage of a long-dead Laurence Olivier), who attempts to scare them away. Through Dex's technological savvy, the team disarms the hologram and other defenses to reveal that Totenkopf—true to his German name—is already dead. Significantly, the hologram scene is an obvious homage to the *most* well-known cinematic fantasy featuring the technological hero in an American context: 1939's *The Wizard of Oz*, based on L. Frank Baum's 1900 novel. Although the film is not typically discussed as a Steampunk fantasy, the technical "wizardry" of Oz—mistaken as magic—helps to highlight the rule of disenchantment that is central to the genre's ideology and the keen interplay between illusion and presumed (scientific) reality.

As most readers will recall in the film, Dorothy and her friends are granted a special meeting with the "wonderful Wizard of Oz," a powerful magician and "Supreme Ruler" who helps her return home to Kansas and provides her nonhuman companions with courage, a heart, and brains, respectively. Oz appears to them as an enormous green head floating in billows of smoke and framed by periodic columns of fire. "I am Oz, the great and powerful!" thunders the wizard; "Who are you?"[35] Dorothy and her friends introduce themselves and make their requests, whereupon the Wizard asks them to return with the broom of the Wicked Witch of the West (in the novel, however, he demands that they kill the witch).

The four succeed and return to the Emerald City for another meeting with the Wizard, which is now depicted in one of the most memorable scenes in narrative cinema: while the ominous talking head attempts to scare the adventurers off, telling them to "come back tomorrow!," Dorothy's dog Toto starts to pull back the velvet curtain in a corner of the hall. "Pay no attention to that man behind the curtain," booms the head of Oz. Then, behind an enclosure, Dorothy pulls back the divide to reveal a portly gentleman operating a twelve-foot machine with various dials, knobs, and switches, which apparently operates an *illusion* of the Wizard as the floating green head amid fire and smoke. The man—dressed in a suit replete with a string tie that signals professional decorum and class affiliation—confesses that he is, indeed, the Wizard of Oz. The Scarecrow calls the man a "humbug" or hoaxer to which the man assents, perhaps in reference to his previous profession as an itinerant illusionist (the original film, however, never clarifies this now assumed reference). Yet the moral power and masculine public comportment central to Steampunk ideology only comes in response to Dorothy's assertion: "Oh, you're a very bad man!" He responds in contrasting humility: "Oh, no my dear. I'm a very good man. I'm just a very bad wizard." The Scarecrow angrily reminds the man of his promises, who responds by arguing that he, the Tin Man, and the Lion already have the qualities that they were seeking. The gentleman, not coincidentally, explains to the Scarecrow that any creature with autonomy has a brain, and that the knowledge and wisdom he had been seeking—such as that taught by "universities, seats of great learning"—were already his. Having wisdom, heart, and courage is discerned by what one *does* and requires no magic. Insofar as magic *is* employed, its Faustian temptation is often too much to resist (as the wicked witches originally outnumbered the good one).

Although the land of Oz features supernatural magic in many ways, the moral righteousness of the *Wizard*—a human—is located in his technical ingenuity and honest heart, skillfully hidden behind a necessary cloak of illusion; witchery or female magic is no match for his (white, male) genius and sense of moral purpose. This frequent contest between magic and technological savvy in Steampunk cinema is amplified more strongly in Disney's moderately successful yet widely panned 2013 "prequel," *Oz the Great and Powerful*, directed by Sam Raimi. In this backstory to the original *Wizard of Oz* film (which is also derived somewhat liberally from Baum's many Oz books), the traveling magician Oscar Diggs escapes an attack from an angry circus strongman in a hot air balloon, only to be caught up in a tornado that whisks him away to the Land of Oz. Oz is ruled by a pair of sister witches who, it is eventually revealed, are evil, and Diggs is mistaken for a great wizard who, prophecy asserts, will come and restore peace and harmony to the land. Motivated by the promise of riches (and implicitly sex), Diggs pretends that he is a masterful practitioner of preternatural feats, until he is finally forced to admit to Glinda the Good Witch (sister to the wicked witches) that he is—in fact—not a wizard. Although she nevertheless believes that he can help the denizens of Oz and provides him with an army to defeat the reign of evil, Diggs insists that the wicked sisters' magic is too powerful for him to overcome and secretly schemes to give everyone the slip. While tucking a companion into bed at her request, China Girl asks if he can grant wishes, as the previous wizard—and father to the sisters, wicked and good—had done. "I'm sorry, I can't grant wishes," says Diggs. "I'm not that kind of wizard." At this very moment, however, the protagonist begins to realize his prowess—and assumes the moral sensibility of a man of technical ingenuity and righteous comportment in the public sphere:

> DIGGS: Uhm, you see, where I come from, there aren't any real wizards. Although, there is one: Thomas Alva Edison, the Wizard of Menlo Park. A truly great man.
> CHINA GIRL: Did he grant wishes?
> DIGGS: No. But he could look into the future and make it real. He created the electric light, the phonograph, he created a camera that could take moving pictures.
> CHINA GIRL: Pictures that move?
> DIGGS: Yeah, can you imagine? And all he had was a little bit of wire and some glass. With almost nothing, he made the impossible real.
> CHINA GIRL: Is that the kind of wizard you are?
> DIGGS: It's the kind of wizard I'd like to be.
> CHINA GIRL: Well, you are that kind, I can tell. I'd rather you grant wishes, but, that's a good wizard too. Good night Wizard.[36]

Notwithstanding the screenwriters' glaring ignorance of the history of Hollywood and Edison's ruthless stranglehold on the burgeoning film industry, the evocation of Edisonian wizardry at this point in the diegesis signals the triumph of technological ingenuity, and by extension masculine self-madeness, over magic.[37] With the help of Glinda and a host of engineers or "tinkers," Diggs fabricates an elaborate, fireworks-driven phantasmagoria in the castle square—the original version of the floating head of a wizard in smoke—which ultimately leads to the triumph of good over evil by the film's end. Diggs becomes Oz's Supreme Ruler, not by magic but through technological mastery and the superiority of human ingenuity.

Of course, the rule of disenchantment in the Disney prequel is followed primarily for the spectator and, secondarily, only for select characters in the diegesis. Diggs must maintain the "illusion" of magical power to banish wickedness, safeguard his rule in the Land of Oz, and prolong an optimistic futurity. In one sense, then, the plotting of deliberate deceit breaks with the moral vision of disenchantment. But in another, it continues what Benjamin has characterized as the "phony spell of personality," otherwise known as the star system: like the Wizard of Oz, Thomas Edison is *wonderful*. Inasmuch as technical reproducibility and ingenuity erode the cult and exhibition value of objects of human labor, thereby making them accessible to many, the mechanisms of that erosion—machinery, for example—lend themselves to the secular magic of *fetishism*. The rule of disenchantment in Steampunk, then, occurs in the service of what Adorno termed a "fetishistic attitude" that recalls to memory "early feelings of omnipotence."[38] Such an attitude, coupled with popular audiences' willful exposure to the fantastic, is, of course, why Wells's and Verne's early romance fiction could make them a living. However much we continue to debate what Steampunk might be, or what forms of popular entertainment are included under its banner, there is no denying that Steampunk is, in the end, a Fetish Machine. In this peculiar sense, the genre is a way to banish your magic and eat it too.

Concluding Remarks: Steampunk as Artful Deception

Although Steampunk's cultural expressions span from comics and novels to role playing and music-centered festivals, we have drawn many of our examples of its ideology of Victorian masculinity from film, because—as Benjamin observed more than seventy-five years ago—filmmaking as an industry represents so neatly the technician-hero and the dialectic of (dis) enchantment at its very core. Outside of the story world, the illusions created by the Wizard of Oz through his technological expertise compose a not-so-subtle commentary on the making of films themselves. The cinema is a Fetish Machine par excellence, generating an experience that we know is the product of a complex, technically administered mode of production that still has the power to enchant us and make "the impossible" real. In the world of popular entertainment, this dialectic of (dis)enchantment can be described as a form of "artful deception," however scientistic its style. This deception was made famous in America by the "Prince of Humbug" himself, Phineas Taylor Barnum: we know that the object of our fascination—a film, a magic trick, a mermaid, a steam-powered elephant—may not be authentic, but we willfully wonder nevertheless.[39]

Such is the "moral" of Martin Scorsese's Steampunk masterpiece *Hugo* (2011), which tells the story of a clockmaker's orphan who makes it his early life's mission to repair a writing automaton that was originally fashioned by none other than film pioneer Georges Méliès. Through the vehicle of a boy's quest, Scorsese crafts a dazzling send-up of the craft of filmmaking as a form of artful deception that is nevertheless based on profound technological ingenuity, moral conviction, and (white) masculine resolve. Because of the boy's technical gifts, Méliès rediscovers his love of the *mechanics* of filmmaking and has, by the story's end, his stature as a pioneering inventor recognized by the sustained applause of upper-class Parisian elites. Of all the different manifestations of Steampunk technician-heroes, then, we might say that it is the "cult of personality" surrounding the filmmaker that embodies the ideology of Victorian masculinity most fully today. Like most celebrated public filmmakers of our time—most of whom are men—Martin Scorsese *is* simultaneously heralded as an engineer, explorer, inventor, learned professor, and scientist through the genius of his craft.

Regardless of the parallels that we might discern between the ideology underwriting the Steampunk protagonist and the "real world" filmmaking wizard, Steampunk practitioners and scholars would likely have us return to the default technician-hero, Captain Nemo,[40] the mysterious genius-engineer and commander of the *Nautilus* in Jules Verne's masterpiece, *Twenty Thousand Leagues under the Sea* (1870), and its companion, *The Mysterious Island* (1874).[41] In fact, Maertens considers Nemo to be the "best example of . . . a technician-hero."[42] Exiled from a world overrun by imperialist hubris, he builds a marvelous submarine of unmatched technical prowess and ingenuity and escapes with his crew to the depths of the sea, where they pursue their own antediluvian utopia. He is, however, a man that straddles the "liminal zone of brilliant inventor and misanthropic madman."[43] He is caring and protective of his crew, assists anti-imperialist revolutionary fighters, saves divers from accidents, and rescues castaways from death. Although the relationship between Nemo and his crew is predicated on a kinder, gentler version of the Victorian class system, he manages to fashion a new society sustained by genuine regard for his fellow man. At the same time, however, he continuously violates maritime and international law by sinking warships and killing those who place his scientific secrets and idealized world in peril. Nevertheless, it is Nemo's brilliance as an engineer, helping him create a new techno-utopian world, and as a hero, helping him rid the world of oppression (whether or not his actions are ultimately morally defensible), that continues to attract the culture of Steampunk to this individual. And who does not absolutely look dashing in a navy peacoat and captain's white hat? Like that of the visionary filmmaker, Nemo's philosophical stance—a kind of techno-heroism as reservoir of emancipatory potential—is best summarized by Nemo's last words in the 1954 cinematic adaptation by Walt Disney Pictures.[44] Fleeing from enemy forces, the *Nautilus* hits a reef, begins to flood, and ultimately sinks after several violent explosions. As the submarine disappears beneath the waves, Nemo says to his guest, Professor Pierre M. Aronnax, these immortal final words: "*But there is hope for the future. When the world is ready for a new and better life, all this will someday come to pass, in God's good time*" (our emphasis).

Notes

The final writing of our chapter took place near Fort Snelling, across from Minneapolis–Saint Paul International Airport. According to an enduring legend, a "daredevil young German nobleman," in his official capacity as a foreign military attaché, visited the fort about 1863 and observed the use of a captive hot air balloon. The Union Army had been experimenting during the Civil War with balloons as military observation posts. The German took a short flight in one such balloon, ascending to several hundred feet above the fort, and immediately became fascinated with the practical possibilities of lighter-than-air vehicles. Nearly forty years later, this soon-to-be technician-hero—Count Ferdinand von Zeppelin—built his first eponymous rigid airship: an awe-inspiring vehicle that continues to play a key iconographical role in the popular imaginary of Steampunk. For a fascinating and critical account of this event, see Rhoda R. Gilman, "Zeppelin in Minnesota: A Study in Fact and Fable," *Minnesota History* 39 (Fall 1965): 278–285.

1. Wave-Gothic-Treffen, at http://www.wave-gotik-treffen.de/english/.

2. We take the term "technician-hero" from James Warren Maertens, "Promethean Desires: The Technician-Hero and Myths of Masculinity in Nineteenth-Century Literature," 2 vols. (PhD diss., University of Minnesota, 1993). We would like to thank Maertens for providing us with a copy of his dissertation. Although Maertens's term is very helpful for articulating our interest in the figure of the Steampunk genius-adventurer, his psychoanalytically influenced study is largely concerned with a different focus: namely, how such a hero is a "psychotic and paranoid subject, radically fragmented and unable to deal with its ultimate inability to achieve omnipotence" (abstract).

3. For a synopsis of fashion styles in Steampunk (such as the "tinker" and the "explorer"), see Libby Bulloff's "Steampunk Fashion: Four Styles" in *The Steampunk Bible: An Illustrated Guide to the World of Imaginary Airships, Corsets and Goggles, Mad Scientists, and Strange Literature*, ed. Jeff VanderMeer and S. J. Chambers (New York: Harry N. Abrams, 2011), 138–141; and—the rather amusing—Calista Taylor, *Steampunk Your Wardrobe: Easy Projects to Add Victorian Flair to Everyday Fashions* (East Petersburg, Pa.: Design Originals, 2012).

4. Dru Pagliassotti, "Does Steampunk Have an Ideology?," *The Mark of Ashen Wings*, February 13, 2009. At http://drupagliasotti.com/2009/02/13/does-steampunk-have-an-ideology/.

5. Due to space limitations, we do not attempt to provide a comprehensive historical survey of this genre. For historical definitions, origins, and perspectives on Steampunk, see VanderMeer and Chambers, *The Steampunk Bible*; and Julie Anne Taddeo and Cynthia J. Miller, eds., *Steaming into a Victorian Future: A Steampunk Anthology* (Lanham, Md.: Scarecrow Press, 2013). Unfortunately, the anthology became readily available only after the completion of our chapter.

6. See, for example, Pagliassotti, "Does Steampunk Have an Ideology?"; and Professor Calamity, "SteamPunk: Colonizing the Past So We Can Dream the Future," *LiveJournal*, November 27, 2004. At http://prof-calamity.livejournal.com/277.html.

7. VanderMeer and Chambers, *The Steampunk Bible*, 9.

8. For a concise overview of Benjamin's historical materialist project, see Michael Löwy, *Fire Alarm: Reading Walter Benjamin's "On the Concept of History"* (New York: Verso, 2006).

9. Pagliassotti, "Does Steampunk Have an Ideology?"

10. German critics Max Horkheimer and Theodor W. Adorno recognized that—notwithstanding some powerfully persistent social inequalities—there existed enough material wealth and progressive political freedoms to care for everyday people in the twentieth century. See Theodor Adorno and Max Horkheimer, *Towards a New Manifesto*, trans. Rodney Livingstone (New York: Verso, 2011).

11. Rebecca Onion, "Reclaiming the Machine: An Introductory Look at Steampunk in Everyday Practice," *Neo-Victorian Studies* 1, no. 1 (Autumn 2008): 139.

12. VanderMeer and Chambers, *The Steampunk Bible*, 11.

13. For studies on these technological advances and others, see Quentin R. Skrabec, *The Metallurgic Age: The Victorian Flowering of Invention and Industrial Science* (Jefferson, N.C.: McFarland, 2006); and Herbert L. Sussman, *Victorian Technology: Invention, Innovation, and the Rise of the Machine* (Boston: Praeger, 2009).

14. Arthur B. Evans, "The Vehicular Utopias of Jules Verne," in *Transformations of Utopia: Changing Views of the Perfect Society*, ed. George Shusser et al. (New York: AMS Press, 1999), 99–108. For Evans, these vehicles offer the utopian fantasy of unlimited mobility that could explore and colonize—in comfort and autonomy—a new world of possibilities.

15. See Jürgen Habermas, *The Structural Transformation of the Public Sphere: An Inquiry into a Category of Bourgeois Society*, trans. Thomas Burger (Cambridge: MIT Press, 1989).

16. For influential studies on Victorian masculinity, see Robin Gilmour, *The Idea of the Gentleman in the Victorian Novel* (Boston: Allen & Unwin, 1981); Herbert L. Sussman, *Victorian Masculinities: Manhood and Masculine Poetics in Early Victorian Literature and Art* (Cambridge: Cambridge University Press, 1995); and John Tosh, *A Man's Place: Masculinity and the Middle-Class Home in Victorian England* (New Haven: Yale University Press, 1999). Although groundbreaking work on the "suppressed history of masculinities" that departed from cultural expectations, such as male-to-male intimacy, exists, these investigations are not the purview of our study. See, for example James Eli Adams, *Dandies and Desert Saints: Styles of Victorian Masculinity* (Ithaca: Cornell University Press, 1995).

17. See esp. Adams, *Dandies and Desert Saints*, as a kind of foundational text.

18. Ibid., 25.

19. For a thoughtful reflection on queer readings of recent Steampunk literary fiction, see Lisa Hager, "Queer Cogs: Steampunk, Gender Identity, and Sexuality," Tor.com, October 4, 2012. At http://www.tor.com/blogs/2012/10/steampunk-gender-sexuality.

20. Maertens, "Promethean Desires," 4.

21. We will save the various online iterations of a Steampunk Abraham Lincoln—with advanced steam-powered weaponry and an exoskeleton—for another project. See the comic series *Steampunk Lincoln* by Brandon Herren and Chris Paugh, published by Psychotronik Comics, at http://steampunklincoln.webstarts.com/index.html.

22. Walter Benjamin, "Theories of German Fascism," in *Selected Writings*, ed. Michael W. Jennings and Howard Eiland et al., trans. Edmund Jephcott and Rodney Livingstone et al., 4 vols. (Cambridge: Belknap Press of Harvard University Press, 1996–2003), 2:321

23. Graeme Gilloch, *Walter Benjamin: Critical Constellations* (Cambridge: Polity Press, 2002), 2.

24. Theodor W. Adorno, "Transparencies on Film," in *The Culture Industry: Selected Essays on Mass Culture*, ed. J. M. Bernstein (New York: Routledge, 1991), 159.

25. Pagliassotti, "Does Steampunk Have an Ideology?"

26. There are, of course, a number of films in the Steampunk genre that are made in other countries like China (*Detective Dee and the Mystery of the Phantom Flame* and *Thai Chi Zero*), Japan (*Howl's Moving Castle* and *Steamboy*), and the United States (*Wild Wild West*). We only suggest that the Victorian aesthetic—from which the genre arose—tends to foreground *UK* productions in the popular imaginary.

27. It is for this reason that we suspect that Gilliam is (notably) absent from VanderMeer and Chambers, *The Steampunk Bible*.

28. We take this term from Adorno. See Theodor W. Adorno, *The Stars Down to Earth and Other Essays on the Irrational in Culture*, ed. Stephen Crook (New York: Routledge, 1994), 73–74.

29. We discuss the magical, fetishistic quality of the gadget at length elsewhere. See Joshua Gunn and Mirko M. Hall, "Stick It in Your Ear: The Psychodynamics of iPod Enjoyment," *Communication and Critical/Cultural Studies* 5 (2008): 135–157.

30. VanderMeer and Chambers, *The Steampunk Bible*, 30–33.

31. Verne quoted in ibid., 30.

32. Walter Benjamin, "The Work of Art in the Age of Its Technological Reproducibility: Second Version," in *Selected Writings*, 3:101–133.

33. Ibid., 116.

34. There is an interesting tangent on this theme that is worth mentioning: Blackwood is a member of an occult order loosely modeled on the Freemasons, underscoring a frequent critique of secrecy in Steampunk fantasy and a corollary to the critique of magic.

35. *The Wizard of Oz*, dir. Victor Fleming, Metro-Goldwyn-Mayer Pictures, 1939.

36. *Oz the Great and Powerful*, dir. Sam Raimi, Walt Disney Pictures, 2013.

37. In this respect, *Oz the Great and Powerful* also reflects the American dime novel genre of the Edisonade, an important precursor to Steampunk. See VanderMeer and Chambers, *Steampunk Bible*, 41–45. Moreover, if the original *Wizard of Oz* is not properly Steampunk, then this Edison-centric prequel certainly makes it so.

38. Adorno, *The Stars Down to Earth*, 74.

39. See James W. Cook, *The Arts of Deception: Playing with Fraud in the Age of Barnum* (Cambridge: Harvard University Press, 2001).

40. Nemo's true identity as the lost Prince Dakkar from the central Indian region of Bundelkhand must not be overlooked—and this surely serves as a pretext for his deep antagonism to imperialism. Historically, however, he has been portrayed as a white male in popular cinema by actors such as Michael Caine, James Mason, and Patrick Stewart. Although a postcolonial analysis of this phenomenon is not the aim of our essay, we believe that Anglo-European Steampunk enthusiasts "may assume an aristocratic or gentry character and costume without advocating for imperialism." Alferian Gwydion MacLir [James Warren Maertens], "Steampunk at ConVergence Part Two: 'The Steam Panels,'" *The Weekly Owl: Druidery, Masonry, and the Magical Life*, July 2, 2011. At http://weeklyowl.com/2011/07/02/steampunk-at-convergence-part-two-the-steam-panels/.

41. See Pagliassotti, "Does Steampunk Have an Ideology?"; Mike Perschon, "Finding Nemo: Verne's Antihero as Original Steampunk," *Verniana: Jules Verne Studies* (February 1, 2010): 179–182; and VanderMeer and Chambers, *The Steampunk Bible*, 18–45.

42. Alferian Gwydion MacLir [James Warren Maertens], "Steampunk and Its Relation to History," *The Weekly Owl: Druidery, Masonry, and the Magical Life*, July 13, 2011. At http://weeklyowl.com/2011/07/13/steampunk-and-its-relation-to-history/.

43. Perschon, "Finding Nemo," 184.

44. *20,000 Leagues Under the Sea*, dir. Richard Fleischer, Walt Disney Productions, 1954.

Victorians, Machines, and Exotic Others

Steampunk and the Aesthetic of Empire

KRISTIN STIMPSON

⚙

HOUSED UNDER THE CATEGORY "NOT REMOTELY STEAMPUNK" ON THE HU-morous website Regretsy (a spinoff of Etsy) sits the defamed "Steampunk 'Compass Cyborg' Altered Art Plush Teddy Bear" still available for purchase for only twelve dollars. Borrowing many of the stylistic signifiers of steampunk's subculture, the bear is "decorated with a working compass cyborg eye with a brass gear, brass and black chain on his arm, connected to silver and brass gears on his chest."[1] Below the shamed "steampunk" teddy bear are eighty-one comments highlighting the laughability of this steampunk imposter, and with a whole category dedicated to "things that aren't steampunk" on the Regretsy site, it appears that steampunk wannabes have infiltrated Etsy's community of do-it-yourself artisans, sparking a protective and defensive response from doorkeepers, resulting in a struggle over style.

Etsy is not the only place one can find steampunk derivatives. From steampunk-themed restaurants and bars, to references in film, to Halloween costumes available for purchase online, there's no question, steampunk has gone mainstream. In an editorial from *SteamPunk Magazine*, Dylan Fox laments the growing trend:

> At the moment, the path of least resistance for Steampunk is for it to become an aesthetic: A meme devoid of meaning. It's a path that leads to buying Steampunk Halloween outfits in Wal*Mart and Tesco in five years time, and yet another song about Victoria's glorious Empire conquering Mars playing on MTV. Individuality in steampunk is paramount. We're not insisting everyone obey our "vision" of Steampunk, but if I ever see anyone in a "sexy clockwork automaton" costume they picked up off a supermarket shelf I'm going to beat them to death with their plastic cog mini-skirt.[2]

19

In a largely anticommercial subculture, the commercialization of steampunk has inevitably taken hold. Justin Bieber borrowed the steampunk aesthetic in his 2011 music video "Santa Claus Is Coming to Town," and that same year Macy's holiday windows featured the neo-Victorian steampunk aesthetic of cogs, wheels, gears, Victorian garb, and flying machines.[3] Although many worried that steampunk was dead after Bieber co-opted its look, its continued presence in material and popular culture demonstrates the perseverance of this growing trend. While those who identify as steampunk bemoan the encroaching appropriation and mass production of their aesthetic, I am left to wonder what the implications of its growing aesthetic appeal could be. This aesthetic is not a "meme devoid of meaning," for the aesthetic is never neutral or value free. In connecting rhetoric with aesthetics, Barry Brummett writes: "Whatever creates and manages meaning, whatever influences people, whatever results in power gained or lost through signs and symbols is ... considered to have a rhetorical dimension."[4]

Corsets, bustles, top hats, vests, goggles, and time travel accessories are just a few of the sartorial styles that come to mind when one thinks of the growing subculture known as steampunk. The aesthetic of the tinkerer, the explorer, the pioneer, the Edwardian, and the Victorian dominate steampunk imagery. Steampunk style is less about the industrial era working class and more about the upper echelons of Victorian society. The fabrics, clothing styles, accessories, constructed personas, and demeanor projected in steampunk's aesthetic all recuperate the aesthetic of nineteenth-century high society. In addition to Victorian fashions, technological innovation and visions of steam-powered locomotives, airships, and futuristic guns also figure prominently in the subculture's style. Exposed gears, oxidized metals, and antiqued machinery are contrasted with the more effete Victorian garb as a machine aesthetic represents a grimier, steamier side to steampunk's more polished fashions. The two looks are juxtaposed to form an aesthetic that reflects fantasies of pioneering the American West and exploring exoticized lands through a homology between fashion and technology. Other than a few mechanized accessories, the ruling-class fashion of steampunk and its machine aesthetic don't have much in common, yet a close rhetorical analysis will connect these seemingly disparate styles through a shared ideology of empire.

This chapter will explore how the material and visual culture of steampunk functions as an aesthetic of empire through a close analysis of steampunk styles accessed through magazines, blogs, online forums, and books. I explore the aesthetic by focusing on steampunk's stylistic elements rather than its literary canon, as the steampunk style seems to be what is most recognizable and prevalent in popular culture. Even Jeff VanderMeer concedes that "many of the people who today call themselves Steampunks have not read the literature, taking cues instead from history, visual media, and the original fashionistas who sparked the subculture in the 1990s."[5] It is essential to note that for the purposes of this essay, by "style" I mean the objects, adornments, and especially fashions of the steampunk subculture. While I am careful to limit my analysis to steampunk style itself, it must be noted that the style cannot be extrapolated from the genre's other aesthetic expressions. Steampunk literature, film, fashions, and material culture all place significant value and importance on what I am labeling as style. Thus, to speak about the rhetoric of steampunk style is to speak about its literature and films as well as its politics and ideologies. These elements are relentlessly intertwined. Rebecca Onion underscores this point, highlighting that steampunk ideology and aesthetic intersect to form a counterculture where "no matter how much it has spread through more traditionally literary/textual representations, steampunk culture is perhaps most defined by the object-based work of its fans."[6] Style is stitched into steampunk narratives, employed to portray empire and for some "a pretty way of coping with [the] truth."[7] Might steampunk's materiality, DIY ethos, and old-fashioned aesthetic reappropriate traditional symbols of power to resist and critique modern institutions? Or does its aesthetic of empire (and its inherent reference to racial politics and colonialism) ultimately reproduce the ideological power relations it claims to leave in the past? VanderMeer suggests that "many see their efforts as a way to repurpose the best of that time while correcting for the worst,"[8] a nostalgic sentiment, but what of steampunk's rhetorical work in the present? In this chapter, I argue that a closer look at the rhetoric of steampunk style reveals a complex and conflicted visual and material culture, which concomitantly resists, but ultimately reproduces, the ideology of empire.

Steampunk promotes itself as more than just a fad or fashion, but a lifestyle, a philosophy, and a politics of presentation. While this may be at its core, I focus on the steampunk aesthetic, and fashion in particular, to explore its rhetorical nature. A fashion that is growing in popularity, the symbols steampunk employs and the history those symbols evoke have rhetorical power and have attracted many to partake in its aesthetic sensibilities. Its fashions have been both hotly debated and uncritically adopted, but to what effect? In this chapter, I hope to examine the rhetorical work that takes place in recalling the style of a different era—a time when the romance of discovery, adventure, and craftsmanship collide with conquests, violence, and empire.

This chapter proceeds in three sections. First, I describe the ways in which empire is already an inherent facet of steampunk subculture. Second, I argue that style is the grounds on which empire is expressed and explore three styles prevalent in steampunk. And finally, I conclude with a discussion of steampunk's rhetorical influence and suggest that its fashion warrants more thoughtful critique. To begin this analysis, we must begin with empire, the dominant aesthetic of steampunk.

The Steampunk Empire

The connection between steampunk and empire is an explicit part of the steampunk aesthetic. Some suggest that the symbolic references to empire help combat and critique a dark past, while others contend that it reproduces and even celebrates a history of conquest and colonialism. Whichever side one stands on in the debate, there is no question, steampunk "explicitly remakes the Victorian but rarely imagines a new version of the nineteenth century without empire in it."[9] Empire is central to the steampunk aesthetic and sometimes unapologetically so. The editorial in the steampunk zine *Gatehouse Gazette*'s final issue is worth quoting at length:

> Neo-Victorianism isn't imperialist revival but does recreate the style and storytelling of an era in which England ruled a quarter of the world's population. The romance of empire has been part of the steampunk ethos for more than a decade. Whether it's imperialist adventure in the colonies or megalomania in old Blighty, the empire is always there, prominently or lurking in the shadows, when you're entering the nineteenth century.
>
> Rather than trying to hide it because we're anti-colonialists now, let's be honest and upfront about the fact that we admire the pomp and spirit of the globetrotting Victorians. Once we identify what we like, we can confidently either discuss or ignore what we don't. The Victorians perpetrated a lot of wrongs after all but it's ridiculous to pretend that steampunk wants nothing to do with empire because of it.[10]

Not necessarily characteristic of steampunk discourse, but an element of steampunk style, this sentiment is described by Diana Pho as an unabashedly nostalgic view of steampunk's pro-imperialist attitudes.[11]

Many in the steampunk community put a positive valence on its neo-Victorian aesthetic, claiming that steampunk revises history to account for the offences of the Victorian era. In some cases, the steampunk subculture claims to redress historic wrongdoings, while in other cases, proponents claim that steampunk addresses current issues inherited from an imperial and colonial past in order to change the present. Ekaterina Sedia sees steampunk as a noble pursuit, arguing that it works to "confront an uneasy past with its history of oppression and science that serves to promote dominance, where women are chattel and where other races are deemed subhuman and therefore fit to exploit, where we can take all things because we feel like it, where the code of moral conduct does not apply to treatment of lower classes."[12] She locates this political ambition in the "punk element" of the genre, citing its "examining and interrogation of the past, the search for alternative turns, imagining what would happen if technology were used to uplift rather than oppress." Sedia goes on to argue that "by reimagining how things could've gone, we can hold up a mirror to our present, and by extension our future."[13]

Jeannette Atkinson shares a similar view: "Revisioning history is a fundamental aspect of steampunk. Steampunks are not interested in acting out the Victorian age, with its colonial aspirations and lack of equality, but in recreating aspects of it and reinventing or reimagining others."[14] Cynthia Miller and Julie Anne Taddeo echo this sentiment in the introduction to their steampunk anthology and suggest that "steampunk reflects the possibilities for subversion; it is not mere nostalgia for corsets or fantasies of goggles and dirigibles, but another lens through which to examine the racial, class, and gender politics of both the past and present." They go on to add: "We look to the Victorians—so familiar yet strange—not necessarily to escape the mundane of the present or romanticize the past, but to understand and negotiate contemporary problems."[15] VanderMeer concurs, "more than just an aesthetic movement, Steampunk focuses on the Victorian era not only because of its aesthetic and technology, but because it recognizes within that epoch issues similar to those facing society in the twenty-first century."[16] Still others suggest that steampunk invites participants to "safely and triumphantly play with and transgress [nineteenth-century] boundaries,"[17] creates dialogue and "open[s] up communicative possibilities,"[18] is socially aware, and "has always been conscious of the nineteenth century's less inspiring moments."[19] Scott Westerfeld bids his readers to think of steampunk as an interruption to the social mores of the Victorian era and likens it to "bringing a flamethrower to a tea party." For Westerfeld, steampunk stories "expand the role of the colonized and otherwise subjugated in that era."[20]

While acknowledging the element of empire in steampunk's machine aesthetic, Gail Ashurst and Anna Powell see the possibility to combat steampunk's problematic ideological and political implications and offer: "The broad political spectrum of Steampunk includes imperialist nostalgia; however, a self-reflexive irony often questions the neo-conservative potential of this position."[21] Suzanne Barber and Matt Hale praise the critical possibilities of steampunk in their study of a theatrical panel at a steampunk convention and write,

> many steampunks confront the complex issues that were part and parcel of the historical time frame from which they construct their alternate worlds (the maltreatment and murder of the native princess motif, for instance). Within these counterfactual play frames, such concerns become centers of gravity for critical discourse. By recentering the nineteenth century within a twenty-first century context, the steampunks are able to confront issues relating to gender inequality, colonization and human/object relations, and so on.[22]

In another example, Jay Strongman, author of *Steampunk: The Art of Victorian Futurism*, briefly breaks from romanticizing the steampunk aesthetic and referential historicity to suggest that, "while some find the days of Empire fascinating and accept colonialism and imperialism as facts of life and just the way things were at the time, others are determined to challenge these past assumptions. The thinking is that by confronting the transgressions of the past, we can learn how to change the politics and socio-economics of the present."[23] Strongman does little to offer how exactly past transgressions are confronted, but he highlights the contemporary anxieties of capitalism and consumerism that steampunk's DIY ethos resists. However, as Pho points out, "the occupation of an anticonsumerist stance is not necessarily a politically progressive position. . . . Left-wing makers, anarchists, and nostalgically imperialist steampunks alike all claim the DIY, anticommercial ethos as part of their political philosophy."[24]

Critical readings of the steampunk subculture are starting to emerge as scholars and steampunk practitioners alike have started to question the subculture's unreflexive, even celebratory portrayal of empire. In her analysis of neo-Victorianism and steampunk, Elizabeth Ho explores the ways in which steampunk offers itself *as* memory. While Ho allows that steampunk may have progressive political potential, she also questions "the visual vocabulary of imperialism that dominates steampunk texts and culture . . . and a certain position toward the Victorian that leaves in place orientalist structures and understandings of 'The East.'"[25] Ho ultimately calls for an "aesthetic that consists of an ethics of appropriation."[26]

Calling steampunk "an uncanny reflection of the West's conflicted legacies of Empire," Marie-Luise Kohlke and Christian Gutleben share a view that "steampunk, including its subcultures and fashion, seems to revel stylistically, even nostalgically in imperial aesthetics from Victorian pith helmets to elaborate weaponry evidently intended for brutal conquest."[27] Sally-Anne Huxtable argues that steampunk as social critique exists, but laments that what actually is consumed by the mainstream is often reduced to nostalgia, escapism, and role playing.[28] This attitude is shared by others who mourn the loss of steampunk's supposed contrarian and subversive political roots. Today, people claim to live a steampunk lifestyle or philosophy, but those who occupy this identity come from the full spectrum of political ideologies; that is to say, a cohesive politics of steampunk simply doesn't exist.[29] With that said, a cohesive steampunk style and aesthetic is more easily identifiable and always already infused with meaning. Ferguson agrees that steampunk's "participants vary widely in their motivations, ideological identifications, and levels of involvement. . . . [P]erhaps the only definitive trait shared by most steampunks seems to be an aesthetic one."[30] Much of what I have discussed so far comes from analyses of steampunk literature, but examining steampunk's style and aesthetic (arguably its most recognizable, popular, and mainstream features) may give us more insight into its rhetorical effects.

Steampunk's Different Engine of Empire

When we think about empire, fashion and technology may not always come to mind, but when we think about steampunk, the idea of empire is ever present. Books like *Rise of the Steampunk Empire, Gears of Empire: A Steampunk Survival Guide,* and *Stars of Empire: A Scientific Romance Set during the Victorian Conquest of Space* are few among many in the steampunk genre that evoke empire, but it isn't only the literary realm where empire is employed. The technologies of steam-powered guns and trains that forged Victorian-era imperialism are complemented by the styles of the colonizer's pith helmet or the capitalist's top hat, monocle, and timepiece. In a combination of its system of aesthetics and style, steampunk, it would seem, is fueled by a different engine of empire. How can steampunk's aesthetic be an engine of empire? To begin to answer this question, I first connect steampunk to a rhetoric of style. Following this, I identify three stylistic modes that are predominant in steampunk culture: the aesthete, machine aesthetics, and exotic aesthetics. Neither a comprehensive list nor mutually exclusive, these stylistic modes overlap in significant ways throughout steampunk fashion, material culture, and aesthetics. In his book *The Rhetoric of Empire: Colonial Discourse in Journalism, Travel Writing, and Imperial Administration*, David Spurr identifies twelve rhetorical modes for writing about non-Western peoples and argues that these modes help maintain colonial authority. His modes, easily translated to other forms of representation (e.g., fashion and aesthetics), offer a helpful tool for analyzing the influential role of steampunk style. Using Spurr's categories of the rhetoric of empire, these examples will show that, while different, when combined these styles form a system of signs and meanings that ultimately reflects a selective version of history and reproduces the ideology of empire.

Steampunk and the Rhetoric of Style

As already mentioned, steampunk's style is readily identifiable. Cogs, gears, pistons, Victorian-era aesthetics, and references to technology are plentiful. Brummett describes style as "a complex system of actions, objects, and behaviors that announce who we are, who we want to be, and who we want to be considered akin to. It is therefore also a system of communication with rhetorical influence on others. And as such, style is a means by which power and advantage are negotiated, distributed, and struggled over in society."[31] Generally speaking, style is the way in which we do something.[32] As such, steampunk style involves how people dress, decorate, craft, move, speak, and more generally aestheticize experience. A range of texts in the form of fiction, film, artwork, functional pieces, clothing, accessories, and adornments speak to steampunk's style.

Style is rhetorical—it works like a language and can be read—and it is influential. Important to the purposes of this study, "[s]tyle's aesthetic organizes such value-laden dimensions of the social as gender and sexual identity, class, time, and space."[33] Additionally, style "is not neutral. . . . Style organizes the social and does so by also expressing values and judgments about people and groups," and this creates rhetorical effects.[34]

Not only does style express values, it is also a site of identification and struggle. Struggle over the meanings of style is certainly a part of debates in the steampunk community.[35] Claims about what constitutes authentic steampunk style and the meanings associated with steampunk's Victorian imagery are often the topic of conversation on steampunk discussion boards and blogs. As the meanings of steampunk style are struggled over, it too is politicized, as "control over meaning is control over politics."[36] With steampunk, a style of the empowered classes is juxtaposed with the appropriation and exoticization of Others, and not without consequence. Style is diffuse with political implications,[37] and "invocations of the nineteenth century in British and American macro-media are rarely accepted as ideologically unaffiliated."[38] Pho asserts, "steampunk, because it deals with the dynamics of history and its alternatives, can never, ever be considered apolitical." She goes on to state: "Even something that seems frivolous like fashion has political ramifications."[39] To analyze the rhetorical work of steampunk style, I first turn to one of its most identifiable stylistic modes: a particular style I refer to as steampunk's aesthete.

STEAMPUNK'S AESTHETE

Probably the most recognizable and often-used, the first category of steampunk style, the aesthete, dons the garb of the ruling-class Victorian. In terms of fashion, top hats, fasteners, and derby hats decorate heads, while vests and corsets dress the aesthete's body. Petticoats, long-tailed overcoats, waxed mustaches, and the aura of a dandy gentlemen and demure lady accompany this look. The richness of this look is attributable to the lavishness of the materials; bold colors, metallics, velvet, and baroque and jacquard fabrics feature in both the clothing and interior designs. The look of the aesthete evokes the image of the capitalist, a colonizer in his own right, and his corresponding interest in "economic mastery over the world."[40] Falling under Spurr's category of aestheticization, the style of the aesthete seems to revel in this mode of colonial discourse. As the classical Victorian era is aestheticized in such a way, fantasy is invoked and history is displaced by story, creating a distance between the costumed community and the reality it represents. The rhetorical effects of this move keep the aesthete "at a safe remove from reality" while stimulating pleasure in a past that wasn't so pleasant for all.[41] Empire is buried under the costumes of the steampunk aesthete but is still there nonetheless.

Typical of the look, "the Victorianness of steampunk usually involves the incorporation of stylized Victorian era objects or costumes."[42] The Victorian curio cabinet, an expression of fascination with nature and a mode for controlling it, is reflected in steampunk artworks, and jewelry pieces fashioned as scarabs, wings, octopuses, and feathers decorate many of these pieces. The look of the aesthete is also about individuality and customization, harking back to a time when clothing for the highest classes was not made in factories or available off the rack but was custom made, expressing the wearer's individualism and status. In the world of steampunk, everything from clothing to lamps to laptops can (and, as is often remarked, *should*) be aestheticized and customized.

The stylistic mode of the aesthete may be said to reflect what Strongman calls a "yearning for an age of elegance and politeness," which he suggests is missing from contemporary society.[43] This feature of the aesthete might be likened to Spurr's category of affirmation, where a rhetoric of empire is evoked through self-idealization and where demonstrations of moral superiority prevail. Spurr writes: "This rhetoric is deployed on behalf of a collective subjectivity which idealizes itself variously in the name of civilization, humanity, science, progress, etc., so that the repeated affirmation of such values becomes in itself a means of gaining power and mastery."[44] Steampunk's role in the colonial discourse of self-idealization and affirmation is articulated by Strongman, who writes,

> the grandeur of the British Empire and its military might is another part of the steampunk equation. The biggest Empire in human history and the colonial apparatus that maintained its global might holds a deep fascination for a large swathe of the movement. And there's something about the idea of a tiny island nation exporting its language and customs to the far-flung corners of the world that fires the imagination.[45]

Often characterized by an aristocratic nostalgia, the combination of moral goodness and material wealth are central to the category of affirmation in the discourse of empire.[46] The look of the aesthete not only evokes this attitude through its aesthetic, but reflects it as well.

In the aesthetic conjured by those describing this stylistic mode, a certain romanticism is evoked. Strongman describes a world of steampunk that "encompasses the romance of flickering glass lamps, foggy streets bustling with horsedrawn [hansom] cabs, men dressed in frock coats and top hats, women in bustles and corsets."[47] The past is reimagined as a dreamworld, creating a sense of nostalgia for a time that never was. The fantasy, too, is extended into steampunk subculture as objects are given histories; adopting an alter ego or steampunk identity is typical of the subculture. A trope of the discourse of empire, the construction of a persona and preoccupation with personal style are categorized by Spurr as a form of insubstantialization, which functions rhetorically to create a "slight ironic distance between the subject and his discourse."[48] We see this in the style of the aesthete, as personas of doctors, professors, and mad scientists abound while the aesthete speaks and dresses in a style that marks the persona he embodies. Although the style may flirt with the realm of fantasy, it is still tethered to a reality that warrants critique.

The stylistic mode of the aesthete seems to render steampunk's style complicit in a rhetoric of empire, but it isn't the only style often exhibited in this costumed culture. Next, we move to steampunk's machine aesthetic as text for analysis.

STEAMPUNK AND THE RHETORIC OF MACHINE AESTHETICS

One significant aspect of steampunk style incorporates machine aesthetics. Whether taking the form of a flying airship or the seafaring *Nautilus*, inscribed on the body of a steampunk cyborg or infused in the arts and products of steampunk's material culture, machines and technology are a major part of the steampunk aesthetic and offer another rhetorical dimension to its style. According to Barry Brummett, "[m]achines, discourse about machines, and aesthetic dimensions of machines have long been understood to contain potential rhetorical power."[49] Regardless of the era from which the machine derives, the all-powerful machine is an inherently rhetorical product creating aesthetic experiences that influence us. The rhetoric of machines can contain both intentional and unintentional dimensions, but regardless of intent it can have profound effects.[50] Brummett describes his theory of machine aesthetics as follows: "By the *rhetoric of machine aesthetics*, then, I mean the ways in which the categories and dimensions of the aesthetic experience of machines and machine-like signs might be put to use so as to influence meanings, attitudes, values, politics, and distribution of power."[51]

In his theoretical connection between aesthetics, machines, and rhetoric, Brummett lays out a number of categories that characterize machine aesthetics: dimensionality, machine as subject, machine as commodity/object, aesthetics of production, gender, persona, dominant relationship, the exotic, and motivating context.[52] Most closely linked with steampunk's technological proclivities, "mechtech" or classical machine aesthetics is best applied to this analysis. Brummett defines mechtech as "a machine aesthetic keyed to gears, clockwork, lawn mowers, revolvers, pistons, hard shiny metal, oiled hot steel, thrumming rhythms, the intricately choreographed blur of a spinning cam-shaft, and the utilitarian shafts and pipes running through the steel box of a factory." In sum, "what people think of when they think of a 'machine' grounds this aesthetic,"[53] and I would add, what people think of when they think of steampunk.

Steampunk machine aesthetics are perpetrated by the personas of the tinkerer, the inventor, the industrialist, and the aviator, to name a few. Their styles are keyed to the ideologies of progress and innovation. The steampunk scene "celebrates and performs scientific culture,"[54] "is a chance for artists to build with their hands and their imaginations, just as the great innovators of the industrial revolution did,"[55] and represents "a longing for an age in which machines were awe-inspiring steam-powered engines and magnificent clockwork mechanisms of gleaming brass, polished wood, and shining steel."[56] Technology, scientific advancements, and machinery are celebrated and aestheticized in this stylistic mode and are a prevalent aesthetic in steampunk films, books, meet-ups, and conventions.

From colorful zeppelins to the train and the *Nautilus*, machines of transportation weigh heavily in the steampunk aesthetic. For Cynthia Miller, the extraordinary transportation machines that are signatures of steampunk serve as icons of progress and symbols of frontiers old and new.[57] Brummett also makes this link, stating that the "historic alliance between machine and an ideology of progress occurs largely through the use of mechtech aesthetics as the feel and look of progress."[58]

Elements of the machine aesthetic also figure prominently in steampunk fashion. Signature brass goggles recall an industrial era, jewelry is adorned with bits of clockwork and gears, and mechanical prosthetic limbs are a common element of steampunk cosplay. The mechanized prosthetic limbs, for example, display a rhetoric of mechtech machine aesthetics whereby the machine is eroticized by "the desire to exert power by extending the body through machines."[59] Arms and legs that appear to be bionic and made of brass and steel are typical accessories in steampunk's machine aesthetic; it isn't uncommon to see a steampunk man or woman with some mechanized body part. The interplay between bodies, machines, and power connects steampunk to empire. This aspect of mechtech's machine aesthetic is also reflected in steampunk's fascination with the automaton and the steam man.

Technology also functions as an aspect of steampunk's machine aesthetic. For Atkinson, steampunk "offers a revisioning of history, one that is inspired by Victorian technology."[60] Victorians were fascinated with technology, and their aesthetic provides a visual vocabulary for steampunk's machine aesthetics today.[61] One feature of that vocabulary is the look of exposed parts, in which the technology of machinery is not hidden behind the surface but "seeks to expose mechanization and make it tangible."[62] From computers and phones to fashion accessories, steampunk's machine aesthetic often uses wood, brass, and gears to expose the technology within. An aspect of Brummett's mechtech, the revelation of the machines' internal workings is a form of dimensionality that informs the aesthetics of the tinkerer and paves a path to knowledge.[63] Rebecca Onion underscores this point, noting that "Steampunks express the sense that, when one is in the act of communing with a machine, one can access the pure pleasure of understanding. This steampunk striving for complete comprehension . . . enthusiastically echoes aspects of Victorian thought."[64]

This mechanical exposure, according to Ashurst and Powell, connects workers with the products of their labor.[65] The ultimate rhetorical effect is one of control and power.[66] In fact, Brummett's analysis of mechtech aesthetics suggests that the essence of control and order (a characteristic of mechtech's aesthetics of production) "can easily become a model of social organization," and those who revel in this aesthetic may even prefer such a world.[67] Elsewhere, Brummett argues that the dominant relationship reflected in mechtech is that of violence, for "the mechtech machine does violence in that it imposes control and mastery over an object, over nature, over people."[68] Mechtech is prevalent in steampunk's machine aesthetic, and the elements of control and violence connect it to empire in significant ways.

In another aesthetic that seems to reflect labor, some machine aesthetic styles reference the industrial era by adding a look of dust and grime to clothing. In an iconic image, Kit Stolen, one of the creators of steampunk fashion, is dressed in the Victorian era's finest apparel but also wears goggles around his neck, appears to have steel wiring wrapped around his wrist, and is putting on heavy-duty gloves; his jacket and vest are dusted with a chalky substance (as if to suggest that he has just performed hard labor).[69] This look, not uncommon in steampunk culture, is one of aestheticized (and romanticized) industry, a feature that Brummett's mechtech classifies under the motivating context of the factory.[70] While this look may serve to "re-enchant the world"[71] and "recapture the wonder and excitement" of an era gone by while also "acknowledging the grime, soot, squalor and chaos of the 'dark satanic mills' of the Industrial Revolution,"[72] the image (and its accompanying aesthetic) is mostly beautified and does little to invite us to consider the era's shadowy, less palatable history. This is not a new development unique to steampunk, however; as Brummett points out, machines in the Industrial Age were often stylized in appearance, an effect that presumably worked rhetorically to pacify workers.[73]

According to Spurr, "the aesthetic stance itself is taken from within a position of power and privilege."[74] Under Spurr's category of aestheticization in the discourse of empire, the rhetorical effect is to reproduce privilege, as the power to add an aesthetic dimension to the kind of labor indicative of the Industrial Age is a privilege that would not be granted to those actually performing the work. This kind of aestheticization is not without consequence, as "suffering evokes not pathos but an easily commodified sentimentality."[75]

Steampunk's costumes and material culture are unquestionably beautiful art, but that doesn't mean they can't have "wider effects. People enjoy the sensory experience of machines, but that enjoyment can lead to further attitudes, actions, and commitments."[76] While machines may represent the technological frontier, the geographical and cultural frontier is another element of steampunk style exhibited in the style of the exotic.

STEAMPUNK AND THE EXOTIC

The final stylistic category of steampunk evokes the exotic. Often characterized by the look of the adventurer, explorer, world traveler, and colonizer, this look might feature a blend of neutral colors or appropriate the aesthetic of some far-off land. In explaining the fashion of the steampunk explorer, Libby Bulloff encourages her readers to "think tailored garments, but more military influenced," consider "silk, linen, tall boots, pith helmets, flying goggles," and "borrow Middle Eastern and Indian flair from belly dancing fashion or take inspiration from pioneer garb."[77] In this example, Middle Eastern and Indian peoples are reduced to aesthetic objects, and "the tendency to treat certain subjects as having inherently aesthetic value has consequences."[78] The trope of exploration is not a "disinterested revealing of the world's wonders" but "a mode of thinking . . . wherein the world is radically transformed into an object of possession."[79]

The exotic look seems to serve as a form of escapism, in which steampunks function as tourists in the worlds they create.[80] As another style that seems to wax nostalgic for the days of empire, the ethos of steampunk's exotic aesthetic seems to uncritically long for the days of exploration and pioneering. Strongman enthuses: "There is also in Steampunk a nostalgic hunger for a period in recent history when much of the world, for the West, was still an unexplored, exotic mystery waiting to be discovered and space travel was just a fanciful dream."[81] Such a notion is common in the writings of steampunk and is worn on the sleeve of its exotic aesthetic. The idea of discovery, exploration, and exoticization works rhetorically to place the West at the center, while other places and peoples are Othered and turned into objects and lands to be discovered, as if their "discovery" brings them into existence. This exoticization reflects what Spurr refers to as the rhetoric of empire's trope of insubstantialization, the rhetorical implication being that non-Western worlds are transformed into enchanted lands, "as easily dissolved as they are conjured up."[82]

The nostalgia so central to steampunk's exotic aesthetic was heavily critiqued upon the publication of the "Victorientalism" issue of *Gatehouse Gazette*. The editorial from that issue reflects a sort of historical amnesia that seems to go along with this particular aesthetic: "[S]teampunk allows us to reject the chains of reality and all the racism and guilt associated with it to explore anew this imagined world of sultans and saber-rattling Islamic conquerors; harems and white slavery, samurai, dragons and dark, bustling bazaars frequented by the strangest sort of folk."[83] Even in this short section, a rhetoric of empire is present and perpetuated in contemporary culture. Rejecting the chains of reality and racism is certainly a privilege not everyone can fantasize about, evoking guilt reveals that whiteness is central to steampunk culture, and non-Western people and places are depicted as dangerous, strange, and, yes, exotic.

Pho's critique of the issue is particularly salient as she problematizes the aesthetic, suggesting that "believing [that] the word 'Victorientalism' implies a positive, transcultural blend is misguided." A steampunk herself, Pho's critique underscores the rhetorical influence of this style, arguing:

Fashion, just like any form of art, is a reflection of society, and art movements like Orientalism have [a] complex political history that members of the dominant culture may not recognize as something negative or hurtful. . . . Do not claim that you are re-living a past that never was because you're not; your fantasy is merely replicated attitudes from a very real present.[84]

As steampunks attempt to valorize Victorientalist style, they concomitantly serve a rhetoric of empire that Spurr categorizes under the tropes of surveillance, aestheticization, and idealization. In classic colonial discourse, the body of the other was a source of valorization and the "essential defining characteristic" of the Other. As a result, bodies were transformed into an object to be viewed (and judged) by the colonizer.[85] Turning culture into an object of beauty works rhetorically by turning culture into an object to be consumed, transformed, and displaced. For Spurr, this kind of aestheticization is "a mode of representation by which a powerful culture takes possession of a less powerful one" and "can be understood quite literally as colonization."[86] Spurr adds that when cultural Others become the subjects of Western idealization and beauty, it serves as a form of compensation for non-Western cultures, otherwise destroyed by the political and economic processes of colonization.[87]

Ho sums it up well: "The genre highlights the persistent problems of colonial relations but does not often erase them." The exotic aesthetic appears to present a problematic style "still haunted and seduced by colonial structures of privilege and suggests that decolonization may be a profound forgetting of the conditions of colonialism that preceded it" (11).

Conquering Empire

Having reviewed several of steampunk's primary styles, it seems that empire is not just ever present in its aesthetic but is reproduced as well. A rhetorical analysis of the steampunk aesthetic reveals that its styles may function to perpetuate a rhetoric of empire. While its literary and filmic manifestations may serve the social functions that so many claim steampunk exhibits, it would appear that steampunk style may require a more critical lens, particularly in light of the fact that steampunk style is the subculture's most mainstream feature.

Steampunk attracts people because of its beautiful aesthetic, but the beautification and aestheticization of the Victorian era have consequences for today. Steampunk style does not seem to grapple with today's racial and class tensions, but rather ignores or reproduces them. Blogs like *Beyond Victoriana* and *Silver Goggles* are powerful interrogators of steampunk's Eurocentric aesthetic, but stronger critique is necessary. From steampunk conventions and gatherings to Justin Bieber and aestheticized teddy bears, steampunk is everywhere. Because of its growing popularity, steampunk may have the potential to influence us in positive ways, but we must consider its style as a nonneutral, political, and strongly rhetorical element of the subculture.

Notes

1. Regretsy. "Things That Are Not Steampunk #27," Regretsy.com, last modified September 14, 2012. At http://www.regretsy.com/category/not-remotely-steampunk/.
2. Dylan Fox, "Editorial," *SteamPunk Magazine* 7 (April 2010): 4.
3. Margaret Hartmann, "Justin Bieber Accused of Ruining Steampunk," last modified December 12, 2011. At http://jezebel.com/5867504/justin-bieber-accused-of-ruining-steampunk.

4. Barry Brummett, *Rhetoric of Machine Aesthetics* (Westport, Conn.: Praeger, 1999), 23.

5. Jeff VanderMeer and S. J. Chambers, *The Steampunk Bible* (New York: Harry N. Abrams, 2011), 9.

6. Rebecca Onion, "Reclaiming the Machine: An Introductory Look at Steampunk in Everyday Practice," *Neo-Victorian Studies* 1, no. 1 (2008): 139.

7. Bruce Sterling, "The User's Guide to Steampunk," in VanderMeer and Chambers, *The Steampunk Bible*, 13.

8. Ibid., 11.

9. Elizabeth Ho, *Neo-Victorianism and the Memory of Empire* (London: Continuum Books, 2012), 144.

10. Nick Ottens, "Farewell to Empire," *Gatehouse Gazette* 21 (November 2011): 3.

11. Diana M. Pho, "Objectified and Politicized: The Dynamics of Ideology and Consumerism in Steampunk Subculture," in *Steaming into a Victorian Future: A Steampunk Anthology*, ed. Julie Anne Taddeo and Cynthia J. Miller (Lanham, Md.: Scarecrow Press, 2013), 200.

12. Ekaterina Sedia, "Steampunk: Looking to the Future through the Lens of the Past," in *The Mammoth Book of Steampunk*, ed. Sean Wallace (London: Constable & Robinson, 2012), 16.

13. Ibid., 16–17.

14. Jeannette Atkinson, "Engagement and Performance: Created Identities in Steampunk, Cosplay, and Reenactment," in *The Cultural Moment in Tourism*, ed. Laurajane Smith, Emma Waterton, and Steve Watson (London: Taylor & Francis, 2012), 118.

15. Cynthia J. Miller and Julie Anne Taddeo, introduction to Taddeo and Miller, *Steaming into a Victorian Future*, xviii.

16. VanderMeer and Chambers, *The Steampunk Bible*, 42.

17. Julie Anne Taddeo, "Steampunk's Reimagining of Victorian Femininity," in Taddeo and Miller, *Steaming into a Victorian Future*, 45.

18. Suzanne Barber and Matt Hale, "Upcycling the Past, Present, and Future in Steampunk," in Taddeo and Miller, *Steaming into a Victorian Future*, 167.

19. VanderMeer and Chambers, *The Steampunk Bible*, 39.

20. Scott Westerfeld, "Scott Westerfeld on *Leviathan*," in VanderMeer and Chambers, *The Steampunk Bible*, 66.

21. Gail Ashurst and Anna Powell, "Under Their Own Steam: Magic, Science, and Steampunk," in *The Gothic in Contemporary Literature and Popular Culture*, ed. Justin D. Edwards and Agnieszka Soltysik Monnet (New York: Routledge, 2012), 160.

22. Barber and Hale, "Upcycling the Past," 177.

23. Jay Strongman, *Steampunk: The Art of Victorian Futurism* (London: Korero Books, 2011), 11.

24. Pho, "Objectified and Politicized," 200.

25. Ho, *Neo-Victorianism*, 148.

26. Ibid., 149.

27. Marie-Luise Kohlke and Christian Gutleben, "The (Mis)shapes of Neo-Victorian Gothic," in *Neo-Victorian Gothic: Horror, Violence, and Degeneration in the Re-Imagined Nineteenth Century*, ed. Marie-Luise Kohlke and Christian Gutleben (New York: Rodopi, 2012), 20–21.

28. Sally-Anne Huxtable, "Steampunk Design and the Vision of a Victorian Future," in Kohlke and Gutleben, *Neo-Victorian Gothic*, 214.

29. Anarchist, conservative, liberal—steampunk's aesthetic is employed by all. One need only consider Steampunk Sarah Palin in conjunction with the work of steampunk anarchists to see that steampunk truly has a broad spectrum of political influences. See, for example, VanderMeer and Chambers, *The Steampunk Bible*, 10.

30. Christine Ferguson, "Surface Tensions: Steampunk, Subculture, and the Ideology of Style," *Neo-Victorian Studies* 4, no. 2 (2011): 67.

31. Barry Brummett, *A Rhetoric of Style* (Carbondale: Southern Illinois University Press, 2008), xi.

32. Ibid., 1.

33. Ibid., 43.

34. Ibid., 50.

35. Ferguson describes the debates over steampunk's sartorial meanings as "highly charged rifts" within the steampunk community; "Surface Tensions," 68.

36. Brummett, *A Rhetoric of Style*, 112.

37. Ibid., 104.

38. Ferguson, "Surface Tensions," 70.

39. Diana Pho, "#17 The Semantics of Words & the Antics of Fashion: Addressing 'Victorientalism,'" *Beyond Victoriana*, last modified March 7, 2010. At http://beyondvictoriana.com/2010/03/07/beyond-victoriana-17the-semantics-of-words-the-antics-of-fashion-addressing-victorientalism/.

40. David Spurr, *The Rhetoric of Empire: Colonial Discourse in Journalism, Travel Writing, and Imperial Administration* (Durham: Duke University Press, 1993), 57.

41. Ibid., 45–48.

42. Atkinson, "Engagement and Performance," 117.

43. Strongman, *Steampunk: The Art of Victorian Futurism*, 41.

44. Spurr, *The Rhetoric of Empire*, 110.

45. Strongman, *Steampunk: The Art of Victorian Futurism*, 8.

46. Spurr, *The Rhetoric of Empire*, 116–117.

47. Strongman, *Steampunk: The Art of Victorian Futurism*, 7.

48. Spurr, *The Rhetoric of Empire*, 154–155.

49. Brummett, *Rhetoric of Machine Aesthetics*, 24.

50. Ibid., 25.

51. Ibid., 28.

52. Ibid., 19.

53. Ibid., 29.

54. Ho, *Neo-Victorianism*, 142.

55. Dr. Grymm [Joey Marsocci] and Barbe Saint John, *1,000 Steampunk Creations: Neo-Victorian Fashion, Gear & Art* (Beverly, Mass.: Quarry Books, 2011), 7.

56. Strongman, *Steampunk: The Art of Victorian Futurism*, 8.

57. Cynthia Miller, "Steampunk's Fantastic Frontiers," in Taddeo and Miller, *Steaming into a Victorian Future*, 146.

58. Brummett, *Rhetoric of Machine Aesthetics*, 50.

59. Ibid., 46–47.

60. Atkinson, "Engagement and Performance," 116.

61. Amy Sue Bix, "Steampunk, Design, and the History of Technology in Society," in Taddeo and Miller, *Steaming into a Victorian Future*, 235–254.

62. Ashurst and Powell, "Under Their Own Steam," 158.

63. Brummett, *Rhetoric of Machine Aesthetics*, 34–35.

64. Onion, "Reclaiming the Machine," 144.

65. Ashurst and Powell, "Under Their Own Steam," 159.

66. See, for example, Atkinson, "Engagement and Performance," 117; and Brummett, *Rhetoric of Machine Aesthetics*, 35.

67. Brummett, *Rhetoric of Machine Aesthetics*, 42.

68. Ibid., 46.

69. VanderMeer and Chambers, *The Steampunk Bible*, 132.

70. Brummett, *Rhetoric of Machine Aesthetics*, 47.

71. Ashurst and Powell, "Under Their Own Steam," 162.

72. Strongman, *Steampunk: The Art of Victorian Futurism*, 7.

73. Brummett, *Rhetoric of Machine Aesthetics*, 30.

74. Spurr, *The Rhetoric of Empire*, 47.

75. Ibid., 53.

76. Brummett, *Rhetoric of Machine Aesthetics*, 2.

77. Libby Bulloff, "Steampunk Fashion: Four Styles," in VanderMeer and Chambers, *The Steampunk Bible*, 139–141.

78. Spurr, *The Rhetoric of Empire*, 46.

79. Ibid., 27.

80. Atkinson, "Engagement and Performance," 114.

81. Strongman, *Steampunk: The Art of Victorian Futurism*, 7.

82. Spurr, *The Rhetoric of Empire*, 155.

83. Editorial, *Gatehouse Gazette* 11 (March 2010): 3.

84. Pho, "The Semantics of Words," n.p.

85. Spurr, *The Rhetoric of Empire*, 22.

86. Ibid., 59.

87. Ibid., 132.

Liberation and a Corset

Examining False Feminism in Steampunk

MARY ANNE TAYLOR

⚙

IN A RECENT CONVERSATION ABOUT THE INCREASING PRESENCE OF WOMEN in steampunk culture, a writer for Steampunk Empire, one of the more prominent online forums for the steampunk community, said that it would be hard to identify a more egalitarian or democratic cultural forum than steampunk. This progressive notion of a democratic and equal ideal was followed by a posting claiming that "the result of an increase in women is welcome because it means I get to see more hot chicks at conventions."[1] Even if this gendered posting is not representative of the treatment of women in steampunk culture, any notion of equality that is tied to a self-proclaimed "distinctly progressive"[2] cultural aesthetic warrants further investigation. Although the presence of women has been steadily increasing in steampunk literature and steampunk conference culture, I am apprehensive to base equitable contributions to a subculture solely based on an increase in number. To explore the claim of an egalitarian ideal, first it is necessary to examine the underlying tension of steampunk's call for neo-Victorian ideology through an appropriation of a Victorian aesthetic. Followers of steampunk advance the notion that performing a steampunk aesthetic promotes a progressive do-it-yourself, anticonsumerist ideology that begins with the best parts of Victorian literature and matches that with the best parts of industrial development.[3] The steampunk movement arguably sees the subculture as a neo-Victorian response to industrial design, meaning, steampunks value the appropriation of Victorian style as an aesthetic that thwarts mainstream culture.[4] As neo-Victorian, the movement drops the regressive politics associated with the Victorian Era and Victorian literature and can adopt an aesthetic that is simultaneously nostalgic and subversive. In order to unpack the utopian ideal of steampunk as a "lived aesthetic"[5] that promotes progressive and ethical ideas of industrial, gender, and consumer responsibility, this discussion is interested in the notion of gender performance as it relates to a steampunk aesthetic, and the mediated perception of gender performance as it relates to steampunk subculture.

Steampunk is an aesthetic in which gender dichotomies are blurred, gender bending is privileged, and women are written in steampunk literature beyond traditional gender roles, which is to say beyond the cult of domesticity where women are relegated to the private sphere only. For these reasons, and although not a universal sentiment, many have argued that steampunk exists as an egalitarian ideal where the subculture is inclusive of women. This chapter will argue against the steampunk notion of gender equality. I will also argue against the steampunk advancement of neo-Victorian style, where "neo" refers to a subversion of the Victorian Era while simultaneously appropriating Victorian style as the dominant aesthetic. First, I will define a steampunk aesthetic for women. In investigating gender empowerment through steampunk and exploring feminist possibilities through the aesthetic, it is necessary to ask if a Victorian aesthetic can indeed be feminist. Julie Anne Taddeo argues that Victorian style and the steampunk corset go beyond feminist critiques of "straightjacket style" because steampunk focuses on what the corset can do "for" women, instead of "to" women, thereby expanding the traditional notions of femininity.[6] It is a recurring notion in steampunk literature that the feminine aesthetic, specifically the reappropriation of the corset, can traverse disciplining restrictions of the Victorian Era. Steampunks argue that the aesthetic goes beyond being derivative of Victorian style and is reinventive, constantly reinterpreting and revising the regressive politics and style of the era.[7] Although the advancement of the utopian aesthetic has progressive potential, steampunk's inability to recognize the material gendered ties to the Victorian Era is an irresponsible advancement.

In steampunk lore, the notion of "neo" and "progressive" seem to be consistently tied to a theme of "choice." Taddeo argues that "when a steampunk puts on a corset, she or he does so by choice—making a fashion statement—but more importantly functions as a resource of resistance critiquing and reimagining Victorian gender norms and roles."[8] It is problematic to claim the choice of a corset as progressive ideology without concern for the material and bodily constraints of the Victorian Era, or concern for the way women were portrayed in Victorian literature. This essay will reconsider the notion that "Victorian" can also be feminist or, at the very least, feminist in style. I will draw on several resources in steampunk fashion as well as the representation of women on fan sites, in media portrayals, and in steampunk fan culture. Using the comic *Steampunk* [Sarah] *Palin* as my primary text, I will argue that steampunk feminine style is incomplete and ignores historical material implications for women of the Victorian Era and women in Victorian literature.

The Ties That Bind Victorian Fashion and Steampunk

Many contributors in this anthology have reviewed the machine aesthetic that guides fashion choices in steampunk. In short, steampunk style is related to the Victorian Era, specifically an aestheticized myth of the industrialized nineteenth century. The aesthetic uses technology, and the word "steam" derives from the steam-powered machinery that predominated at that time. Jeff VanderMeer, in *The Steampunk Bible*, argues that the "punk" in steampunk "highlights a reactionary response that is distinctly progressive . . . where steampunks seek to reject the conformity of the modern, soulless, featureless design of technology while embracing the inventiveness and tech origins of Victorian machines."[9] The rejection of conformity that is tied to consumer behavior is central to steampunk ideology and is communicated through a neo-Victorian aesthetic, where the style is represented by do-it-yourself and organic reapplications of the Victorian Era. The *New York Times* dedicated a Style Section column in 2008 to growing fashion trends that incorporate steampunk style. As interpreted by that article,[10] the aesthetic could be understood as taking visuals that the public associates with the Victorian Era (top hats, coattails, corsets, mourning dresses, high-button shoes) and matching them with fashion-forward contemporary design. Also a big part of the aesthetic is military dress, in which a steampunk wears trousers, high boots, a couture military jacket or vest, with a top hat and fuses that style with mechanical buttons, brass goggles, and clockwork accessories.[11]

For our purposes, it is important to describe steampunk fashion for women, particularly as it is guided by Victorian style. G. D. Falksen of the blog Steampunk Fashion argues that the fundamental rule in dressing for steampunk is that, when in doubt, dress Victorian and then add to it. He states that "the Victorians were the first people to fully capitalize upon steam technology in a way that affected everyday life. . . . [I]f you are afraid that your outfit is too Victorian, then you are probably doing it right."[12] The most noted image for women in Victorian Era fashion is the elaborate gown. These dresses were designed for modesty rather than functionality and often featured puffed sleeves and high collars. The gowns were thick and almost always had layered, restrictive undergarments. These undergarments, often categorized as corsets, were worn to cinch the waist of women, creating a sleek feminine silhouette in which a woman's waist was the narrowest part of her body.[13] According to the Victoria and Albert Museum in London, a museum of design and style, wealthy women from the 1830s to the 1860s usually wore skirts supported by petticoats (which is what gives skirts their bulge at the bottom). The petticoats were often fitted with a pliable steel hoop, so the dress would maintain its form. Undergarments would have consisted of very tight bodices, often boned or made of steel. The sleeves of women's dresses usually extended to the wrist in casual wear, and long gloves covering the arm would be worn for formal wear. According to the museum's archive of clothing, dresses from 1860 to 1890 became sleeker but more restrictive, often dispensing with the petticoat in lieu of a corset to project the appearance of a slim waist. Many of the bodices and blouses had high necks, which were stiffened with bones or wire. Hats were common in this era, and evening dresses were made for luxury, often with heavy silk and boned bodices and corsets. The Victoria and Albert's dress collection also shows that styles were differentiated by class. Although poorer women would often wear second-hand clothes that would need to be patched, such apparel was still modest and made of restrictive material.[14] Steampunk's modern interpretation of this style is often achieved through blending, or mixing styles that yearn for a nostalgia of a wealthy Victorian Era, but also have functionality. The most recognizable fashion choice for women in steampunk is the blending of Victorian tropes, the corset for example, with modern accessories and jewelry.

Karen Christians writes that the beauty of steampunk is that it is a merger of low and high tech in which historical objects can transform the body into a work of art.[15] Christians adds, "until recently, much of steampunk jewelry simply involved watch gears, hearts, lockets and keys, but new advances are pushing the boundaries of metaphoric art, with intricate attention to detail, thoughtfulness, and fabrication; which combines historical reference and metaphor."[16] Steampunk style blends the aesthetics of femininity with practical application that is inherently read as masculine. For example, San Francisco artist Nifer Fahrion designed and created a "work corset," a laced corset blended with a construction work belt complete with a drill holder, tool clips, and hammer belt.[17] The corset is marked by femininity, but the notion of a work belt or tool belt is marked by masculinity.

Further representations of steampunk style for women is the blending of couture (high-end, hand-stitched fashion) with do-it-yourself adjustments. An article appearing in the design magazine *VivaLaModa* argues that, much like punk style, "steampunk style combines an ethos of deconstruction (unraveling seams, torn lace, distressed leather) to update the dress of the past in an entirely postmodern style."[18] Also a classic representation of Victorian style is the tailcoat. A blending style for steampunk might accessorize a tailcoat with gear-shaped buttons, or pair stereotypically masculine styles (steel-toed boots) with stereotypically feminine Victorian styles (the bodice or corset, for example). Central to the steampunk aesthetic is the countercultural appeal that often supports people insular to the movement. There are websites, message boards, and new media that give tips on how to steampunk a wardrobe. It is considered the opposite of mainstream fashion to piecemeal a wardrobe to achieve the intended style, as practiced by steampunks. For example, Steampunk Workshop and *SteamPunk Magazine* have DIY postings that show viewers through YouTube videos and detailed pictures how to put together an ensemble, and how to do it cheaply.[19] A move away from the DIY aesthetic would conflict with the subculture's ideology. However, as steampunk style is growing in popularity in new media, it is also being drawn into mainstream fashion. Steampunk Workshop, a website and guide for how to steampunk one's life, recently posted an article on how steampunk couture, "consisting of clockworks, corsets, cogs, goggles, boots and bustles, with the return of material such as wood, metal, velvet, leather and lace," has now infiltrated high fashion.[20] According to the writers of Steampunk Workshop, Prada is the first major name in high fashion to create an entire steampunk line, which was released as men's clothing, complete with double-breasted vests, long trench coats, accentuated collars, tailored suit jackets, and mixed materials including leather and fur. Prada's campaign included print ads featuring respected actors Gary Oldman and Willem Dafoe, driving home the notion of mainstream couture and the possibility of the subculture being co-opted for consumer interests.

Along with the "steam" aesthetic, which has been described as blending the form of Victorian fashion with the functionality of advanced industrial society, steampunk also incorporates the notion of "punk" for women. The word "punk" suggests subversion and counterculture. It is empowering in that it allows for community in a subculture while simultaneously pushing against mainstream or dominant cultural expectations. Steampunks argue that one critical aspect of steampunk is the tremendous diversity of appeal it presents, which allows it to offer something to nearly everyone.[21] The egalitarian ideal that has been promoted for women in steampunk literature, and steampunk fashion, is that women can do, or be, whatever they choose. Suzanne Lazear, a writer of steampunk fiction, argues that the world of steampunk creates a place where women can become inventors, explorers, or engineers, and she can do this in a lacy bodice if she chooses. The argument from Lazear is that "women and girls can be anything in steampunk—from ladies to air pirates. They could be pushing social norms or they could be the norm. . . . [A] woman in a steampunk story could wear trousers like Madame Lefoux in *Changeless* or could be Captain Octavia Pye in *Steamed* who captains in a skirt and corset."[22] The troubling binaries in Lazear's example notwithstanding, she argues that women have options and choice in steampunk, which is far more progressive in fiction than it is in modernity. Lazear's argument, in line with those who advance steampunk as an egalitarian ideal, is that women can be anything they choose. The notion that "[steampunk] women can have it all," as contended by Lazear and others, suggests that steampunk has been able to create equitable space for women that they have not been able to find in traditional arenas such as politics. Although this suggestion is fair and to some degree justified, it is incomplete. In Lazear's argument, as in most steampunk social media, there is no discussion or complication of the sexualized nature of steampunk aesthetic prescriptions.

Some also argue that steampunk fashion can be transgressive. For example, Jake von Slatt and Libby Bulloff have spoken extensively about steampunk style as it relates to nineteenth-century feminism. At the Steamcon II conference in November 2010, they chaired a panel called "Queering Steampunk Fashion" where they argued that steampunk style is more than costume, it is fashion that can traverse confining social norms. Von Slatt and Bulloff argued that steampunk fashion can be transgressive, as it is represented through gender bending and playful application. They argued, "gender-bending fashion and re-mixing gender-typed garments presents a great opportunity in Steampunk fashion and personal expression."[23] Rather, "androgyny should be a gender smorgasbord, not an absence of gender."[24] Von Slatt argues that gender bending, not to be confused with blending fashion, has been prominent in steampunk literature from its inception. Steampunk uses the terms "androgyny" and "gender bending" interchangeably, but writers in steampunk such as Judith Butler tend to prefer the latter, because the term "androgyny" privileges masculinity as it relates to power.[25] A big part of steampunk is how to subvert gender dress codes and allow transformations of style to represent rebellion and resistance against dominant and pervasive gender norms.[26] However, it is problematic that VanderMeer, Taddeo, Pho, and other writers of steampunk do not reconcile that their counterculture movement has now entered mainstream high fashion and that the aesthetic is tied to the Victorian Era, which cinched and relegated women to the private sphere. Also lacking in the discussion of gender bending is what constitutes masculine or feminine. To explore these problems, it is necessary to historicize the Victorian Era, in literature specifically, and then address how gender and the performance of gender challenge the assertion that reappropriating Victorian style in steampunk is progressive or subversive.

In the next section, I will draw from the speculative lens of style and performativity, where a rhetoric of style can help us investigate steampunk as an egalitarian, or even feminist endeavor. As we have navigated steampunk fashion to this point, specifically as it relates to women, choice in fashion is valued as empowering. Interestingly, however, steampunks explain and critique the style in a way that positions the aesthetic within restrictive binaries. Specifically, a woman can choose to be a lady through her style, or she can perform masculinity, but she cannot do both. This paradox is noted in a conversation between steampunk authors writing about the potential for steampunk to empower young girls.[27] Steampunks argue that the costuming, conference pageantry, and now even high fashion of steampunk have made headway in the ability to create a feeling of empowerment. Pushing boundaries of conformity and patriarchy are welcome endeavors, but the interventions are at best lacking and at worst paradoxically troubling. What I want to investigate in the remainder of this essay is whether steampunk style has created a false empowerment for women, particularly given that gender performativity within steampunk has material implications for the perception of feminism and equity within this subculture.

Performing Victorian Style

Although corsets, petticoats, and bodices historically represent oppression, steampunk fashion has attempted to reapply Victorian style. Some argue that this reappropriation is done in a satiric way, attempting to reevaluate women's place in Victorian history. Robin Blackburn of the web series *The League of S.T.E.A.M.* said that she liked wearing a corset because "it gives me a waist." She also noted that in "the real Victorian Era, women were second-class citizens. But the steampunk aspect of it allows us to be strong, powerful women. So while Victorian women didn't often get the opportunity to be scientists or world travelers, women in steampunk can imagine a world where they could do those things while still embracing a Victorian aesthetic."[28] The notion here is that because she chooses to wear a corset, she is freed from the mandated and restrictive Victorian laws dictated for women of the Victorian Era.

Robert Hariman argues that "style becomes an analytical category for understanding a social reality; in order to understand the social reality of politics, we can consider how a political action involves acting according to a particular political style."[29] Rhetorical style goes beyond the traditional rhetorical canon of discourse and allows a critic to interpret and understand meaning through symbols. The perception of meaning is created through a shared understanding of signs, which is to say that art and satire do not work without a popular understanding of signifiers. For example, the theme of the Metropolitan Museum of Art's 2013 annual gala was "Punk: Chaos to Couture." The MET gala is a famous gathering of models, fashion designers, film stars, and other icons of popular culture. It is lavish, and a representation of high fashion. A punk theme for this gala was a blending of high culture and subversive culture. Perhaps even with a limited understanding of the punk aesthetic, attendees managed to blend their couture dresses and tuxedos with platinum blonde hair, dark heavy eye makeup, visible piercings, and a deconstruction of high fashion. This blending of styles was achieved because participants at the gala had a rudimentary understanding of punk signifiers. Barry Brummett argues, "style is the text we all wear on our backs like a shell. It is explicitly designed to be read and noticed by others."[30] We understand Victorian signifiers through old photographs and through descriptions in Victorian literature. Although the steampunk aesthetic is intentional in its premeditated fascination with the Victorian Era, shared meaning of Victorianism is complicated.

Because so much of Victorian culture was informed by overtly sexist signifiers, the corset for example, it is unclear if Victorian style can be reappropriated to create a meaning or feeling of empowerment. In order to explore whether Victorian style can also be feminist, it is important to historicize implications of the Victorian Era for women. A shared understanding of signs and symbolic meaning from the era often comes from Victorian literature.[31] Kate Millett has introduced a notion that the struggle for women's economic and legal rights in the Victorian Era first played out in literature. She argues:

> While the Victorian period is the first in history to face the issue of patriarchy and the condition of women under its rule, it did so in a bewildering variety of ways: courageously and intelligently as in Mill and Engels; half-heartedly as in the tepid criticism of the novelists who describe it, with bland disingenuousness as in Ruskin; or with

turbulent ambivalence as in the poets Tennyson, Rossetti, Swinburne, and Wilde.[32]

Ellen Rosenman writes about the disciplining of the female body in Victorian literature, showing that the representation of female sexuality in this era was swiftly followed by punishment. Rosenman argues that, through Victorian literature, the female body is objectified and sexualized for the male gaze.[33] She gives the following historical perspective:

> Looking back over the novels about the unchaste woman written between 1835 and 1860 we see, with few exceptions, a field littered with broken bodies; the survivors are on their knees to God. . . . At best, a fallen woman may retire to a convent so that, in the words of one such character, she is hidden from the world, and no longer permitted to contaminate the pure and virtuous. . . . Whatever sexual desires provoke transgression must be disclaimed, and sensuality appears almost exclusively as a dreadful illusion. Whatever consciousness these characters have of their bodies is coded as a dangerous and unacceptable vanity that paves the way for their fall. . . . For these female characters, "fallenness" is the vanishing point of subjectivity; sexuality and selfhood appear as mutually exclusive terms, overdetermining the exile or death of the sexual woman.[34]

Donald Stone finally argues that the Victorian novel "characteristically mirrored the prevailing sentiments of the age, which took a harsh stand, generally, against active women."[35] The myths and tropes associated with the Victorian Era are inherently gendered, and the traits of purity, chastity, and modesty were associated with women. It follows, then, that the style of dress would mirror the restrictions of societal norms. In explaining norms of the nineteenth-century Victorian novel, Stone discusses the characterization of women as inevitable victims, unassuming, and submissive. These characteristics are written throughout Victorian literature by men (Byron) and women (Austen, the Brontës), with one common theme: the idealization of the home and private responsibilities. Millett argues: "The Victorian belief in marriage—nearly an article of faith—is an attempt to beautify the traditional confinement of women at any cost. The cloying sweetness, the frenetic sentimentality, all conspire to hide the fact that this is only candy-coated sexual politics."[36] Women in Victorian literature exist in a cult of domesticity and are relegated to a private sphere, separate from public discourse and activism.

The place of women in this society is relevant in painting a picture of the obstacles that women face in steampunk, specifically as they reappropriate or reclaim attributes from the Victorian Era. Taddeo and Pho link feminine steampunk style as an aesthetic response to how women were described in Victorian literature. Taddeo argues that feminist critics of Victorian literature are shortsighted. For example, feminist criticism of this era has not acknowledged that the corset has the ability to "not only aid in the refined appearance, but also [allow] women to conceal pregnancies and to transgress prevailing moral restrictions."[37] Also problematic here is the implication that pregnancy, as it relates to femininity, needs to be hidden to preserve order. Theresa Meyers, in her post "An Ode to the Corset" at the fan-fiction steampunk website Steamed!, traces how the corset has developed as a tool for empowerment beginning with Victorian literature and carrying through to present-day high fashion. She argues that, starting as a tool of restraint intended "to create an hour-glass shape," the corset has developed over the decades into a fashion statement and a sign of empowerment.[38]

The rejection of the corset as a straightjacket relies on the assumption that the corset can be a symbol for subversion, "where the interrogation of gender issues connect past and present."[39] Steampunks argue that the corset and other gendered markers of the Victorian Era represent more than mere nostalgia, but a need for "historical relevance that blurs the Victorian binary of angel/whore."[40] Taddeo argues that the binaries are blurred because steampunk is built from an alternative history in which steampunks can "enjoy cinching our waists while still enjoying our liberty since we lace up by choice."[41] If steampunk sees its subculture as one that frees women from the regressive politics of the Victorian Era through the reapplication of a Victorian aesthetic, it seems first that steampunks would do a better job of explaining how the reappropriation of gendered style markers lifts women from the private sphere. The notion of "choice" is not enough to show how neo-Victorian style is transgressive of the Victorian Era.

Steampunks also discuss gender bending, found in Victorian literature as well, as a transgressive aesthetic and arena for empowerment. Lauren Goodlad, an English scholar, argues that although many Victorianists count the domestication of women as a socialized truth, mid-Victorian literature can be rich with theories of "androgynous ethical competence, for such literature is both historically implicated in and deeply hostile to the bourgeois developments most often described in Victorian literature."[42] Goodlad argues that although the term "androgyny" has been eclipsed by more precise concepts such as transgender, gender preference, and gender performativity, "androgyny has the potential to speak to the ethical deficiencies of post-enlightenment gender and sexuality in ways that postmodern substitutes do not."[43] Steampunk is an open canvas for gender bending, particularly in the ability to blend traditionally masculine styles with stereotypically feminine styles.[44] In a video posted by Jake von Slatt at Steampunk Workshop, androgynous performance comes from men appropriating traditional feminine styles of skirts, corsets, makeup, and jewelry, and from women appropriating masculine styles of tool belts, short hair, tailcoats, and top hats. As an empowering advancement in steampunk, Gayle Rubin argues that androgyny is not a "prescribed mixture of masculinity and femininity, but the entire absence of gender: an androgynous society is genderless, for in it, one's sexual anatomy is irrelevant to who one is, or what one does."[45] Gender bending in steampunk is empowering because of the absence of gender rules. However, gender bending in steampunk still finds itself operating within a masculine/feminine binary, meaning that gender bending as shown in von Slatt's video and as described by Bulloff has men applying feminine markers of style, and women taking on masculine traits. The markers are clearly differentiated by gender and exist within normative expectations; at no time is a corset associated with the masculine, or a top hat with the feminine.

Steampunks argue that their attempt to revise a regressive past is made through performativity. Performing steampunk is a cornerstone of the subculture, and steampunks claim that performing a revised neo-Victorian aesthetic is a way to thwart normative constructions of gender. Catherine Siemann argues that performativity "is manifested in steampunk by the representation of problems in new and proactive ways."[46] Siemann argues that performing steampunk and writing steampunk are about creating possibilities, not creating solutions. Adopting and reappropriating Victorian style is a way of bending and breaking stylistic expectations. Look no further than websites like Steampunk Emporium and How to Dress Steampunk for ideas on matching the subculture's aesthetic genres. Steampunk Fashion,[47] another site for understanding how to blend steampunk styles, shows how the performance of reappropriation can be subversive through neo-Victorianism. For example, while a female character in a Victorian novel would never be permitted to wear trousers or coattails, bending these historical references are inherent to the steampunk aesthetic.

Judith Butler says that "to say that gender is performative is to say that it is a certain kind of enactment; the 'appearance' of gender is prompted by obligatory norms to be one gender or the other, and thus the reproduction of gender is always a negotiation of power."[48] For women in steampunk, the female character is something that can be developed, as if an avatar in video gaming. She can start from scratch and build a blended style that thwarts conventional norms. Ashley Strickland goes as far to say, "[c]rack open a clockwork [steampunk] tale about a teenage steampunk sweetheart and don't be surprised if she's shucking her skirts for pants, piloting air-based contraptions or generally giving all proper Victorian societal conventions a kick in the rear."[49] Strickland is arguing that female characters can perform roles that are typically disconnected from mainstream expectations of women. She uses the work of Scott Westerfeld, author of the *Leviathan* series, to show how the performance of steampunk in costuming, and the literature of steampunk, are ways of reclaiming a history that was unkind to women. Westerfeld is known for gender bending. One of his most famous characters is a woman who dresses as and pretends to be a man in the "British Air Service" in 1914. Westerfeld sees this as an opportunity to give women a voice at a time when social and political restrictions on women bound them to the home. Steampunks argue that the ability of steampunk authors to alter history through the inclusion of women is an empowering step for women of the subculture. Writing about women from this time period also gives steampunk authors a new canvas on which to elaborate steampunk style. Aesthetic archetypes are explained at the website Chronicles of Harriet,[50] and illustrate that the style is most successful when a steampunk starts with an archetype and builds in accessories. For example, a woman could choose a traditionally masculine archetype like hunter/fighter, which would assume the use of weapons and canvas clothing, but could add femininity through lace or a corset.[51] Similarly, a man could choose a traditionally feminine archetype like dandy/ femme fatale and add a top hat or coattails over the traditional archetypal requirements of "form-fitting and revealing clothing."[52] Again, any notion of "blending" in these steampunk examples is limited, as the stylistic markers are drawn from two distinct columns of masculine and feminine, creating the very same ideological dichotomy that steampunk is trying to leave behind.

Donna Haraway, in her "Cyborg Manifesto," argues that "the cyborgs populating feminist science fiction make very problematic the status of man or woman, human artifact, member of a race, individual entity, or body," challenging the very restrictive dichotomies that create private/public binaries in which women are restricted to "structural arrangements of home/ market/paid work place/state/and school."[53] Steampunks argue that female protagonists in steampunk literature are often at odds with the restrictions of the Victorian Era, which propagate what Haraway calls gendered structural arrangements. For example, this can be seen in Kady Cross's young adult Steampunk Chronicle series. In her novel *The Girl in the Steel Corset*, her protagonist is a young girl "chasing down bad guys, tinkering in her work-shop, and basically doing things normally reserved for a male protagonist."[54] Steampunks argue that what literature has been able to do for female pro-tagonists is tell the stories of women who were ignored by history. That said, binaries remain in descriptions of how female leads break from perceived gender conventions, especially how they use fashion and style to challenge cultural gender norms. There is a clear dichotomous position of fashion, outlined for instance in Balogun's archetypes, in which trousers, pants, and coattails are marked as masculine and gowns, corsets, and jewelry are marked as feminine.

This paradox warrants further investigation. Nisi Shawl draws on two problematic characteristics of steampunk culture: the overtness of sexual and gendered style markers, and the lack of same-sex relationships in steampunk fiction. The gendered markers in online forums notoriously draw attention to and exploit women's bodies. There are certainly forums where women talk about style and empowerment through Victorian dress, for instance Gail Carriger's comment at the 2012 ComicCon Convention: "If you have large boobs, corsets are more comfortable than a bra."[55] There are also online forums that work to subvert gender dress codes, like *SteamPunk Magazine*. However, some online forums are used exclusively to exploit women and ste-ampunk fashion choices, Steamgirl for example. Judith Butler argues that "performativity of gender is bound up with the differential ways in which subjects become eligible for recognition. . . . [W]e think of subjects as the kind of beings who ask for recognition in the law or in political life; but per-haps the more important issue is how the terms of recognition—of gender and sexual norms—condition in advance who will count as a subject, and who will not."[56] In asking who conditions or defines the subject within rec-ognition, Butler points to an interesting gap in steampunk, where men have been the primary audience. With more women entering the subculture and appropriating style that related to an oppressive historical era, it is necessary to investigate the perception of women's bodies with the style markers of the culture.

Regarding gender performance, Butler argues that "it is the constitutive failure of the performative, this slippage between discursive command and its appropriated effect, which provide the linguistic occasion and index for a consequential disobedience."[57] This is to say that as women enter steampunk, heretofore defined and written predominately by men, they may not be able to reappropriate a style than represents nothing less than the material oppression and marginalization of countercultures. Rather, "how is it that those who are abjected [in steampunk] come to make their claim through and against the discourses that have sought their repudiation?"[58] Within Victorian literature, which provides the blueprint for adapting Victorian style to steampunk culture, female characters are disciplined if they depart from the conventions of virtue, passivity, and chastity. Rosenman, in her exploration of women tropes in Victorian literature, argues that sexual marks for women are irredeemable, stating that "although the stories and morality of sexually transgressive heroines vary widely, sex is generally fatal and female characters often don't survive sexual irregularity."[59]

There is also a paradox in the relationship between technology and women in the Victorian Era. We think of technology as a mechanism that allowed greater egalitarianism in this era, especially in the re-creation of art, an activity that was reserved almost exclusively for men. Moving to contemporary art and performance in steampunk, it is through technology, gadgets, and the steam aesthetic that women strive for equitable conventions beyond normative social restraints. Steampunks argue that new media is a platform that can create greater egalitarianism, just as photography and other channels did for Victorian women. However, new media, according to Pho, "can simultaneously galvanize individual opinions while also dividing an international fandom, thus the tools of Web 2.0 serve as both a platform and as a micro-media by which current ideological fluctuations within steampunk can be gauged."[60] Even in the steampunk subculture, there is a distinction between what is valued and what is not. Whereas *SteamPunk Magazine* and Steampunk Fashion show how to build a progressive steampunk identity, Steamgirl and the Tumblr account for *Your Boobs Are Not Steampunk* are websites that objectify and sexualize women's bodies.

Rosenman points to how Victorian women became more objectified and sexualized as they were "consumed within the economy, both visual and monetary, especially when aided by the new technology of photography."[61] Fastforward to twenty-first-century new media channels for steampunk, and one finds websites and blogs that objectify women's bodies as a recruiting tool. Steampunks view the reappropriation of feminine Victorian style as a performative revision that offers a better future for women, with that future never being fully explained or problematized. Images found on Steamgirl,[62] a website and photo gallery for steampunk erotica, make no differentiation between a steampunk-blended aesthetic and pornography, yet these images claim empowerment. Although steampunk is growing and even entering mainstream popular culture through technology and social media, and although women in steampunk have grown in number, it is unclear how equality is defined by steampunks, or whether equitable treatment actually exists.

One of the more interesting texts that has popped up in steampunk comics and online forums is *Steampunk Palin*, namely Sarah Palin, former governor of Alaska and 2008 Republican vice presidential nominee. *Steampunk Palin*, as Chris Murphy explains, hopes to capitalize in two ways: to "tell a story of the beauty queen and media celebrity that has captivated a nation, and create a literary genre that borrows the notions of cyberpunk and transplants them into an alternate history past or fantasy world, usually influenced by the works of H. G. Wells or Jules Verne."[63] This comic is decidedly not satire and is a representative anecdote for why claims of equity for women in steampunk are premature. *Steampunk Palin* centers around a story "somewhere in the near future, where after a huge war makes the Earth's oil dry up, politicians and policy makers must gather to figure out a new power source." Palin, as an energy expert, suggests that "steam power should run the world's generators, as a replacement for now long gone oil."[64] Along with this story, the comic book includes eight pin-up photos of a steampunked Sarah Palin. In the words of Lisa Derrick, a columnist for the *Huffington Post*, the fan boys and creators of *Steampunk Palin* "really like Palin's breasts, a lot." The pin-ups are stylized with traditional markers of the steampunk aesthetic, including goggles, guns, and corsets. Most notably, the photos are highly sexualized. Safa S., a columnist for Care2 Make a Difference, an online forum promoting global gender equity, argues that "not only does the comic book objectify women in the drawings, most notably through steampunk Palin's steam-powered breast enhancement, it also depicts a degraded American public as a sea of robots controlled by a female politician's DD body."[65]

Steampunks argue that the website suggests a "feminist stance criticizing Palin's fetishization by the public."[66] In this comic, created by Antarctic Press, Sarah Palin is a hero. This form of comic fits most steampunk literature in that the authors can argue that they have created a strong female protagonist. Steampunk Sarah saves the day. However, what happens next is what Safa S. calls "punishment through eight objectifying pages of steampunk Sarah Palin pin-up drawings."[67] The comic proclaims progressive politics through its reimagining of Palin, but the pin-ups alone suggest that the comic pays tribute to her attractiveness, while exploiting her political inexperience. When flipping through the comic, the overt message to the reader is that it is okay that Palin is inept at politics and government because she is so attractive, complete with her ornate bodice and gun holster.

Safa S. argues that although the comic book is not Palin propaganda, or propaganda for any one political party, it is more troubling as a "commentary on and contribution to the already growing library of fetish politics through commodification."[68] What started as a subculture has now entered high fashion, an industry based on the commodification and exploitation of female bodies. Analysts at IBM have called steampunk a "new retail trend in the making," predicting that steampunk is poised to break through as a full-fledged fashion trend in 2013.[69] Using analytics to provide data for the fashion industry, IBM found that from 2009 to 2012 steampunk conversations on social media websites increased elevenfold, useful information for fashion conglomerates making choices about high-cost mass production of clothing.[70] The IBM analysts further predicted that "steampunk will be a major trend to bubble up, and take hold, of the retail industry, where major fashion labels, accessories providers and jewelry makers are expected to integrate a steampunk aesthetic into their designs in the coming year."[71] So what was once a subculture, striving for an egalitarian ideal, has now become a commodified style that makes money for fashion elites. For Stuart Ewen, the attention that mass culture has begun to pay to style and surface is problematic, particularly when it involves the female body.[72] Although Ewen can be shortsighted in his attempts to separate popular culture from politics or public policy, he gives us an understanding of how to critique steampunk's blending of styles. Even though a female politician is the hero in *Steampunk Palin*, she is no more a representation of feminism or progress for women than Sarah Palin herself.

Steampunk Palin gives us an interesting opportunity to explore the problematic nature of assigning styles through gender performance. The postmodern interpretation of Palin as an energy hero is an interesting, and even progressive, reappropriation of Sarah Palin's real politics. However, there are very real material implications of Sarah Palin the politician, especially her views on human and women's rights. In 2004, Judith Butler wrote: "I confess that I am not a very good materialist. Every time I try to write about the body, the writing ends up being about language."[73] This statement is applicable to steampunk in that steampunk may seek an egalitarian ideal, but is still uncertain about the application of style as it relates to feminism and the female body.

Steampunk Discussion

Steampunks argue that gendered stylistic markers like the corset offer a way that women can participate in a neo-Victorian fashion statement in order to represent contemporary progress. Taddeo writes: "[O]n any steampunk-themed website, at conventions, at fairs, and of course, on the jackets of romance novels, the corseted female—also outfitted in the obligatory goggles, perhaps a pistol at her waist—makes her appearance, while the corset, worn outside rather than underneath the weighty Victorian-styled clothes, rejects any notion of the garment as 'straitjacket.'"[74] Scott Westerfeld argues that the "steampunk movement is partly about messing up the stuffy ways of the Victorians," adding that "in many steampunk works, history is rewritten in a very positive way with women—and other people who suffered under imperialism—given roles and powers beyond their historical station."[75] For steampunks, the corset and other markers of Victorian fashion go beyond erotica and are much more than sexualized applications of the female body. The revisionist approach of Victorian style for women is empowering for Taddeo, who argues, "for any woman who has qualms about donning this restrictive garment, there are plenty of reassurances from fellow corset devotees, where corset fanciers can enjoy cinching our waists while still enjoying our liberty since we lace up by choice."[76] There it is: a statement of style and choice that negates the materialist implications of neo-feminism. There is no better example in steampunk than *Steampunk Palin* to show the problematic assumptions of steampunk reapplication. A style is not feminist because a sub- or counterculture deems it feminist.

Taddeo spends a chapter trying to talk women into a corset because it represents "a well worn glove," a "buxom beauty," and the "support of the fainting couch in the Victorian boudoir."[77] The deconstruction of the body, and the performance of gender bending, has given insight to how steampunk can be egalitarian and progressive. However, the performativity of steampunk leaves us lacking in any answers as to how we might traverse restrictive gender binaries, specifically what constitutes masculine and feminine style. Lauren Goodlad, in her attempt to explore gender bending and gender performativity, asks a key question: how will calculated stylistic choices liberate us, and how will subversive styles bring on the kind of change we want to see in our political culture? The *Steampunk Palin* text demonstrates that this question has no easy answers. The ability to reappropriate style, specifically in a way that represents empowerment, is important for women, but not without recognizing the material implications of that reappropriation. In a critique of Butler's arguments about gender performance, Samuel Chambers argues that "bodies undo us because their significance exceeds our reach; their meaning derives from the norms of gender and sexuality, norms that get (re)articulated in culture, in society, in politics."[78] So can steampunk be feminist? Although steampunk is a burgeoning trend in popular culture, based on limited research relegated to message boards, conference culture, and pop-culture images, I argue that feminist and egalitarian ideals are tied to greater materialist benchmarks than those offered by the steam aesthetic. Steampunk is not feminist, yet.

Notes

1. Sky Marshall, "Steam Chart 15000," Steampunk Empire, March 2, 2013. At http://www.thesteampunkempire.com/photo/steam-chart-15000.

2. Jeff VanderMeer and S. J. Chambers, *The Steampunk Bible: An Illustrated Guide to the World of Imaginary Airships, Corsets and Goggles, Mad Scientists, and Strange Literature* (New York: Harry N. Abrams, 2011), 99.

3. Diana M. Pho, "Objectified and Politicized: The Dynamics of Ideology and Consumerism in Steampunk Subculture," in *Steaming into a Victorian Future: A Steampunk Anthology*, ed. Julie Anne Taddeo and Cynthia J. Miller (Lanham, Md.: Scarecrow Press, 2013), 192.

4. Ibid., 185.

5. Ibid., 186.

6. Julie Anne Taddeo. "Corsets of Steel: Steampunk's Reimagining of Victorian Femininity," in Taddeo and Miller, *Steaming into a Victorian Future*, 43.

7. Ibid., 56.

8. Ibid.

9. VanderMeer and Chambers, *The Steampunk Bible*, 99.

10. Ruth la Ferla, "Steampunk Moves between Two Worlds," *New York Times*, Fashion and Style, May 8, 2008. At http://www.nytimes.com/2008/05/08/fashion/08PUNK.html?_r=0.

11. "Steampunk Style," *New York Times*, Fashion and Style, May 8, 2008. At http://www.nytimes.com/slideshow/2008/05/07/style/0508-PUNK_index.html.

12. G. D. Falksen, "A Sense of Structure," Steampunk Fashion (blog), August 15, 2008. At http://steamfashion.livejournal.com/929255.html.

13. Victoria and Albert Museum, "Victorian Dress." At http://www.vam.ac.uk/content/articles/v/victorian-dress-at-v-and-a/, accessed June 16, 2013.

14. The Victorian dress collection of the Victoria and Albert Museum breaks up the Victorian Era into ten-year increments. The museum also differentiates styles between wealthy women, middle-class women, and poor women; the latter often wore second-hand clothes, but still of modest and restrictive material. Pictures and descriptions of each era can be found at the museum's website, http://www.vam.ac.uk/content/articles/v/victorian-dress-at-v-and-a/.

15. Karen Christians, "Steampunk Future Past," *MetalSmith* 31, no. 3 (2008): 18–20.

16. Ibid., 19.

17. Jake von Slatt, "Work Corset: Inspired by Carhartt Work Clothing," Steampunk Workshop (blog), September 8, 2009. At http://steampunkworkshop.com/articles/ fashion?page=3.

18. "Style Insight: Steampunk," *VivaLaModa*, March 11, 2009. At http://steampunkwork shop.com/vivalamoda-does-steampunk.

19. Libby Bulloff, "Quaintrelles, Dandies, and Flâneurs #3," Steampunk Workshop (blog), January 29, 2010. At http://steampunkworkshop.com/quaintrelles-dandies-and-flâneurs-3.

20. "Steampunk Couture Hot on the Runway (and We're Not Talking Airships)," Steampunk Workshop (blog), March 6, 2013. At http://steampunkworkshop.com/ steampunk-couture-hot-runway-and-were-not-talking-airships.

21. G. D. Falksen, "Steampunk 101," Tor.com (blog), October 7, 2009. At http://www.tor .com/blogs/2009/10/steampunk-101.

22. Suzanne Lazear, "Women in Steampunk," Steamed! (blog), August 16, 2010. At http:// ageofsteam.wordpress.com/2010/08/16/women-in-steampunk/.

23. Jake von Slatt, "Sub-culture Friendly Gender Playful Marketplace," Steampunk Workshop (blog), December 6, 2010. At http://steampunkworkshop.com/sub-culture -friendly-gender-playful-marketplace.

24. Ibid.

25. Judith Butler, *Bodies That Matter* (New York: Routledge, 1993).

26. Nisi Shawl, "The Steampunk That Dare Not Speak Its Name," Tor.com (blog), October 5, 2011. At http://www.tor.com/blogs/2011/10/the-steampunk-that-dare-not -speak-its-name.

27. Ashley Strickland, "Steampunk Powers Female Characters Forward," CNN.com, November 16, 2011. At http://geekout.blogs.cnn.com/2011/11/16/steampunk-powers-female -characters-forward/.

28. Anna North, "5 Steampunk Fashion Tips for Women," BuzzFeed, July 13, 2012. At http:// www.buzzfeed.com/annanorth/5-steampunk-fashion-tips-for-women.

29. Robert Hariman, *Political Style: The Artistry of Power* (Chicago: University of Chicago Press, 1995), 9.

30. Barry Brummett, *A Rhetoric of Style* (Carbondale: Southern Illinois University Press, 2008), 119.

31. Cynthia Miller, Julie Anne Taddeo, and Diana Pho link the understanding of Victorian women's fashion to the explanation of women in Victorian literature. Each description can be found in Taddeo and Miller, *Steaming into a Victorian Future*.

32. Kate Millett, *Sexual Politics* (Urbana: University of Illinois Press, 2000), 89.

33. Ellen Bayuk Rosenman, "Spectacular Women: The Mysteries of London and the Female Body," *Victorian Studies* (Autumn 1996): 31–64.

34. Ibid., 36.

35. Donald Stone, "Victorian Feminism and the Nineteenth-Century Novel," *Women's Studies*, no. 1 (1972): 65–91.

36. Ibid., 79.

37. Taddeo, "Corsets of Steel," 44.

38. Theresa Meyers, "An Ode to the Corset," Steamed! (blog), June 22, 2010. At http://ageof steam.wordpress.com/2010/06/22/an-ode-to-corsets/.

39. Taddeo, "Corsets of Steel," 45.

40. Ibid., 46.

41. Ibid.

42. Lauren Goodlad, "Toward a Victorianist's Theory of Androgynous Experiment," *Victorian Studies* (Winter 2005): 219.

43. Ibid., 217.

44. Von Slatt, "Sub-culture Friendly Gender Playful Marketplace."

45. Gayle Rubin, "The Traffic in Women: Notes on the Political Economy of Sex," in *Toward an Anthropology of Women*, ed. Rayna R. Reiter (New York: Monthly Review Press, 1975), 204.

46. Catherine Siemann, "Some Notes on the Steampunk Social Problem Novel," in Taddeo and Miller, *Steaming into a Victorian Future*, 4.

47. Steampunk Emporium is a clothing retail site found at http://www.steampunkemporium.com/steam.php. Steampunk Fashion is a website that details how to perform steampunk through accessorizing, found at http://steamfashion.livejournal.com/. How to Dress Steampunk is a blog that explores the reattribution of Victorian looks, found at http://howtodresssteampunk.com/.

48. Judith Butler, "Performativity, Precarity and Sexual Politics" (lecture delivered at the Universidad Complutense de Madrid, June 8, 2009). Butler's lecture revisited the notion of sexual politics introduced and discussed in two of her famous works, *Bodies That Matter* and *Gender Trouble*. The lecture can be found at http://core.kmi.open.ac.uk/display/5487119.

49. Strickland, "Steampunk Powers Female Characters Forward."

50. Balogun [Balogun O. Abeegunde], "Putting the Funk in Steampunk: For the Mahogany Masquerade and Beyond!," Chronicles of Harriet (blog), October 21, 2012. At http://chroniclesofharriet.com/2012/10/21/putting-the-funk-in-steampunk/.

51. Ibid.

52. Ibid.

53. Donna Haraway, "Cyborg Manifesto: Science, Technology, and Socialist-Feminism in the Late Twentieth Century," in *Simians, Cyborgs, and Women: The Reinvention of Nature* (New York: Routledge, 1991): 149–181.

54. Strickland, "Steampunk Powers Female Characters Forward"; see also http://www.kadycross.com/.

55. North, "5 Steampunk Fashion Tips."

56. Butler, "Performativity, Precarity and Sexual Politics," iv.

57. Butler, *Bodies That Matter*, 82.

58. Ibid., 170.

59. Rosenman, "Spectacular Women," 35.

60. Pho, "Objectified and Politicized," 188.

61. Rosenman, "Spectacular Women," 37.

62. Drawing from this argument, photography featuring women, steampunk, and the reapplication of Victorian style can be found at http://www.yourdailymedia.com/post/women-of-steampunk and http://www.steamgirl.com/home.html.

63. Chris Murphy, "*Steampunk Palin*: Comic More Insane Than You Imagined," Comics Alliance, January 20, 2011. At http://www.comicsalliance.com/2011/01/20/steampunk-palin-comic/.

64. Lisa Derrick, "Sarah Palin Goes Steampunk," *Huffington Post*, January 23, 2011. At http://www.huffingtonpost.com/lisa-derrick/sarah-palin-goes-steampun_1_b_812655.html.

65. Safa S., "Steampunk Palin Is as Two Dimensional as the Real Thing," Care2 Make a Difference (blog), January 31, 2011. At http://www.care2.com/causes/steampunk-palin.html.

66. Pho, "Objectified and Politicized," 197.

67. Ibid.

68. Ibid.

69. Carol Pinchefsky, "Fashion's Biggest Trend in 2013–2015 (as Predicted by IBM)? Steampunk," *Forbes*, January 15, 2013. At http://www.forbes.com/sites/carolpinchefsky/2013/01/15/fashions-biggest-trend-in-2013-2015-as-predicted-by-ibm-steampunk/.

70. IBM Social Sentiment Index, "Analytics Points to the 'Birth of a Trend,' Steampunk Aesthetic to Pervade Pop Culture in 2013," January, 14, 2013. At http://www-03.ibm.com/press/us/en/pressrelease/40120.wss.

71. Ibid.

72. Stuart Ewen, *All Consuming Images: The Politics of Style in Contemporary Culture* (New York: Basic Books, 1999).

73. Judith Butler, *Undoing Gender* (New York: Routledge, 2004), 98.

74. Ibid., 45.

75. Scott Westerfeld, "Leviathan Series," CNN.com, November 16, 2011. At http://geekout.blogs.cnn.com/2011/11/16/steampunk-powers-female-characters-forward/.

76. Taddeo, "Corsets of Steel," 46.

77. Ibid., 48.

78. Samuel Chambers, "'Sex' and the Problem of the Body: Reconstructing Judith Butler's Theory of Sex/Gender," *Body and Society* 13, no. 47 (2008): 69.

A RHETORIC OF
STEAMPUNK
SEMIOTICS

Antimodernism as the Rhetoric of Steampunk Anime

Fullmetal Alchemist, *Technological Anxieties, and Controlling the Machine*

ELIZABETH BIRMINGHAM

ANIMATION IS A PERFECT VEHICLE TO CARRY THE AESTHETICS OF IMAGINED worlds: pasts that never quite were and futures that may never quite come to be. Animation creates the Rube Goldberg machine that, no matter how overengineered, always delights viewers in its perfect completion of its task. It animates the tin man, the floating island, the clockwork girl, the moving castle. Animation, especially of imagined machines, reveals to viewers not how things do work, but how they could work, alternatively. In the same way, alternative, animated worlds reveal the horrors that could occur without care and tending, and amazing possibilities that generous attention could bring to the future. The rich and varied history of animation in Japan, therefore, includes many imagined worlds: pastoral utopias and automated dystopias. Exploring the version of steampunk depicted in anime helps bring into focus that Japan's experience of modernization was different from that of the West, occurring in a compressed timeline and therefore engendering shifts in "nature, culture, and religion" that were exponentially more tumultuous. Economic historian Harry Harootunian describes the Japanese experience as being "overwhelmed by modernity,"[1] and the steampunk response is not so much in a consistent aesthetic but in a rhetoric of antimodernism.

The central question the articles in this book address is: "When images and themes of the nineteenth and early twentieth centuries are used aesthetically today, what social and political messages are urged upon audiences?" This essay argues that the messages of Japanese anime steampunk are profoundly antimodern, critiquing both contemporary technologies and consumer culture. It describes Japan's experience of modernization and the ways in which anime is an antimodern medium, one that is effective for embodying an antimodern message. Using the rhetoric of Victorian anti-modernism as a lens, I examine the preoccupations of Japanese steampunk anime, particularly the animated series *Fullmetal Alchemist*. Although not all steampunk texts—whether fiction or film—embrace a rhetoric of antimod-ernism, this essay will argue that *Fullmetal Alchemist*, in employing a wide range of Victorian neo-medieval tropes, reinforces the values of antimodern-ist rhetoric. Steampunk, whether framed as a postmodern, antimodern, or aesthetic movement, is occasionally criticized for idealizing a Victorian past, glossing over histories of imperialism and colonialism; however, many of the Japanese texts associated with steampunk, such as *Fullmetal Alchemist*, are highly critical of the rationalist modernism that shaped both the colonial enterprise of the Victorian era and the global fascism[2] that erupted between the world wars.

Japanese Modernity

Japan has a reputation of being among both the most advanced technologi-cal societies in the world and the most historically anxious about those tech-nologies. Certainly, Japan's experience of World War II, as the only nation in the world to have had atomic warfare brought to its soil, shaped an an-timodern response to the technologies of war. As Thomas Lamarre argues: "War and technologies of military destruction . . . present a challenge to the idea that modernism is all about rationality, progress, and productivity. . . . there is always something irrational and empty in scenarios of progression to destruction."[3] Yet the Japanese progression in developing tools of war has not been a story of teleological evolution but one of punctuated equilibrium.

Noel Perrin's *Giving Up the Gun* describes "an almost unknown incident in history. A civilized country, possessing high technology, voluntarily chose to give up an advanced military weapon and return to a more primitive one."[4] Perrin's book, although ostensibly about the three and a half centuries of Jap-anese history during which the island nation "forgot" the Western firearms technology it had once mastered, more centrally questions the inevitability of technological "progress." Japanese history, as told by Perrin, is profoundly antimodern, and, through this history, Perrin is primarily concerned with denaturalizing the teleologies of capitalism and progress. He concludes by telling readers that his story means two important things: "that a no-growth economy is perfectly compatible with a prosperous and civilized life"[5] and that humans are not "the passive victims of their own knowledge and skills."[6]

Similarly, David Nye employs the "giving up the gun story" of Japan's anti-modernization, suggesting that the shogunate alone could not have restricted guns once introduced; samurai warriors rejected them because guns carried little symbolic value for them.[7] In both cases, scholars suggest a Japanese "choice" about technology, a notion that is highly contested because it projects an anachronistic rationality about technologies and their uses.

While both Perrin and Nye share this story, claiming that it reveals essentially "Japanese" cultural values, Lamarre frames the same story as a critique and rejection of modernism's tenets, as he refuses to embrace an inaccurate perception of homogeneous Japanese cultural values—values that were imposed later by the nation-state and did not exist in the centuries before the Meiji Era. He argues that human history is not one of choosing one or another technology, but rather of being enmeshed in "a technological condition . . . or more precisely, a techno-cultural field of actions potentialized by a machine."[8] Lamarre's description especially matters because this notion of a technological condition privileges the "scene" in a Burkean sense, constraining (but not dictating) actors and actions that may occur within it.[9] While this difference may seem trivial, Lamarre denies technological determinism and creates a theoretical space in which a literary genre like steampunk can offer political and social critique by depicting alternative histories that question the teleologies of continuous progress and expansion.

Steampunk's Antimodernism as Victorian Neo-medievalism

When critics write about steampunk, especially in literature, art, music, or film, they typically write about two interconnected things: subcultural aesthetics and the politics of those aesthetics. The aesthetics of steampunk have been visited in a number of academic articles, including many in this book. Jeff VanderMeer and S. J. Chambers's *Steampunk Bible* illustrates the subculture and its preoccupations,[10] and Julie Anne Taddeo and Cynthia Miller's *Steaming into a Victorian Future* contains numerous essays describing the literary, artistic, and subcultural fashion aesthetics of steampunk makers, the do-it-yourself retrofitters of contemporary culture.[11] In the first issue of *SteamPunk Magazine*, Cory Gross encapsulates the ways in which the discussion of steampunk aesthetics is always already political, too, describing works that both re-create "the Victorian Era as a Romantic myth infused with utopian desires" and also acknowledge "the corruption, the decadence, [and] the imperialism" of the era, not as a retrocriticism of the turn of the twentieth century but as "an indictment" of our own times.[12] *SteamPunk Magazine*'s vision is of putting the "punk back into steampunk"—a move that values the handmade object and the process of its creation over the literary products or popular film that often more broadly disseminate contemporary notions of "steampunk."

In addition to the aesthetic of the handcrafted object, the material of its construction is important for both aesthetic and political reasons. Rebecca Onion's seminal article in the first issue of *Neo-Victorian Studies* describes the material aesthetic thus: "The steampunk ideology prizes brass, copper, wood, leather, and papier-mâché—the construction materials of a bygone time. Steampunks fetishise cogs, springs, sprockets, and hydraulic motion."[13] These aesthetics are political in that they attempt to reenvision a world untainted by the internal combustion engine, and they describe communities of artist-makers who create through recycling, upcycling, repurposing, and adopting eco-friendly practices. The "punk" of steampunk is countercultural, aesthetically and politically.

While theorists like Dru Pagliassotti posit steampunk as a postmodern movement based on its ironic stance and preoccupations with intertextuality, pastiche, and bricolage,[14] others such as Onion suggest that steampunk is a more thoroughly aesthetic and materialist movement, as it "stands outside of chronological periodisations of modes of thought—such as 'modern,' 'anti-modern,' or 'postmodern'—and defies categorisation within the ideologies of previous technology-based social movements."[15] She acknowledges that there is something analogous between steampunks and the "anti-moderns of the late nineteenth and early twentieth century, who, through the Arts and Crafts movement, advocated a return to a premodern 'middle' landscape." The difference, Onion claims, is that contemporary steampunks value the technological world over a pastoral one.[16] However, it is in this claim that anime may most break with Western steampunk sensibilities, as the machines of steampunk anime tend to be worrisome things, found and repurposed objects that need to be controlled and contained—they are not part of a utopian future but are more often remnants of a dystopian, weaponized (and capitalist/fascist) past. The steampunks of anime are less interested in the modernism of the steam age than in the antimodernism of the period's romantic medievalism.

This Victorian medievalism grew from what T. J. Jackson Lears describes as a "feeling of overcivilization" carrying with it "a dissatisfaction with modern culture in all its dimensions: its ethic of self-control and autonomous achievement, its cult of science and technical rationality, its worship of material progress."[17] The Arts and Crafts movement and its key authors, John Ruskin and William Morris, desired to place control of production back in the hands of individual artists and workers, arguing for a return to the guild as resistance to capitalist oppression.[18] (Similar to some steampunks, they were criticized for glossing over the deep social inequities of the feudal world in order to develop what some claimed was an essentially aesthetic—as opposed to political—response.) Control over the machine, in this instance, was not about the fetishistic desire for the machine over the natural, as Onion asserts of some contemporary steampunks; it was the desire to regain control over the means of production, taming the machine as a tool for workers rather than as a weapon through which captains of industry controlled workers and stole the dignity of their work. Steampunk anime, then, is a response to Marx's commodity fetishism, not Freud's fetishes of desire.

Anime as an Antimodern Medium

In visual texts, viewers often begin to recognize steampunk through aesthetic cues. In Japanese animation, or anime, such cues are often subtly present and are highlighted by an antimodern rhetorical stance in the texts' content. Imagine anime as drawing together low-tech or machine production (as opposed to computer production), an antimodern rhetoric in content, and a steampunk aesthetic in style. Through that low-tech process of creation, anime embraces a mode of production that is mechanical, handmade, and decidedly "other" than the production techniques of contemporary film, demonstrating a synchronicity of medium and message. As Lamarre, a media ecologist and East Asian scholar, puts it, anime, as a medium, "minimizes the narratives of technology"[19] shaping films that question modernism's techniques and teleologies, not simply in content but in form. The anime films of Hayao Miyazaki are well-known artifacts that illustrate this confluence of antimodern rhetoric, technological anxiety, and a medium that both looks different and "looks" differently. As film, it directs the viewers' looking, and that gaze is decidedly not cinematic, but, as Lamarre calls it, a "primordial form of panoramic perception."[20]

Miyazaki's medium, hand-drawn cel animation, literally reflects a Japanese medieval style and is related to twelfth-century scroll "animation." Moreover, anime uses the composition and stylistic techniques of Edo-period woodblock prints, including hand layering color in animation compositing, which is similar to the hand inking techniques used to tint woodblock prints.[21]

While some contemporary anime has resorted to employing sweatshop labor outside Japan, Miyazaki's studio retains a "guild" approach to production, according to Helen McCarthy.[22] Lamarre extends this view further, describing Miyazaki's production company as a "combination of artistic hierarchy and cooperation, with energetic youth under the guidance of charismatic leaders in the service of preserving and sustaining a brand of animation and a worldview, [calling] to mind some of the quasi-feudal communities evoked in Miyazaki's animations."[23]

Not only is the medium born of antimodern techniques and ways of looking, but the message, too, carries antimodern concerns. Colin Odell and Michelle Le Blanc note: "The struggle between tradition and modernity, and between craft and technology is a theme in many of Miyazaki's films."[24] Lamarre writes that Miyazaki's films, like William Morris's philosophy a century earlier, "imply that modern technology is not just dangerous in its applications but in its effect on human perception and human thought."[25] Miyazaki suggests that antidotes to modernism might be found in a return to tradition and a reacquaintance with the natural world. Although Miyazaki is perhaps the best-known anime director among Western followers of the genre and has a long history of steampunk references, he and other directors consistently add to steampunk's style through antimodern rhetoric, making specific arguments about the dangers of the modern condition to societies and individuals.

Steampunk Anime

Although much anime represents a profoundly technophobic and antimodern position, only a small subset of that anime would be considered "steampunk" in any traditional sense. VanderMeer notes that a number of Miyazaki's films are explicitly steampunk and that Miyazaki himself articulates a sympathy with the Arts and Crafts aesthetic, applying it to the machines he envisions, which "are not products of mass production, rather they still possess the inherent warmth of handcrafted things."[26] Miyazaki's work, from *Nausicaä and the Valley of the Wind*, which celebrates communion with the natural world as an antidote to industrialization, to *Kiki's Delivery Service*, which acknowledges the role of tradition in welcoming a new age, have hints of steampunk in their Victorianesque settings and otherworldly retrotechnologies. But Miyazaki's *Princess Mononoke*, a medieval, mythic retelling of the "giving up the gun" saga; *Spirited Away*, a story of a little girl who discovers the traditional world of spirits in a bathhouse; and *Howl's Moving Castle* all employ a steampunk look with their antimodern theme.

In addition to Miyazaki's work, several scholars identify a constellation of steampunk anime. Rick Klaw, in his contribution to *The Steampunk Bible*, identifies several anime as steampunk: *Fullmetal Alchemist, Steam Detectives* (1989–1990), *Last Exile* (2003), and *Samurai 7* (2004), a retelling of *Seven Samurai*, Akira Kurosawa's film classic.[27] In addition, the 2004 films *Cassburn* and *Steamboy* both combine overt steampunk references and a strong antiwar stance, questioning the role of science in a militarized future. The other primary academic text on steampunk, Taddeo and Miller's *Steaming into a Victorian Future*, does not mention anime or Japanese steampunk in any of its fourteen chapters.

One article that considers the differences between Western and Japanese steampunk is Michaela Sakamoto's "The Transcendent Steam Engine: Industry, Nostalgia, and the Romance of Steampunk." Sakamoto considers two Japanese films, *Steamboy* and *Spirited Away*, and the anime series *Fullmetal Alchemist*, arguing that Japanese steampunk combines a pending (but not yet arrived) utopian future with Confucianist ideas of social hierarchy. She notes that Miyazaki's films "show a sophisticated sense of the idea of physical paradises and the threats of social destruction of those Arcadias through human greed and ambition."[28] That greed and ambition are most often the primary traits of steampunk villains, who in Sakamoto's estimation "are little more than capitalists"[29] who damage the natural world or misuse technologies and people to maximize profits. In contrast to Onion's notion of a Western steampunk aesthetic that fetishizes technology, Sakamoto suggests that Japanese steampunk, despite its fascination with the mechanized, is nostalgic for a romantic and pastoral past, in the future. She writes that these worlds "are nearly Utopian, but only on the verge of Utopia, not in it. The tension of these narratives derives from the potential for evil within humanity and how that potential can assert itself."[30] Nowhere is that tension more fully realized than in the neo-medieval philosophy of *Fullmetal Alchemist*.

Reading *Fullmetal Alchemist* as an Antimodern Text

One of the most popular anime series ever on Japanese television, the series *Fullmetal Alchemist* (fifty-one episodes that originally aired from October 4, 2003, to October 2, 2004) shares many of the surface preoccupations of steampunk (alternative and blended histories, a clash between science and religion, the fetishization of the mechanical, and a strange, continental Edwardian style in a fascist military state, Amestris). In addition, stock steampunk characters abound: the girl genius tinker who makes and repairs metal prosthetic limbs; the metal boy who ponders whether, lacking an organic body, he "is"; the deeply flawed hero, a true believer in the "science" of the craft he practices; and a variety of villains representing the seven deadly sins. Yet this anime's connection to steampunk lies less in its aesthetic choices of its "look" and plot—both marginally steampunk, as Rick Klaw points out[31]—than in its embrace of antimodernist rhetoric. Although the plot and characters reveal the series' neo-medievalism, the specific anxieties surrounding technologies of war and mass destruction create a nexus of antimodernist messages, urged on the viewer.

Like much anime, the series' plot is complex and includes a cast of hundreds. The central action of the series involves the fortunes of two orphan brothers, both prodigies of alchemic craft, over the course of about five years. Edward Elric, the elder of the two, misuses his alchemic abilities in a misguided attempt to "play god" and bring the boys' dead mother back to life. The act completely destroys his younger brother Alphonse's body (forcing Ed to outfit Al's soul with a handy medieval suit of armor). Ed lost his own arm and leg as a result of his hubris and has these limbs replaced with "automail," a kind of high-tech metal bioprosthetic device. Ed is introduced to the audience as a true believer, a practitioner who believes that the world will be made better through alchemy. The story revolves around the boys' journey to find or create the fabled philosopher's stone that will enable them to restore their bodies.

As with much anime, there is little literature that directly addresses *Fullmetal Alchemist*. Lesley-Anne Gallacher discusses monstrosity in the text, those many creatures, including Ed and Al, that inhabit the borders between humanity and something else. Benjamin Chandler addresses questions of Japanese culture and the role of the hero in his close reading of the anime series. Dylan E. Wittkower, in "Human Alchemy and the Deadly Sins of Capitalism," reads *Fullmetal Alchemist* as a cautionary tale about capitalism, one that illuminates the ways in which human beings are repeatedly sacrificed for profit and progress.

Wittkower's argument is especially supported by the series' consistent point-of-view character, Alphonse Elric, a lumbering, empty suit of medieval armor inhabited by a child's soul. Al provides the story's narration and its consistently antimodern voice, questioning his older brother Ed's teleological worldview and offering instead a critique of Ed's craft along with his own decidedly antirational angst. Al's narration frames the story as a missive written to a girl, Rose, whom the brothers meet in the first episode. Much of the story is told in flashback, as a letter from Al to Rose, entreating her to "not make the same mistakes we did." Each episode begins with this narration from Al to Rose: "Humankind cannot gain anything without first giving up something in return. To obtain, something of equal value must be lost. That is Alchemy's First Law of Equivalent Exchange. In those days, we really believed that to be the world's one, and only, truth." The boys believe that the philosopher's stone is the only way around that truth, only to discover, to their horror, that the sacrifice required of the stone is massive loss of human life. Al gives up on the rational "truth" of equivalent exchange sooner than his brother Ed, and the series is a narration of his journey to a new understanding.

At first blush, Ed might seem to be the series' protagonist; he is the more active and older brother, and he becomes a state alchemist, working for the military industrial complex, although always assuring his brother and the audience that he has not sold out to the fascist state. However, the anime, through Al's narration, offers a very different rhetorical position than the one Ed espouses; Ed is regularly shown to be arrogant and flat-out wrong. In fact, like any modernist worth his salt, he continues to make the same mistakes, based upon the same rational processes, from the beginning to the end of the anime. To read *Fullmetal Alchemist*'s rhetoric as antimodernist, the argument that follows teases apart the neo-medieval motifs that are used to critique the modernist capitalism and technological progress that the series aggressively undermines through Al's narration and Ed's grudging moral choices.

Medieval Motifs as Metaphor

Reading the alchemy in *Fullmetal Alchemist* as not just a plot device but a literary conceit, a fully developed metaphor with a complex logic that gives shape and meaning to the text, offers a path through the complicated tangle of medieval motifs that carry rhetorical and cultural meaning. Mary Baine Campbell explains that "[m]etaphor is a figure of resemblance, even if its literary charm and pedagogical power depend on the kick of difference. In the period immediately preceding the seventeenth century's grand eschewal of metaphor . . . the fundamentally metaphorical process of alchemic transformation fascinated many of those who considered the natural world in ways we might now consider precursors to the 'properly' scientific."[32] Alchemy, in this series, becomes a metaphor for various modernist teleologies of progression: science (especially the science of war), capitalist growth, and colonial exploitation.

The metaphor is an effective conceit because alchemical processes are themselves teleological—they function on the notion that the chemical states of elements can be perfected (lead to gold being but one narrow example) through chemical processes such as sublimation or distillation, whereby elements are refined (through boiling, burning, and recombining) to ever higher states of perfection. Alchemy shows interest in biological processes as well, and its scholarly texts describe the creation of near-human creatures: parthenogenetic clones, chimeras, homunculi, and golems. All of these creatures occupy the world of *Fullmetal Alchemist*, and much of the work of the show is a Victorian hierarchical ordering of these near-human species and the creatures' coming to an understanding of their place in the hierarchy. Alchemy, therefore, becomes a metaphor for modernism's teleology: a critique of rhetoric of optimism that progress leads to a perfected society. Al's ultimate rejection of the "law" of equivalent exchange that introduces each episode becomes a rejection of that teleology.

Al himself is in many ways a golem figure[33] in that he is an empty and inorganic shell animated by a glyph or cipher, a transmutation circle written in his brother's blood inside a medieval suit of armor. His only frailty is that mark—the written characters that animate him by tying his soul to the suit of armor. Should that mark be erased or destroyed, he would cease to be animated, like the medieval golem, who is animated and destroyed through writing or erasing Hebrew letters. Without a corporeal body, Al has, in fact, been living the promise of the philosopher's stone: immortality. The immortality was purchased at a terrible price; after his physical body was destroyed, his brother literally gave his right arm in exchange for Al's soul, a weightless slip of nothing that Ed tied to the only anthropoidal form in the room—a suit of armor. Throughout the series, other characters comment of Al's fortune: he can live forever, he cannot be irreparably injured, he does not even "need" to eat or drink.

While the many warriors and villains of the series envy Al's strength and immortality, Al perceives Lears's notion of "over-civilization" and Nietzsche's conception of "weightlessness,"[34] an experience of being untethered, in response to his inability to feel (even pain). As a result, Al encounters what Lears refers to as "modern doubt," a late Victorian psychic and moral disruption that "destroys the sense of reality."[35] In nearly every episode, Al's lack of a corporeal self is highlighted: he is offered food he cannot eat, smell, or taste, and when those he loves touch him, he cannot feel their presence. At one point, Ed lays his head against Al's leg, remarking how good the cool metal feels. Al replies that he is glad, at least, that he can give someone comfort in the form he now inhabits.

Although the series is very clear in its telling of Al's origin story, Al himself has moments of intense doubt; when his memory occasionally fails, in a very human way he begins to wonder if he is all golem and no soul, animated by his brother's alchemy and fed with stories of a past that did not "really" exist. His anxieties are verbalized and reinforced after he meets a soul attachment like himself, Barry the Chopper, who stirs the pot of Al's anxieties: "What a naive worm you are! What if you're a fake, an imitation? How would you know the difference? Your brother's the one who crafted you in this form. How do you know you don't love him because he made it so you would, tailored your memories and personality to suit him best?"

Al's response to this anxiety of existence and authenticity mirrors a particular Victorian response to modernism, the now largely debunked neurological condition known as neurasthenia, characterized by "immobilizing, self-punishing depressions."[36] Through Al, the series argues that the promise of the philosopher's stone, life everlasting, is a metaphor for modernism's promise of ease and plenty without physical pain or struggle, and demonstrates that such a promise simply carries new and different anxieties.

In contrast to Al, whose lack of a physical body forces him into "belief" (and anxieties of doubt) that a world he cannot empirically verify indeed exists, Ed represents the voice of scientific positivism. Although alchemy functions as a metaphor for science, Ed voices a positivistic stance: a consistent rejection of metaphysics and a reduction of knowledge to the observable and the measureable. In the very first episode, he confronts Rose, a young woman with the strong religious belief that a faith healer will bring her dead lover back. Ed responds to her faith with a sigh, and recites:

Water: 35 l. Carbon: 20 kg. Ammonia: 4 l. Lime: 1.5 kg. Phosphous: 800 g. Salt: 250 g. Saltpeter: 100 g. Sulfur: 80 g. Fluorine 7.5 g. Iron 5 g. Silicon 3 g. and trace amounts of 15 other elements. . . . It's all the ingredients of the average adult human body down to the last speck of protein in your eyelashes. And even though science has given us the entire physical breakdown, there's never been a successful attempt at bring a human to life. There's still something missing. So what makes you think that hack job priest with his parlor tricks is going to be able to? And in case you're wondering, all those ingredients can be bought on a child's allowance. Humans can be built on the cheap. There's no magic to it. . . . Science will find a way. Science is the answer to everything. If I were you, I'd drop the scriptures and pick up an alchemy book. We're the closest thing to gods there are.

Ed's speech, although delivered in the first episode of the series, comes chronologically three years after he destroyed his brother's body in an effort to bring a human being back from the dead. Not only does he not tell Rose of his transgression, he assures her that such a feat is possible through the progression of scientific knowledge.

In the series' final episode, Ed is killed, and Al successfully restores his life, using himself and the philosopher's stone for an equivalent exchange. Ed wakes to discover that he has been restored (with an arm and leg that are newly flesh), but his brother has been taken, and he refuses his brother's gift. Ed shows that he has gained almost no insight into his belief that the law of equivalent exchange is irrefutable, despite his brother's assurance that sometimes one could sacrifice everything and get nothing. Ed says: "Maybe no life has equal trade. Maybe you can give up all you've got, and get nothing back. But still, even if I can't prove it's true, I still have to try, for your sake, Al." He attempts human transmutation, offering his own life. Al returns to his child's body, losing all memory of the years he spent in close companionship with his brother. Ed is pulled through the gate of truth, not to his death but to a parallel world, where he will continue to search for his brother, using a new science, physics, for this work.

Online fan critics regularly cite Ed's lack of emotional or intellectual change or growth (he doesn't grow physically, either) as *Fullmetal Alchemist*'s central flaw. He loves his brother, but not enough to let his brother sacrifice for him; he searches for his brother, but simply substitutes a new science for the old one. The lack of change—Ed is as egotistical in the series' last episode as he was in the first—is only troubling if viewers read Ed as the series' central character and his positivism as the show's central philosophy. However, I choose to read Al as the show's central character and his antimodernism as the series' central philosophy. At the end of the series, Al *believes* and trusts an experience he does not remember, a feeling of connection and brotherhood with Ed. He closes the series by reframing the law of equivalent exchange, acknowledging that the law cannot explain or predict everything and that, moreover, it is not an unchanging law but a promise, metaphysical rather than positivistic, with ebbs and flows of commitment and belief:

But the world isn't perfect, and the law is incomplete. Equivalent Exchange doesn't encompass everything that goes on here, but I still choose to believe in its principle, that all things do come at a price, that there's an ebb and a flow, a cycle, that the pain we went through, *did* have a reward, and that anyone who's determined and perseveres, will get something of value in return, even if it's not what they expected. I don't think of Equivalent Exchange as a law of the world anymore. I think of it as a promise, between my brother and me. A promise that someday, we'll see each other again.

Al's narration ensures that this is not Ed's story, and his final denial of equivalent exchange not only recovers a sense of religiosity and belief without evidence, it also refutes the capitalist progressive conception of economic equivalence.

Wittkower reads *Fullmetal Alchemist* as an anticapitalist allegory, interpreting Al's concluding remarks as acknowledgment that "[f]ree and fair equivalent economic exchange brings about conditions that are not fair, and in which we are not free. . . . [T]he power to profit without work is to disobey the law of equivalent exchange, only because capital is built on human sacrifice."[37] Wittkower's analysis is consistent with Lears's claims about capitalism and modernization: "Modernization has never been a neutral or inevitable process; it has nearly always been furthered by particular classes at the expense of others."[38] There is nothing natural about the progress of modernism; in fact, it represents an unnatural marriage of science's wartime technologies with capitalist economic progress into a military industrial complex. The "punk" of steampunk becomes the countercultural wedge that attempts to regain control of science and its machines for individual use.

The *Fullmetal Alchemist* character most clearly a steampunk type is Winry Rockbell, the Elric brothers' childhood friend and neighbor, a tinkering girl genius who wears a bandana over her blonde hair and coveralls over her tube top and who sleeps with a wrench. It is she who lovingly crafts Ed's automail, and she is depicted as a consummate gearhead—there is nothing she can't take apart and put back together. She alone among the characters fetishizes the machine and the mechanical, asking Ed, when he explains his desire to get his original arm and leg back, "Seriously, Ed, why go to all this trouble just for human limbs? You've got the smell of oil, the creak of synthetic muscles, the hum of spinning bearings. Who needs natural when you've got automail?" Ed's response is to call her a "loser machine junkie," a comment that highlights her near addiction to the smell and feel of the machines with which she works.

Although these predilections would seem to align Winry philosophically with Ed's science of alchemy, she is wary of, if not hostile to, the fascist military, and she questions Ed's desire to join the state alchemists, uncertain whether he can maintain his individuality while serving the state apparatus. She is the true steampunk—self-sufficient in her ability to build or repair all she needs, a symbol of the early modern entrepreneurial spirit rather than a tool of corporate capitalism. Her craft was passed down to her from her grandmother through a matriarchal apprenticeship, and despite the applied science of their work, neither Winry nor her grandmother, Pinako, accept or value an alchemic worldview. They are William Morris's independent makers, offering viewers a countercultural political position as they drop out of the industrial economy and control their own means of production through knowledge of machinery.

Several other medieval preoccupations inhabit *Fullmetal Alchemist* as antimodern metaphors. Homunculi, or "little men" artificially created outside the womb, represented an alchemic challenge for hundreds of years. Medieval alchemists sought to gently heat human semen with warm horse dung in a vessel for forty weeks (the period of human gestation), in an effort to produce homunculi.[39] In *Fullmetal Alchemist*, homunculi are the by-products of failed human transmutation. Because they were born of the sin of transmutation, each was named for one of the seven deadly sins and is, in many ways, a mirror image of Al. They are bodies that have lost their human souls. Like Ed and Al, they search for the philosopher's stone, in an effort to become fully human by gaining a soul. Some of them are more effectively made than others, depending perhaps on the skill of the alchemist who attempted to craft them. While most of them lack human ethical grounding, most are no more evil than many of the state alchemists the series depicts.

The series begins with clear demarcations of what is human and what is other, but as it progresses, the lines between human and other become more blurred. For example, the viewer immediately accepts Al, the narrator and moral compass of the show, as human, although he is little more than a disembodied child's voice. In contrast, Dante, the story's antagonist, is no doubt fully human, and she has the power to control and use other people and acts upon it. Her amorality, however, marks her as something less human than several of the homunculi, who die heroic deaths opposing the state's use and abuse of them.

The central question, though, concerns the contemporary rhetorical value of the seven deadly sins in this anime. In a 1968 article, Siegfried Wenzel notes the lack, among his contemporaries, of scholarship on the seven deadly sins, arguing that it is perhaps "due to their lack of appeal and interest for modern man as a meaningful pattern in the analysis of human behavior."[40] "Modern" man, Western corporate capitalist human, might find the seven deadly sins unappealing as a pattern for analysis of human behavior, as, following Thomas Aquinas, they see greed as the root of evil in that "by riches, man acquires the means of committing any sin whatever."[41] In *Fullmetal Alchemist*, the "capital" sins are those that are born of greed and hubris, the greed consistently articulated by the voice of the state and the hubris voiced by Ed, whose unwavering belief in the myth of progress draws him inexorably away from home, family, and tradition to his life in the city.

A final voice for antimodernism in *Fullmetal Alchemist* comes from the Ishbalan people, whose fundamentalist religious beliefs led them to decry alchemy as a sin against nature. During the early episodes of the series, Ed and Al see the Ishbalans as the state military has depicted them: as culturally backward terrorists. Winry's parents, doctors, were killed during an Ishbalan uprising. While initially it seems as though they were killed by Ishbalan rebels, it becomes clear that they were providing medical aid to local people terrorized by Amestris invaders. For that caring choice, they were executed by the state military; a young state alchemist, Roy Mustang, who will later be Ed's commanding officer, is forced to murder them. As the series progresses, both Al and Ed come to see Ishbal as a victim of their own state's expansion, and Roy sends Ed to locate Roy's former partner, who reveals the story of the Rockbells' murder to Ed. The story is framed as a confession, though secondhand, and it gives Ed insight into Roy and a new understanding of the ways the machinery of nation operate unchecked.

The series associates the fascist state apparatus primarily with modernist rhetoric and an imperialist and colonialist teleology that includes genocidal wars of conquest. Steampunk images are perhaps most prevalent in depictions of the nation-state: the steam trains that move the military to the edges of empire and return goods from the colonies to the center, called, unsurprisingly "Central." Central functions as both central headquarters for the military and the metropolitan center of the nation-state. Steampunk images abound in the blue, double-breasted, neo–Crimean War uniforms; the rows of gleaming, firing weapons shown close up in such a way that human actors are blocked from the scene; and Amestris's fascist leader's—the führer's—richly detailed uniform, lined with rows of military honors. But perhaps the most powerful signifier of steampunk aesthetics is the silver pocket watch, the weapon carried by state alchemists to amplify their already considerable power. The accoutrements of steampunk operate as merely a backdrop to conjure up an otherworldly, different-time scene for the action: a technological condition of early industrial modernity.

The anime employs that scene to implore viewers to search for rhetorics alternative to those that naturalize progress. It positions itself strongly against the kinds of progress that perfect society through state-sanctioned genocide, covered up by a state military claiming terrorism and dangerous religious infiltration as pretenses for the expansion of power. It positions viewers to look in the mirror.

Fullmetal Alchemist may be read in a variety of ways, but one that is especially fruitful is as a neo-medieval morality tale, using antimodernist rhetoric to question the very possibility of progress through its depiction of the title character, Edward Elric, the Fullmetal Alchemist, who does not grow during the five-year duration of the story. Likewise, his more sympathetic younger brother, Al, reunited with his ten-year-old body and his memories at the story's end, is incapable of having "learned" a lesson, although he expresses faith that he did.

In contrast, the end of the program lands Ed in an alternate world, 1930s Germany, where the new alchemy is physics, and he begins again, attempting to master the new alchemy for his own purposes while avoiding being exploited by the fascist nation-state in which he finds himself enmeshed. Ed has not yet learned how things might work—differently. The viewer, of course, knows where this will lead. The Japanese viewer, no doubt, might have an even more anxious response to this moment. Although the rhetoric of steampunk might most often refer to the aesthetic of a contemporary subculture or a style of alternative future fiction, I want to suggest that it can also offer a rhetorical antidote to the demoralizing cultural effects of industrialization, colonization, consumerism, and mass production. However, for the antidote to work effectively, we must see ourselves reflected in an alternative past and be willing to embrace an alternative future.

Notes

1. Harry Harootunian, *Overcome by Modernity: History, Culture, and Community in Interwar Japan* (Princeton: Princeton University Press, 2000), x.
2. Ibid., xii.

3. Thomas Lamarre, *The Anime Machine: A Media Theory of Animation* (Minneapolis: University of Minnesota Press, 2009), 118.

4. Noel Perrin, *Giving Up the Gun: Japan's Reversion to the Sword, 1543–1879* (Jaffrey, N.H.: David Godine, 1988), ix.

5. Ibid., 91.

6. Ibid.

7. David Nye, *Technology Matters: Questions to Live With* (Cambridge: MIT Press, 2006), 21.

8. Lamarre, *The Anime Machine*, 95.

9. Kenneth Burke, *A Grammar of Motives* (Berkeley: University of California Press, 1969), 3.

10. Jeff VanderMeer and S. J. Chambers, *The Steampunk Bible* (New York: Harry N. Abrams, 2011).

11. Julie Anne Taddeo and Cynthia J. Miller, *Steaming into a Victorian Future* (Lanham, Md.: Scarecrow Press, 2013).

12. Cory Gross. "Varieties of Steampunk Experience," *SteamPunk Magazine*, no. 1 (2006): 62–63.

13. Rebecca Onion, "Reclaiming the Machine: An Introductory Look at Steampunk in Everyday Practice," *Neo-Victorian Studies*, no. 1 (2008): 139.

14. Dru Pagliassotti, "Does Steampunk Have an Ideology?," *The Mark of Ashen Wings*, last modified 2009. At http://drupagliassotti.com/2009/02/13/does-steampunk-have-an-ideology/, accessed July 20, 2011.

15. Onion, "Reclaiming the Machine," 142.

16. Ibid.

17. T. J. Jackson Lears, *No Place of Grace* (Chicago: University of Chicago Press, 1994), 2.

18. Ibid., 63.

19. Lamarre, *The Anime Machine*, 6.

20. Ibid., 38.

21. Tze-Yue G. Hu, *Frames of Anime: Culture and Image Building* (Hong Kong: University of Hong Kong Press, 2010), 13–23.

22. Helen McCarthy, *Hayao Miyazaki: Master of Japanese Animation* (Berkeley: Stone Bridge Press, 2002), 32–40.

23. Lamarre, *The Anime Machine*, 100.

24. Colin Odell and Michelle Le Blanc, *Studio Ghibli: The Films of Hayao Miyazaki and Isao Takahata* (Harpenden, Herts., England: Kamera Books, 2009), 81.

25. Lamarre, *The Anime Machine*, 91.

26. Quoted in VanderMeer and Chambers, *The Steampunk Bible*, 182.

27. Rick Klaw, "Obscure Steampunk TV Moments," in VanderMeer and Chambers, *The Steampunk Bible*, 198–199.

28. Michaela Sakamoto, "The Transcendent Steam Engine: Industry, Nostalgia, and the Romance of Steampunk," in *The Image of Technology in Literature, Media, and Society* (proceedings of the 2009 Conference of the Society for the Interdisciplinary Study of Social Imagery, Colorado Springs), ed. Will Wright and Steven Kaplan, 130.

29. Ibid., 128.

30. Ibid.
31. Klaw, "Obscure Steampunk TV Moments," 199.
32. Mary Baine Campbell, "'Artificial Men': Alchemy, Transubstantiation, and the Homunculus," *Republics of Letters: A Journal for the Study of Knowledge, Politics, and the Arts* 1, no. 2 (2010): 4.
33. Moshe Idel, *Golem: Jewish Magical and Mystical Traditions on the Artificial Anthropoid* (Albany: SUNY Press, 1990), 3–8.
34. Lears, *No Place of Grace*, 41.
35. Ibid., 42.
36. Ibid., 47.
37. Dylan E. Wittkower, "Human Alchemy and the Deadly Sins of Capitalism," in *Anime and Philosophy: Wide Eyed Wonder*, ed. Josef Steiff and Tristan Tamplin (Chicago: Open Court Press, 2010), 217.
38. Lears, *No Place of Grace*, xix.
39. Campbell, "Artificial Men," 5.
40. Siegfried Wenzel, "The Seven Deadly Sins: Some Problems of Research," *Speculum* 43, no. 1 (1968): 22.
41. Quoted in Wittkower, "Human Alchemy," 212.

Works Cited

Bartlett, Robert Allen. *Real Alchemy: A Primer of Practical Alchemy*. Lakeworth, Fla.: Ibis Press, 2009.

Burke, Kenneth. *A Grammar of Motives*. Berkeley: University of California Press, 1969.

Campbell, Mary Baine. "'Artificial Men': Alchemy, Transubstantiation, and the Homunculus." *Republics of Letters: A Journal for the Study of Knowledge, Politics, and the Arts* 1, no. 2 (2010): 4–15.

Chandler, Benjamin. "Alchemic Heroes." In *Anime and Philosophy: Wide Eyed Wonder*, ed. Josef Steiff and Tristan Tamplin. Chicago: Open Court Press, 2010.

Condry, Ian. *The Soul of Anime: Collaborative Creativity and Japan's Media Success Story*. Durham: Duke University Press, 2013.

Gallacher, Lesley-Anne. "(Fullmetal) Alchemy: The Monstrosity of Reading Words and Pictures in Shonen Manga." *Cultural Geographies* 18, no. 4 (2011): 457–473.

Gross, Cory. "Varieties of Steampunk Experience." *SteamPunk Magazine*, no. 1 (2006): 60–63.

Harootunian, Harry. *Overcome by Modernity: History, Culture, and Community in Interwar Japan*. Princeton: Princeton University Press, 2000.

Hu, Tze-Yue G. *Frames of Anime: Culture and Image Building*. Hong Kong: University of Hong Kong Press, 2010.

Idel, Moshe. *Golem: Jewish Magical and Mystical Traditions on the Artificial Anthropoid*. Albany: SUNY Press, 1990.

Irving, Helen. "Guilds, Corporations and Socialist Theory." *Economy and Society* 15, no. 1 (1986): 123–144.

Klaw, Rick. "Obscure Steampunk TV Moments." In VanderMeer and Chambers, *The Steampunk Bible*, 198–199.

Lamarre, Thomas. *The Anime Machine: A Media Theory of Animation*. Minneapolis: University of Minnesota Press, 2009.

Lears, T. J. Jackson. *No Place of Grace*. Chicago: University of Chicago Press, 1994.

McCarthy, Helen. *Hayao Miyazaki: Master of Japanese Animation*. Berkeley: Stone Bridge Press, 2002.

Nye, David. *Technology Matters: Questions to Live With*. Cambridge: MIT Press, 2006.

Odell, Colin, and Michelle Le Blanc. *Studio Ghibli: The Films of Hayao Miyazaki and Isao Takahata*. Harpenden, Herts., England: Kamera Books, 2009.

Onion, Rebecca. "Reclaiming the Machine: An Introductory Look at Steampunk in Everyday Practice." *Neo-Victorian Studies* 1, no. 1 (2008): 138–163.

Pagliassotti, Dru. "Does Steampunk Have an Ideology?" *The Mark of Ashen Wings*, last modified 2009. At http://drupagliassotti.com/2009/02/13/does-steampunk-have-an-ideology/, accessed July 20, 2011.

Perrin, Noel. *Giving Up the Gun: Japan's Reversion to the Sword, 1543–1879*. Jaffrey, N.H.: David Godine, 1988.

Sakamoto, Michaela. "The Transcendent Steam Engine: Industry, Nostalgia, and the Romance of Steampunk." In *The Image of Technology in Literature, Media, and Society* (proceedings of the 2009 Conference of the Society for the Interdisciplinary Study of Social Imagery, Colorado Springs), ed. Will Wright and Steven Kaplan, 124–131.

Taddeo, Julie Anne, and Cynthia J. Miller. *Steaming into a Victorian Future*. Lanham, Md.: Scarecrow Press, 2013.

VanderMeer, Jeff, and S. J. Chambers. *The Steampunk Bible*. New York: Harry N. Abrams, 2011.

Versluis, Arthur. "Antimodernism." *Telos*, no. 137 (2006): 96–130.

Wenzel, Siegfried. "The Seven Deadly Sins: Some Problems of Research." *Speculum* 43, no. 1 (1968): 1–22.

Wittkower, Dylan E. "Human Alchemy and the Deadly Sins of Capitalism." In *Anime and Philosophy: Wide Eyed Wonder*, ed. Josef Steiff and Tristan Tamplin. Chicago: Open Court Press, 2010.

Jumping Scale in Steampunk

One Gear Makes You Larger, One Duct Makes You Small

BARRY BRUMMETT

⚙

STEAMPUNK IS AN AESTHETIC STYLE GROUNDED IN THE VICTORIAN ERA, OR the age of steam. It borrows the clothing of that era, but what is most reliably distinctive is its use of a machine aesthetic based on steam engines, locomotives, and early electrical machinery: gears, pistons, shafts, wheels, induction motors, and so forth. The aesthetic was first articulated in literature during that period in the works of Jules Verne and H. G. Wells. The American West has contributed images to the aesthetic, many of them grounded in the revolvers, locomotives, and rifles of the second half of the nineteenth century. It has found common aesthetic cause with Goth style among young people. Steampunk images are found widely in the films of Tim Burton such as *Edward Scissorhands* and other films of that style such as *Coraline*, in the television series (and later film) *The Wild Wild West*, and in many iterations of the television series *Doctor Who*. In many ways, Steampunk imagines what our world might look like were the internal combustion machine never invented, and instead steam power had been refined over two centuries. Steampunk thus makes use of public memory through its appropriation of images of the past, but it changes those memories in its rhetorical applications.

Steampunk has wide popular appeal, even among people who may not have heard that term. A Google search for "Steampunk" generates on average more than twenty million entries. There is also a budding scholarship on Steampunk, some examples of which may be found in the online journal *Neo-Victorian Studies*.[1] There are several scholarly monographs on the subject, including Étienne Barillier, *Steampunk!*;[2] Art Donovan, *The Art of Steampunk*;[3] Jay Strongman, *Steampunk: The Art of Victorian Futurism*;[4] and Jeff Vander-Meer and S. J. Chambers, *The Steampunk Bible: An Illustrated Guide to the World of Imaginary Airships, Corsets and Goggles, Mad Scientists, and Strange*

Literature.[5] However, I can find no record of any study exploring specifically the rhetorical impact of Steampunk. Such a study would explore questions of how Steampunk influences its audience; which attitudes, emotions, and predispositions it facilitates; and what political or social commitments it might encourage. Steampunk is a unique popular culture phenomenon; it is also a unique opportunity for rhetorical criticism. The overall question arises: What rhetorical effects do Steampunk texts have for different contexts and audiences?

A recurring characteristic of Steampunk artifacts is that they often "jump scale" from the original grounding and size of steam engines and related machinery. Steampunk imagines the steam engine grown tiny or huge. Michael Nevin Willard has developed the idea of jumping scale as a useful analytical instrument: "Whenever a place is constructed—both architecturally and socially—" he explains, "scale is also produced."[6] We see this on many levels: "Scale is open-ended and extends in an indefinite series of nested levels from the smallest scale of the body to the largest scale of the global."[7] Scale has rhetorical power, as those in positions of power, in designing public and private spaces, "produce scale that limits the extent of [the disempowered's] social activity and everyday life."[8] Therefore, to jump scale can be a way to challenge the social, physical, and geographic arrangements made by people and institutions in power. Jumping scale is a way to claim a different identity and a different social organization from that which hegemonic power has assigned: "Jumping scale is a process of circulating images of self and community that can be cast broadly to the rest of the social hierarchy. This is the basis for the production of larger scales that insure continued inclusion in, and ability to shape, urban spaces."[9] Willard's specific concern is with urban skateboarders, who refuse the scale that urban planners have assigned to their activities and who can be found skating in a wider, expanded space, in places forbidden to them.

Beyond the example of skateboarders, one can see jumping scale as a way to claim an identity and social construction, sometimes by the empowered and sometimes by the disempowered. The writing of huge graffiti in public spaces, beyond the scale of the human body writing on paper or a computer, jumps scale. The political leader who constructs enormous statues of himself, who speaks in halls and on podiums far larger than needed for the human frame, has jumped scale. The typical consumer delights in the arc of electronics development that produces telephones and computers and so forth that are by now so much smaller than their originals that they have practically jumped scale.

We see many examples of jumping scale in Steampunk. An eBay search for "Steampunk wrist watch," for instance, generates quite a few collections of tiny, used watch mechanisms and parts, evidently for use in making jewelry such as cufflinks (also for sale on Etsy). The watches themselves are made with tiny (often fake or nonfunctional) tubes, hinges, cogs, and other apparatuses copied from the era of enormous steam machinery. Such a search also reveals "skeleton" watches in which gears, levers, and springs that one may find on a much larger scale in steam engines are visible as the clockworks of these watches. On the other side of jumping scale, the aesthetic of a geared engine blown to enormous proportions may be found in the eponymous film, *Howl's Moving Castle*. The film features a steam-powered machine that is as large as a castle. The Corliss "Centennial Engine" built for the 1876 Centennial Exhibition in Philadelphia was based on an ordinary-sized steam industrial engine (large enough on its own terms) that was blown up to tremendous, monumental size. This working engine could be walked through by those attending the exhibition, and reportedly caused the faint of heart to swoon. The aesthetic for both examples is clearly Steampunk.

What is the rhetorical significance of jumping scale? How does it work rhetorically to influence audiences specifically in Steampunk? These are the questions I will address in this essay. To do so, I will engage in a close reading of several elements of Terry Gilliam's film *Brazil* that are clearly Steampunk and have jumped scale "up," to a size beyond the human, beyond the activities contained within them.[10] And I will examine some products offered on eBay that are explicitly identified as Steampunk but have jumped scale "down," shrinking the world of massive steam machinery to the human scale and below. Let me begin with a brief consideration of the aesthetic dimensions of Steampunk so we can know how to understand what happens when scale is jumped.

The Aesthetic of Steampunk

I have previously published a book studying the rhetoric of machine aesthetics.[11] Unaware of Steampunk as a distinct aesthetic at the time, I describe the aesthetics of what I call "mechtech." Clearly, this aesthetic, although it goes beyond Steampunk, subsumes it: "a machine aesthetic keyed to gears, clockwork, lawn mowers, revolvers, pistons, hard shiny metal, oiled hot steel, thrumming rhythms, the intricately choreographed blur of a spinning camshaft, and the utilitarian shafts and pipes running through the steel box of a factory."[12]

Several dimensions of the mechtech aesthetic are found in Steampunk.[13] The first is a "dimensionality" of *depth and surface together*. One can see into a mechtech machine, can see its inner workings. I argued: "Mechtech dimensionality is the machine in context, gears and pistons within the frame of their housing, the dialectic between them being a part of the aesthetic."[14] Key to this aesthetic is *knowledge of how something works*, for "seeing past the skin and into its depth is a revelation, an epiphany, an avenue to knowledge."[15] Therefore, "as a path to knowledge, the dimensionality of mechtech is also a means to order. . . . Knowing what is inside something is an act of ordering what is inside."[16] One may not actually understand the engine, but the ability to see into it with depth gives the illusion of knowledge, and at an *aesthetic* level gives an illusion of understanding the machine.

Another dimension of mechtech aesthetic is the sense of *personal empowerment* one gets from operating a machine. Given the great potential for power in most mechtech, and Age of Steam, machines, the operator of the machine must perforce exercise a great deal of kinetic and psychological identification with the machine. Anyone who has operated heavy machinery knows the feeling of power that comes from merging with the machine, being as one with it, in a kinetic way that is rarely found when operating, say, a computer. Another aesthetic dimension has to do with the mechtech machine as object. It is an object of *precision*, its beauty is *geometric*; there is nothing ambiguous or biological about an Age of Steam machine. A steam engine, unless it malfunctions, does thus and so in precisely the same way each time. This is the ethos of the *factory*, which is the imaginary context for the mechtech machine, where efficiency and precise procedures rule.

The ideal of production in mechtech aesthetics is that of *fragmentation and precision*: the machine is designed to perform one part of a larger overall process of production, but to do that one function with great precision and power. Uniformity and reproducibility of product are important components of this dimension. Finally, in explaining the mechtech machine, I pointed out that machines are gendered with typical gender roles under patriarchy, and that the engenderment of the mechtech machine is *male*, with the persona of the operator being that of a *warrior*. Think of John Henry wielding a hammer. Think of the male driver of a battle tank. Having noted these aesthetic dimensions of mechtech, let me also point out that another kind of machine aesthetic I described as "chaotech," or the appeal of the

Figure 1. Example of steampunk cufflinks. Photo courtesy of Barry Brummett.

decayed machine, overlays much of Steampunk. There is a light wash of decay over the Steampunk machine as object. Many of them show or simulate signs of long use. They are just a bit rusted, just a little brown from age and pollution. Often, this chaotech dimension serves as the bona fides of actual use or its simulation; the machine looks as if it has been in hard use for a long time. The Steampunk machine is thus an aesthetic object of great power with a hint of corruption about it that may reinforce an aesthetic sense that it is a real machine that actually works.

In sum, insofar as Steampunk machines are what I described as mechtech, they are sources of knowledge and personal empowerment, especially on a male dimension, and of the persona of the warrior. A Steampunk aesthetic is one of precision and great power at doing very specific tasks. Add to that a hint of decay, a whisper of rust and age as the bona fides of actual use, and you have the aesthetic potential of the steam engines, locomotives, old revolvers, and so forth that Steampunk borrows from the Age of Steam. I now want to take up the question, what happens to these aesthetic dimensions when scale is jumped? What are the rhetorical effects of a text that shrinks the Steampunk machine and its parts down to a human scale or below, to a scale of easy personal appropriation and use? What are the rhetorical effects of a text that blows up the Steampunk machine to gargantuan proportions, raising these aesthetic dimensions up to monstrous size? I take those questions up first in an analysis of two Steampunk wristwatches and a set of cufflinks, and then in an analysis of scenes from the film *Brazil*.

One more observation before I begin. In *A Grammar of Motives*, Kenneth Burke observes that the scene of an interaction, of a drama, is powerfully definitive of what happens and what may be found within it: "Using 'scene' in the sense of setting, or background, and 'act' in the sense of action, one could say that 'the scene contains the act.' And using 'agents in the sense of actors, or acters, one could say that 'the scene contains the agents.'"[17] When we jump scale, we shift scene. In what follows I want to keep in mind the idea that jumping scale down makes the human and human uses of objects the scene for "tiny" Steampunk. And jumping scale up makes the Steampunk machine or object itself the scene for the human and human actions. This distinction will prove to be useful in understanding the different rhetorical effects of jumping scale.

Jumping Scale Down

If you go to eBay and do a search for "steampunk wrist watches," "steampunk clocks," "steampunk cufflinks," "steampunk jewelry," and the like, you will find hundreds if not thousands of items on offer identical or similar to those that form the texts I am examining here for jumping scale down. Figure 1 shows a pair of cufflinks I purchased on eBay; as you can see, they are old watch movements, case, face, and hands removed, otherwise very little altered other than to be glued or soldered onto a cufflink base. Figures 2 and 3 are two wristwatches I purchased on eBay. These are works of art that are somewhat more manipulated than the cufflinks. They are actually working watches in a manufactured setting cleverly designed to look like Age of Steam engines and mechanical parts. Figure 2 in particular shows tiny, entirely fake, hoses, gears, dials, metal tubes, and the like as if the watch were powered by, or were part of, a tiny steam engine. Both watches are truly tiny, the watch face in figure 2 being smaller across than a dime, the watch face in figure 3 about the area of a nickel.

An aesthetic experience is more than merely representational, it is simulational. To hear the thunderstorm passage in the *William Tell Overture* is not simply to be told of a passing storm, it is to create a simulational experience for the audience. Nonprogrammatic music perforce creates a simulational experience, evoking emotions apart from direct connection to an external

Figure 2. Example of a steampunk watch.
Photo courtesy of Barry Brummett.

context. Aesthetic experiences are powerfully moving, and thus powerfully rhetorical, and this is in large part because of the highly simulational nature of the aesthetic experience. We take moving passages in literature not as factual references to war, love, loss, and so forth; rather, we enter the experiences aesthetically.

In this way, the aesthetic dimensions of mechtech machines, powerful Age of Steam engines, locomotives, and so forth, are re-created simulationally in Steampunk artifacts. When the Steampunk object jumps scale downward, it puts the power of those aesthetics within a frame of the human scale. Clearly, an engine the size of a watch face would in actual experience, were such a thing possible, make very little clatter, roar, and commotion. But the aesthetics of Steampunk jump scaled down to the tiny puts the power, energy, precision, and other aspects of the large mechtech engine simulationally within the human scale and under the control, in the possession, of the human agent.

The aesthetic of precision in a mechtech/Steampunk engine is paradoxically amplified by jumping scale down. The dead clockworks in figure 1 in particular show minuscule gears and cogs, all fitting tightly, all the works tightly packed into a small space. Even this dense array of mechanicals reveals some depth of perception, as we can peer into the machine somewhat even

Figure 3. Example of a steampunk watch. Photo courtesy of Barry Brummett.

if we cannot understand how it works. A dense thicket of otherwise incomprehensible parts is made more comprehensible precisely by the shift of scale, which puts the complexity of machinery into a tiny package that can be borne by the human wrist. It is ours and we subsume it, which gives us a kind of mastery over it even in the absence of actually understanding how a clock mechanism works. In our possession and shrunk to a scale in which *people* are the context for the machine, the clock mechanism of the cufflinks gives a simulation of actual use. One is using it, even if only to close a shirt sleeve, and this aesthetic use is then a simulation of the sense of power that would come from an operator becoming one with a powerful, throbbing machine. Notice too that in the cufflink on the right in figure 1, a faint hint of decay seems brushed over the mechanism. This clockwork is just a bit rusted, not burnished as brightly as the one on the left in a place or two. A hint of use amplifies the simulation of a machine that is powerful and actually harnessing vast energy. A touch of decay tells us that the machine has been used, and is thus usable, thus bolstering a simulation of power. The effect is then one of the power of the Age of Steam machine jumped down below the human scale and put at the simulated disposal of the human. The rhetorical effect is a feeling of micro-empowerment.

If the cufflinks in figure 1 show a dusting of age and wear, the two watches in figures 2 and 3 have been riding the railroad to Birmingham and back for decades. The bona fides of rust and use, telling of a "real" machine in real use, lie heavily on the scuzzy surfaces of these watches. Unlike the cufflinks, however, both are actually working watches. Battery powered, they tell time perfectly. Thus, whenever the wearer checks the time, the wearer is performing a tiny simulation of the merger with the machine that is key to the mechtech aesthetic. The aged appearance of the watches is, of course, entirely simulated. Although each is made by hand in limited lots, each is completely new. But the simulation created by the appearance of age is of a machine in long use, generating great power at the hands of the user for decades.

The aesthetic of surface and depth, of an ability to peer into the machine and achieve some understanding of its parts, is greater in figures 2 and 3 because they are more sculptural than are the cufflinks of figure 1. The actual watch part in figure 2 is cantilevered at an angle up off the plane of the watchband. One wears it so that it sits at about a forty-five-degree angle facing one. One can see beneath and around the actual watch. The plane of the base for the watch, beneath it, is a simulation of hoses, tubes, pipes, steam pressure dials, and the like. None of these actually work, of course, but they contribute to a simulation that one can see into a machine and know how it operates. The watch in figure 3 has hands that actually tell time, but the cogged, barred plate over the face makes telling the time quite a feat. One must peer from more than one angle and discount the movement of the second hand to make out that it might be 2:15. It's not an easy machine to use, and in that way it simulates the difficult mechtech engine barely brought under the control of the operator. An effort must be expended, and the effort is then rewarded by knowledge. If the knowledge is of the time rather than of the engine that gives the time, close enough; a simulation of the mechtech engine is maintained. The watch in figure 3, in contrast to the complicated, simulated machine of figure 2, is fairly simple. An impression is created that the whole thing is one gear, a part of a larger machine pulled out and functioning on its own.

In sum, the sense of controlling and understanding powerful machines that one may obtain by mastering a mechtech engine is made easy, and brought within the sphere of human operation, by jumping scale downward in figures 1 through 3. Simulations of tiny, workable parts—the fact that some parts *do* work, productively—and the appearance of age and use are simulated guarantees of an actual, productive, mechtech machine. Yet this machine, by jumping down in scale, is brought entirely within the domain of the human agent. In simulational rather than real terms, the effect is an impression that one has the power of the locomotive, of the steam engine, literally on one's wrist or in one's hand. The rhetoric of Steampunk aesthetics in jumping scale down is therefore bound up in simulations of empowerment.

Jumping Scale Up

Terry Gilliam's 1985 film *Brazil* is surely one of the most prescient movies ever made. Sixteen years before 9/11 and its aftermath, it depicts a society obsessed with terrorism, dominated by tyrants, where the greatest threat to life and happiness is an overreaching, inefficient, and highly bureaucratized government. Low-level technocrat Sam Lowry realizes that one Harry Buttle has been wrongly arrested, tortured, and killed on suspicion of terrorism—all caused by an insect crawling into the creaky works of a government machine, thus creating an error. As Lowry works to right this wrong, he himself, and the woman of his dreams (literally), themselves fall under suspicion of terrorism. Lowry is arrested and taken to the torture chamber, where the stress is too much and he loses his mind. Images of a society wracked by pollution and never-ending war, willing to settle for cheesy simulations and corrupt politicians, might be taken from today's headlines.

Steampunk images, grounded in a mechtech aesthetic, are plentiful in *Brazil*. The film is constantly threatening to jump scale up. Excess and hyperbole lie around every corner. Everything is bigger than it needs to be. Everything is clunky and mechanical, forming a society developed in a mechtech rather than an electrical direction. It is eerily reminiscent of our world, deviated in the direction of Steampunk a few decades ago. First, I will review the ubiquity of Steampunk images in the film. Second, I will point to many cases of excess in the film, which are consistent with a theme of jumping scale upward, even if they do not technically make such a move. Finally, I will point to the clear cases of jumping scale upward, and the meanings that creates.

Steampunk images permeate the film. If there is one image that dominates, it is that of the duct. Old fashioned, clunky television sets in a shop window all show advertisements for ducts in the opening scene. Ductwork snakes through every room, every building. Ducts are all over the key Ministry of Works building and the Department of Information Retrieval. Otherwise elegant salons have ducts running through them. When walls and ceilings are cut into, coiled ductwork bursts out of them like the intestines of a beast. When Lowry goes back to his apartment after work one day, after it has been sabotaged by a vengeful Central Works team, he finds it unlivable, festooned with ducts of every size and condition, so that one can hardly move through it. The cleaning machines at the Ministry of Information are trailed by enormous long ducts.

Computers are mechanical-electrical devices, the screens distorted magnifying lenses positioned over small, old-fashioned television picture tubes. The keyboards of these computers are from antique typewriters, and one can clearly see into the works of the computers. And these works are unambiguously in a Steampunk register: pipes, hoses, tubes, dials, pressure chambers, and the like protrude from behind the keyboard and beneath the monitors. Often the monitors are held up by clunky iron brackets. Nothing looks quite new, quite shiny; these "electrical" machines seem at least as much mechanical, and they have seen hard use.

Clothing and decoration is from the late Age of Steam, reminiscent of a range from Edwardian times through the 1930s. The bureaucrats wear suits that could be found any time during that period. The clerk who manages the abduction of Buttle early in the film has an Edwardian bowler hat and suit. But the police all wear goggles, a key Steampunk accessory, and their uniforms are covered on the outside by pipes and tubes. The heating and cooling anarchist engineer, Harry Tuttle, is likewise dressed in clothing laced with pipes, tubes, and small ducts. When Sam dreams of himself as an avenging angel, his costume and wings are actually supported by a scaffolding of brackets and steel girders. Similarly, the secretary in the outer office of the torture chamber, typing the screams and cries of the victims as fast as she can, has her hands encased in a scaffolding of steel to enable faster typing. Clothing and other body coverings are often clearly Steampunk. Living quarters often reference Victorian through prewar times as well. Old Mrs. Lowry's apartment is floridly Edwardian. Even the humble Buttle flat looks turn of the twentieth century. Central to the aesthetic of mechtech, shared by Steampunk, is the image of the male warrior, and the film is simply full of such beings, in gaudy and overwrought military uniforms. The Ministry of Information's basement floor is populated by men in exaggerated Nazi uniforms. Women seem largely occupied with shopping and getting elective plastic surgery. This is a male, and thus a mechtech/Steampunk, world.

The film is a riot of excess and exaggeration, a style akin to the spirit of jumping scale upward, even when scale is not actually jumped. Images of Steampunk of *ordinary* scale, or of other mechanicals, abound, and always just on the edge of bursting out of scale into enormity. The terrorist bombing campaign that provides the context for the society of the film is in its thirteenth year, but the insurgents are still experiencing, as a deputy minister says, "beginner's luck." Breaking into living quarters to abduct residents, as with Buttle at the start of the film and Sam Lowry himself near the end, is way overdone: not only are doors rammed in but holes are cut through ceilings, and the police slide down firemen's poles as well as bursting through doors and swinging in through windows. Harry Tuttle, the guerrilla heating expert, comes and goes by sliding down buildings on a zip line instead of simply knocking on doors. Going to the Information Retrieval Office for the first time, Lowry observes a surreal stampede of bureaucrats following their leader as he runs up and down the corridors of the building barking out orders at a staccato pitch. Horrific explosions from terrorist bombs are taken by the characters in their stride; the wounded and bleeding writhe on the floor while the Lowrys and their guests continue to dine in the restaurant that just blew up. In short, everything is just about to burst from absurdity, from excess. Even when the film is not jumping scale physically, it is doing so discursively, with exaggerated and ridiculous scenes.

When the Steampunk images truly jump scale upward, the rhetorical effect is clear. The human characters are swallowed up in the belly of the beast, and it is a mechanical beast. Steampunk pushes one's face into its mechanicals; when the mechanicals are gigantic, then Steampunk inserts the human into the aesthetics of Steampunk. The control, the power, the precision of Steampunk is thus ascribed to the state, and the individual is consumed by it.

The Ministry of Information, which seems to be the very seat of government, is in a building that is enormous, monumental beyond all telling. In the basement of the ministry are the biggest ducts in the entire film, watched over by men in Gestapo uniforms. Twice, Sam must creep along through this wonderland of fantastically large ductwork. Upstairs, the walls of the lobby are covered with television monitors and other machines of surveillance. These machines are clearly Steampunk, exposing their inner workings as much as any Tim Burton film does.

Sam Lowry rides in a ridiculous little car that is barely larger than he is on an errand to the Buttle's apartment complex, and it is nearly run off the road by enormous, grungy vehicles fitted out with ducts, hoses, and pipes. It is in one of these vehicles that he attempts a getaway with Jill Layton, the woman of his dreams, and they are swallowed up by the obvious, visible mechanics of a gargantuan vehicle. Driving into the countryside, we see the human scale dwarfed by acres of enormous pipes, tall industrial towers, and huge storage containers, all of them as rusty and used-looking as the vehicles.

At the end of the film, Sam Lowry is captured and winds up in the mechanical belly of the beast. He is locked in a padded cell that is so huge we cannot see the ceiling. Then he is taken to the torture chamber, a wonder of Steampunk jumping scale up. The distant walls of this chamber look like the inside of a machine, and they show signs of industrial use and wear. Here also, the ceiling is so high we cannot see it. A single catwalk crosses acres of scaffolding out to the platform on which the victim sits strapped into a chair, machines and instruments of torture with their workings, hoses, pipes, and gears clearly visible. The victim is inside a machine, and the machine is the state. Such is the aesthetic power of this image that many of the victims die or, like Sam Lowry, lose their minds in fear and desperation.

Conclusion

Steampunk shares the aesthetics of what I have described as mechtech, an aesthetic of power, of knowledge of the means of power, of control and precise production, of male and military domination. Steampunk uses that aesthetic in two ways: it gives a simulated, entirely aesthetic feeling of dominance and mastery over that power when it jumps scale down and puts simulations of Age of Steam mechanics literally into or on the hands of people. And it cows, warns, and frightens the viewer when it puts the ordinary human into the jumped up scale of truly monumental, enormous aesthetic simulations of that power, knowledge, mastery, and domination. The aesthetics remain fairly constant, the differing results coming from the direction in which scale is jumped. Therefore, part of the news of this essay is to stress the importance of jumping scale, and the direction of the shift, in creating rhetorical effects.

This essay may have served to clarify some of the rhetorical effects of the aesthetics of Steampunk. I hope I have also illustrated the utility of thinking about shifts in scale, and the varying meanings that all sorts of aesthetics and simulations might have as they jump scale up or down. Further research might consider the effect of jumping scale on other aesthetics: Christian, art nouveau, and so forth. Additional research might also consider other examples of jumping scale in Steampunk, and the different rhetorical effects created by shifting scale in other contexts.

Notes

1. *Neo-Victorian Studies*. At http://www.neovictorianstudies.com/.

2. Étienne Barillier, *Steampunk! L'esthétique rétro-futur* (Montélimar, France: Les moutons électriques, 2010).

3. Art Donovan, *The Art of Steampunk* (East Petersburg, Pa.: Fox Chapel Publishing, 2011).

4. Jay Strongman, *Steampunk: The Art of Victorian Futurism* (London: Korero Books, 2011).

5. Jeff VanderMeer and S. J. Chambers, eds., *The Steampunk Bible: An Illustrated Guide to the World of Imaginary Airships, Corsets and Goggles, Mad Scientists, and Strange Literature* (New York: Harry N. Abrams, 2011).

6. Michael Nevin Willard, "Séance, Tricknowlogy, Skateboarding, and the Space of Youth," in *Popular Culture: A Reader*, ed. Raiford Guins and Omayra Zaragoza Cruz (Thousand Oaks, Calif.: Sage Publications, 2005), 466.

7. Ibid.

8. Ibid.

9. Ibid., 467.

10. *Brazil*, dir. Terry Gilliam, Universal Studios, 2007.

11. Barry Brummett, *Rhetoric of Machine Aesthetics* (Westport, Conn.: Praeger, 1999).

12. Ibid., 29.

13. Ibid., 33–48.

14. Ibid., 34.

15. Ibid.

16. Ibid., 35.

17. Kenneth Burke, *A Grammar of Motives* (Berkeley: University of California Press, 1969), 3.

Steampunk and Sherlock Holmes

Performing Post-Marxism

JAIME WRIGHT

JEAN BAUDRILLARD WARNS US OF THE POWER WIELDED BY OBJECTS IN A SYS-tem of meaning.[1] These warnings serve as post-Marxist predictions of un-predictability—that Marx underestimated the power of the object; that the force and vigor of technology are powers beyond the capacity of human management; that the destructive telos of our post-Victorian Industrial Age will continue, by any means necessary, into the foreseeable future. Meeting semiotics with a system of symbolic exchange, Baudrillard provides a method of reading the transformation of tech into a structure of meaning. Basically, he takes high sociocultural theory and applies it to our everyday interactions with various forms of technology; the results, he suggests, are more multidi-rectional than unilateral. We are not as in control of the objects we use as we think we are.

Nowadays, most of these predictions and warnings are dismissed as over-wrought, overdetermined, and overly complex. Theorists argue that the pes-simism with which many post-1968 Marxists greeted the resumption of com-modified business-as-usual and the juggernaut of neoliberal globalization must be read with different lenses. While politicians and citizens continue to try to shrug off the cultural and economic predictions of Karl Marx, we are still functioning in a capitalist structure defined by how much we own and how much we owe. Rhetorically speaking, post-Marxism is dead; long live post-Marxism. However, there are vestiges of Baudrillard's distinctly twentieth-century fears in contemporary popular culture. Our psychosocial concerns about the power of such a system of objects, and our inability to manage such power, reoccur periodically in sweeping stories of apocalypse. The Terminator's Skynet, the Matrix, Kubrick's HAL . . . each of these enti-ties is a lightning rod for old object fears, and they have been examined as such. In this chapter, I look to a slightly different manifestation of those old

primordial suspicions: steampunk. Using the genre of steampunk as a starting point, I interrogate contemporary versions of Sherlock Holmes (in Guy
Ritchie's 2009 and 2011 films and in the modern British TV show *Sherlock*),
looking for rhetorical indicators of Baudrillard's post-Marxist object system.

As with any contemporary adaptation of British Victorian tales, some of
the original elements of the Holmes story are elided. While the current Sherlock replaces understated adages (placed and designed to remind readers of
their shared knowledge and faith in rationality) with slick, often violent re-
sponses, performances of class and the trappings of class remain. Sir Arthur
Conan Doyle was very clear about the inability of the lower classes to comprehend the ways in which technology was changing worlds (an observation I
will demonstrate in a few sentences with *The Hound of the Baskervilles*). In the
contemporary vision of Sherlock, though, class-based foundational assumptions about the nature of knowledge itself—as well as the function of the object in class relations (as a buffer, as a divider, and as a memoir) to put "certain
kinds" of knowing in their place—are removed. For example, in *The Hound
of the Baskervilles*, the quintessential Holmesian revelation is that mechanics
(phosphorous and chemical equations) were used to create a wild horror. This
wild horror, the Hound, long accepted as a curse by the common people of
the day, is revealed by Holmes's science to be another in a long line of cleverly
mechanistic human devices. Typically in Doyle's stories, his rigid classism is
performed obliquely—the people who believe in ghosts and hellhounds are,
clearly, uninformed by the Enlightenment and its objective search for mechanical, objective truth. And, further, while we might like to imagine these
class-driven denouements to be behind us, I suggest that in the contemporary
versions of Sherlock, on both the small and the big screen, the reliance on
objects (of science, of violence, and of the law) performs old classism anew.

I must say that it's not as if theorists are unaware of objective power/the
power of the object, especially as it relates to constructions of the past. Systems of meaning in a technology of history manifest themselves in a variety of
ways: museums (collections of objects), quilts and memorials (constructions
and presentations of objects), books and plays (retellings of objects), and personal collections (objects as markers-of-narrative). Each of these object-uses
demonstrates the form and function of objects-in-history. They help us tell
stories of the past, the present, and the future. Objects function rhetorically
in history as signposts (literally but mostly figuratively), guiding us in the narrative directions most helpful to the telos of that particular story.

Steampunkers are doing exactly that. An intrinsic element of the steampunk aesthetic is the notion that objects carry meaning in various ways—they

can rewrite the past, they can restructure power relationships, they can exhibit different kinds of social and cultural interactions. Into these collections of historical revisionism, steampunk inserts objects constructed and narrativized. So, instead of just making pretty, impossible objects, steampunkers seek to (a) make the object functional (as much as that is possible—for CPUs, yes. For Doctor Who's sonic screwdriver, not so much); and (b) make the object exist in a structure of meaning that may or (preferably) may not fit into the current historical trajectory. Samantha Carroll, writing for *Neo-Victorian Studies*, suggests a reason for the current resurgence in neo-Victorianism: "It is an activity whose nostalgic impulse has been deemed retrograde, yet one that persists in neo-Victorian scholarship where the nineteenth century is often expressed as the present's point of origin—an historical parent to whom the present looks for guidance."[3]

The Theory of Steampunk

Post-Marxist concerns about Marx's failed predictions created a big theoretical discussion in the late twentieth century. While I recognize that we are in a different theoretical and historical mode (perhaps) in the twenty-first century, I think that that conversation still echoes in our popular culture. To that end, I provide a brief discussion of the object-as-reason: essentially, later Marxists suggest that the use-value of an object, while appropriate and understandable at the time of Marx's writing, became outdated—in a current context, the symbolic value of the object is more powerful rhetorically and less predictable politically. Further, some post-Marxist theorists suggest that Marx underestimated the effects the object would have on us and simultaneously overestimated our ability to control the things we make.[2] Instead of freeing us from the manacles of the system of production, the ever-trudging progress of capitalism just turned our use-value against us, shifting the mode of object-use to a symbolic exchange focused on consumption.

In *The System of Objects*, Baudrillard writes about the rhetorical power of objects to create a world. In such a contemporary rhetoric of objects, the practice of consumption is only allowed by a material relationship between objects and subjects. He writes:

> Consumption is not a material practice, nor is it a phenomenology of "affluence." It is not defined by the nourishment we take in, nor by the clothes we clothe ourselves with, not by the oral and visual matter of

the images and messages we receive. It is defined, rather, by the organization of all these things into a signifying fabric: consumption is the virtual totality of all objects and messages ready-constituted as a more or less coherent discourse. If it has any meaning at all, consumption means an activity consisting of the systematic manipulation of signs.[4]

The transformation of objects from use-directed things into signs, for Baudrillard, demonstrates the transformation of human culture into a culture of consumption. Essentially, the world in which humans function, he argues, is no longer controlled by the subjects—but by the objects designed for their comfort and ease. The technological shift of a system of objects from usable to signifying makes the process of consumption central to human life.

Continuing his exploration of the object, Baudrillard writes about the various ways objects obtain value: function, (economic) exchange, symbol, and sign. The functional value of an object is similar to Marx's discussion of uses-value—an object is evaluated based on its instrumental purpose. Pens are valued because they write; swords are valued because they kill. The second mode, the exchange value, is based on the ways in which each object measures up against other objects within that system: a pen may be worth three boxes of chalk; a sharp sword is worth several dull ones. The third, symbolic value, moves up a step on the scale of abstraction because the object becomes a signifier of something else, forming a relationship between itself and another object or event: a pen symbolizes promotion for an executive or tenure for a professor; a sword symbolizes the skills of an assassin. The final stage, the sign, is the most abstract (and is the contemporary function of object valuation in Western sociopolitical structures). In the sign stage, the object gets its value within a system of objects: a certain kind of pen is more prestigious than another kind of pen not because of its intrinsic capabilities but because the multiple levels of relation between the pens, the events, the symbols, and the exchange values of those things alter and affect their value. This is the sense in which a Bic pen is not as valuable as a Montblanc—they both write, but they work differently in the system of objects.

Baudrillard's differentiation between ways of valuing objects lays the foundation for his later claims about the overwhelming power of the object. While Marx recognized the use-value of objects, his reading of their inertness was overreaching. Instead, Baudrillard argued later in his career, the system of objects in which we live is an outgrowth of capital's shift from production to consumption. Here is where we may begin to see the link between contemporary practices of steampunk and the current concerns we feel about the proliferation of objects and our overreliance on them. In the following quotation, Baudrillard interrogates the ideological friction between our assumption of objects' passivity with their obvious and material effects on our everyday lives, our intellectual understanding of those everyday lives, and our interactions with the objects themselves:

> It seemed to me that the object was almost fired with passion, or at least that it could have a life of its own: that it could leave behind the passivity of its use to acquire a kind of autonomy, and perhaps even a capacity to avenge itself on the over-sure of controlling it. Objects have always been regarded as an inert, dumb world, which is ours to do with as we will, on the grounds that we produced it. But, for me, that world has something to say which exceeded its use. It was part of the realm of the sign, where nothing happens so simply, because the sign always effaces the thing. So the object designated the real world, but also its absence—and, in particular, the absence of the subject.[5]

In this world of effaced, erased subjects and all-powerful signs, perceiving the object as a dumb production is not only incorrect, it is dangerous. When the inventors and explorers of the nineteenth century expressed their awe and admiration of the object, most of that expression revolved around the freeing aspects of the object, the ways in which these new productions would improve the lives and livelihoods of the people involved. Now, in the twenty-first century, we know what factory production and technological speed have brought us; we see the horrors of the twentieth century, we breathe the ruined air, we worry about the missing bees. The nineteenth-century notion that the object would save us wasn't totally right—nor was it totally wrong. Steampunk, then, with its contemporary understanding of the object system and its Victorian hope for the object's use, corrects those damages. In their careful and dedicated use of the object, steampunks *re-present* the past . . . as *they imagine* it should have been.

A popular song lyric expresses the desire we all feel to go back to some point in the past with the knowledge we have now. We would have done it so much better! we tell ourselves. Because we can see the harms of our unknowing actions and our unpredictable decisions, we imagine redoing the past as a corrective. In current practices of simulated history, like in steampunk, sometimes this impulse is very clear. Sometimes, of course, it is not.[6] A nostalgic combination of both memory and ceremony, living history was designed in the nineteenth century to demonstrate the activities and objects of the past while simultaneously lending it a more "real" feeling than static museums and exhibitions. Since the middle of the twentieth century, an interest in the performance and reconstruction of the past has grown among both spectators and participants, and those performances have expanded to include all sorts of practices and actions.[7] Steampunk is another variation of that contemporary push to practice the past, but, as I mentioned before, even as the practices may look similar (Civil War reenactments, *Star Trek* conventions, steampunk movies and conventions, living history museums), the rhetorical implications of those practices are not necessarily the same.

Simulated history events share some rhetorical elements: a drive for authenticity, pedagogical designs, and a desire to make history/memory closer. These various performances of simulated history work to *re-present* and *re-member* the past. In this paper, I argue that steampunkers practice the human desire to go back in time with current knowledge—steampunk is a performed do-over, a theoretical mulligan designed to demonstrate our just-now-developing understanding of Object Power. Basically, the differences between steampunk and other kinds of simulated history are not really differences as much as they are shared imaginaries in which the history gets re-known; they are rewritings of the past. This shared space is openly acknowledged in steampunk's rhetorical endeavors—steampunks are eager to demonstrate their devotion to the ways and means of history, while devoting those means to contemporary technological advances. Similarly, Civil War reenactment, on the other side of the simulated spectrum, plays its redesigns of history very close to the vest. In Civil War reenactment and like endeavors, it's anathema to mention the changing effects redoing history might have on our perceptions of the past; in steampunk, it's the reason for doing it. "We want to reimagine the past, as it should have been," might as well be the motto of steampunk.

The Object of Steampunk

The temporal divide between steampunks and the people/eras they seek to improve by representation, then, can be bridged by the use of objects. By putting on the clothes, moving in the same materials, constructing the technology, eliding the time lapse between then and now, steampunk presents us with a rhetorical identification—a myth collapsing the people represented and the people representing. Kenneth Burke, discussing the mechanics of rhetorical identification, writes about the "rhetorical situation": "wherein division may be idealistically buried beneath a terminology of love, or ironically revealed in combination with varying grades of compensatory deference, or where the continuity is snapped."[8] Steampunk's "compensatory deference" focuses on the object of identification—the ways in which contemporary simulational experiences can rewrite, and thus correct, the sins of the past. By doing the past with objects and imbuing those objects with the power of contemporaneity, steampunk gets to retell stories conscientiously that were told by Victorians who were unaware of the impact and import of their object worship.

Another shared space between the steampunk storytellers and the past they seek to reconstruct exists in the ideological underpinnings of each time period. In *Charles Dickens in Cyberspace*, Jay Clayton suggests that there are more links between the nineteenth century and the 2000s than one might at first assume:

> Romanticism and postmodernism share the distinction of being the most significant counter-Enlightenment discourse produced in the West. Indeed, they represent this society's only sustained internal oppositions to Enlightenment. Romanticism's challenge came at the very beginning of the project, while postmodernism's challenge arises at the other end, when some believe that the project has run its course; but the two discourses are united not only in many aspects of their critiques but also in some of the utopian alternatives they propose. Important figures from both eras share counter-Enlightenment attitudes such as an opposition to the hegemony of sight, a critical attitude toward instrumental reason, a preference for undisciplined modes of inquiry, an interest in ad-hoc practices, a relish for hacking, and a reliance on self-reflexive modes of thought.[9]

Clayton draws links between the ontological impulses behind these ideological frameworks, and in those links we see the practical, objective ways those impulses might be performed. These two counter-Enlightenment discourses depend on the object to do the work they need to do—whether that is destabilizing the consumption juggernaut or problematizing the scientific method. Steampunk, then, is a perfect amalgamation of these two discourses. As a practice, steampunk combines the impulses with the use of object, and it takes the use of that object as a foundational method of re-presenting a past filled with object-driven mistakes. Steampunk is the performance of postmodern Romanticism.

Steampunk as postmodern Romanticism focuses very closely on the social aspect of reenacting the past. Twenty-first-century technology becomes a way of performing a Romantic past—the interaction between these two discourses (postmodernism and Romanticism) provides an experiential history that steampunkers work to create and re-present. Experiential tourists like steampunks spend great amounts of time, money, and energy trying to feel the events they reenact by engaging with the time-displaced objects of the Victorian age. Materiality is a persuasive tactic—and, particularly if we are talking about groups of people opposed to the "hegemony of sight," we must see that the tactile engagement with objects from the past works rhetorically to shape their understandings of not only that past but the future in relation to it. These tactile sensations depend upon the persuasion of feeling—in order to agree on a feeling (that the sand is hot, that the waves are cold, that the milk is sour, that the baby's skin is soft, that the rollercoaster ride is fast), we must share the perceptual sensation of that feeling.

Tactility and feeling work together, then, to provide us with a mutual, shareable feeling—a sensation of identification. This emphasis on sensation and tactility—as we see in the previous section—manifests itself in a rhetoric of authenticity. But authenticity is not the only element of this kind of rhetoric; there is also a drive to identify, physically and psychically, with the people reenactors portray. As Burke discusses at length in *A Rhetoric of Motives*, one of the main reasons people talk at all is to feel some connection, some shared substance, with their interlocutors. Below, he describes the human drive to interact—it is because we are separated by space and time, he suggests, that we seek to rhetorically bridge the distance between each other and ourselves.

> Because we are substantially and materially divided, then, we seek rhetorical identification. Identification is affirmed with earnestness precisely because there is division. . . . If men were not apart from one another, there would be no need for the rhetorician to proclaim their unity. If men were wholly and truly of one substance, absolute communication would be in man's very essence. It would not be an ideal, as it now is, partly embodied in material conditions and partly frustrated by these same conditions.[10]

This excerpt explains the rhetorical function of identification: to unify the divided. A particularly appropriate element of this definition is Burke's mention of the material; systems of objects work simultaneously to divide and to unify. The partial embodiment of identification—the materiality of consubstantiality—exists. But, at the same time that embodiment works for identification, it also subtracts from the possibility.

The relationship between their own research—in order to establish and construct the experiences they then seek to simulate—and the actions they perform demonstrates a tension in the relationship between steampunkers and their objects; this tension is performed in movies like *Sherlock Holmes.* Such a tension (between the objects from history and the objects used now) points to the rhetorical claims to authenticity and physical identification—these claims work to bolster the credibility of steampunk while also ensuring that their reversion of the past is believable, at least in the situations they depict. But, even more importantly, the object is itself an actor in this construction—and steampunks are the first to admit that. When Baudrillard wrote about the power of the object, he was lamenting our late awareness of its nonpassivity: "In a first place, one communicates through objects, then proliferation blocks that communication. The object has a dramatic role. It is a fully fledged actor in that it confounds any mere functionality."[11]

As with tourism, the economy of steampunk revolves around the production of simulated experience, and that simulated experience depends on the consumption and use of objects. The greater the consumption, the more a simulation convinces—essentially, I suggest, if we believe that buying things will make us richer or happier or smarter or thinner, then why wouldn't we believe that consumption can tell us something about the past? Or even better, why can't consumption help us *fix* the past? In the performance and practice of steampunk, if the goal is to recognize the action of the object (as opposed to its motion),[12] the past gets corrected and placed—it becomes a thing that we do and was done, instead of a thing that happened. This kind of rhetorical device seeks to control the interpretation of the past while simultaneously rewriting it, using contemporary knowledge of that same past. The method of doing this is through use of objects, but even then, there is an unpredictable, mutable spin of the objects themselves.

Steampunk tries to control the power of the object by locating actions within the frame of known Victorian materials—steam, copper, glass, wood, leather. In the process of defining objects and naming evidence, steampunks rely upon the sign-function of these objects. These objects exist in a clearly delineated, dual-system world—they are both past and present at the same time. Further, the world in which steampunks function, a re-created version of the past, is populated by certain historical actors as well as specific historical objects—an environment divorced from history by time and space. But the steampunk in which reenactors function is realistic, up to a point—it is authentic in its dedication to the rhetoric of consumption. And that dedication produces some of the very effects about which Baudrillard warns us:

> [T]he object slips away, absents itself—all that it retains of the *Unheimlich*, the "uncanny." The exchange, of which it is the medium, remains unconsummated. The object is, admittedly, mediatory, but at the same time, because it is immediate, immanent. It shatters the mediation. It is on both sides of the line, and it both gratifies and disappoints. . . . There is no Redemption of the object. Somewhere, there is a "remainder," which the subject cannot lay hold of, which he believes he can overcome by profusion, by accumulation, and which in the end merely puts more and more obstacles in the way of relating.[13]

The object is a slippery little bugger. It works for us, yes, while also working within and around the system of objects—which is always and already not ours to control. As we seek to control our relation with each other as objects, we accumulate more and more—constantly adding to the excess of meaning (because the object drives this search) while losing any ability to "consummate" our relation with the Uncanny Other. Hence, the uncanniness of steampunk, which is something steampunkers work hard to convey and emphasize, works against them as well. That anti-steampunk work, the creeping omnipresence of commodification and capital, lives in the lenticular logic of any kind of simulated history. The term "lenticular logic," coined by Tara McPherson in *Reconstructing Dixie*, plays on the imagery of a lenticular lens, which is designed in such a way that it magnifies images differently when turned in different directions. Another good conceptualization of lenticular logic, explained by McPherson, is lenticular postcards: two images on one postcard, but, as you turn the postcard in different ways, you see each image separately. It is impossible to see both images at once. Applying lenticular logic to history allows us to explore the many and simultaneous truths of the past while recognizing that those separate "truths" are often impossible to see at the same time. While we are looking at one aspect of history, we cannot see the other aspects, until there is a turn, a space, a breath—and, in that breath, the vaulting power of the object exceeds itself.

Objects in steampunk are used for two reasons: first, to reinforce, through performance, the credibility of the reenactors; and second, to function as lenticular logic. The performance of credibility relies heavily on the use and explanation of objects. As they name certain objects and display particular aspects of the past, reenactors rhetorically perform the part of historians. They use the naming of objects and the performance of past practices (with objects) to define the parameters of the past they claim to know. Lenticular logic relies heavily on the use and explanation of objects as well. Meaning, then, in the culture of steampunk, gets communicated innately via a particular kind of logic: a monocular or lenticular logic. McPherson uses the term "lenticular" to describe the alternating ideological images of race and gender in pop cultural and historical appraisals of the American South. According to McPherson,

> a lenticular lens . . . allows the viewer to see only one of . . . two views at a time. Rotating the picture slightly brings the second image into focus, displacing the first. . . . [T]he structural logic of the [lenticular perspective] makes joining the two images within one view difficult if not impossible, even as it conjoins them at a structural level.[14]

The most familiar example of this kind of illusion occurs in 3-D postcards: "The coating on each card is actually a lenticular lens, a device that makes viewing both images together nearly impossible."[15] Only by turning the cards back and forth can one see the images, and they are always separate—or sort of melting into each other. They cannot exist separately on the same page at the same time.

The images revealed in lenticular logic exist simultaneously, but they do not stand together. Imagining the culture of steampunk as a kind of lenticular logic, a place in which only one story of the past is visible at any given time, allows for the understanding that historical perceptions as performed by reenactment and the identities constructed through reenactment will only reveal certain, one-sided readings of past events. And, as a culture, this kind of logic will be the kind of logic that determines who is and is not authentic, who is and is not an appropriate representative of the culture at hand.

Lenticular logic is the logic of steampunk. The obsession with detail, the myopic focus on material and process, the particularities of image authenticity—each of these concentrations enhances the ability of steampunks to see and create a world in which they get to choose the directions of the tech they employ. The lenticular logic of these practices allows them to imagine that they are in control of the objects—because of time passed, because of contemporary ideological understandings, because of vast amounts of cultural knowledge regarding both the Victorian age and its processes. Lenticular logic describes the inability to see simultaneously all the sides of a many-sided event (or image). Performing the past-as-present, to say the very least, is a many-sided event—other moments re-presented and performed by other kinds of simulated history are as complex. But lenticular logic allows for a very specific focus on a nonspecific practice. The implications and outgrowths of these microscopic views result in a simulated history that both adheres to the "truth" of detail and reimagines the consequences of those object details. Objects perform a lenticular logic in steampunk that works to elide the historical constructs of the Victorian age, even as it reroutes those paths to allow for a more controlled and controlling use of the object. If we are in a stage of object evaluation that exists totally in sign value, then we may acknowledge that sign system. But we may also be able to redirect our energies in directions that Victorians never managed to predict.

The Steampunk Sherlock

Guy Ritchie's 2009 film *Sherlock Holmes* blew the doors off the staid nineteenth-century imaginary of Sherlock Holmes that had long been the standard. The plot is familiar in that it focuses on the perceived mystery of various crimes while always falling back on Holmes's ability to detect and explain the science behind each magical event. We are introduced to Irene Adler (famously adored by Holmes in the stories, even though she is only featured in one of them),[16] Dr. John H. Watson (Holmes's close friend and assistant), and Professor James Moriarty (Holmes's nemesis—who is shadowy and unseen in the first movie but makes a physical appearance in the second). In this analysis, I suggest that Sherlock Holmes is the perfect representative of a steampunk discourse—a discourse that seeks to rewrite the past, using contemporary knowledge of the object as a corrective to centuries of technological advancement in which the development of war machinery always and already outstrips the healing technology it makes necessary. Holmes, the quintessential analyst, embodies a cold understanding of the object that renders its lenticular logic almost obsolete. He sees the various facets of every situation, he predicts and analyzes—he is a scientific object par excellence. To demonstrate the link between Guy Ritchie's Holmes and twenty-first-century steampunks' desire to redo history, I will do two things: first, I will discuss the movie itself—including filming style, plot, and character development; and second, I will investigate the character of Holmes in relation to the movie-as-steampunk-construction.

As a director, Guy Ritchie is known for his fast cuts, a style of direction specifically designed to note the passage of time, convey a large quantity of information in a small amount of time, and/or draw attention to the constructed nature of the movies we watch. Fast cuts are the quick, jerky changes of scene that occasionally make moviegoers feel a bit of motion sickness. Alfred Hitchcock famously used fast cuts in the celebrated shower scene from *Psycho*: "The shower scene was originally written to see only the knife-wielding hand of the murderer. Hitchcock suggested to Saul Bass, who was storyboarding the sequence, a number of angles that would capture screenwriter Joseph Stefano's description of 'an impression of a knife-slashing, as if tearing the very screen, ripping the film.'"[17] Fast cuts, when used successfully, can make a (watched) film feel (physically) visceral; they effect a tangible quality in a visual medium, becoming visual objects, signifiers of the harrowing scenes they represent.

Over the past few years, fast cuts have become ubiquitous. The suggested reasons for this increase in a fast-cut style range from cost to the tastes of twenty-first-century audiences to ADHD. Below is a comment on movie production and fast cuts:

> Consider the modern movie trailer. Very fast cuts with an overpowering sound track. The cuts are so fast you can't really see the composition and art of individual shots. It's a crescendo of shock and awe, almost like being in a war zone. Film scholar Matthias Stork has called this sensory overload Cinema Chaos. . . . In "The Bourne Ultimatum" (2007) the average shot length is 2 seconds. When you combine that fast editing style with "shaky cam" shooting, the sensory overload is too much for some people. Roger Ebert received so many letters about the editing style of the "Bourne" movies that he published them in his column entitled "The Shaky-Queasy-Ultimatum."[18]

Watching films like *The Bourne Ultimatum* and *Sherlock Holmes* creates an object-woozy audience. We are trapped in the theater, subject to the machinations of directors intent on conveying distance or vertigo or speed. The rhetorical implications of this shift in movie style are many, but for the purposes of this chapter (and, in particular, a discussion of steampunk as simulated history), I suggest that Ritchie's style creates a participative audience, a collective that is in on the story with Holmes, carried along the storyline by fast cuts, jump cuts, and handheld cam shots.

This collective construction of the audience contributes to the simulated history of the movies. Sherlock Holmes, as a representative of a past-that-could-have-been, becomes the immutable focus, the unshakeable center of a film filled with fast scenes and head-shaking action. Through the construction of lenticular logic and the application of objective powers (telescopic vision, time prediction, the use of clocks and weapons out-of-time), Ritchie's contemporary Sherlock is a fantastical scientist. He is a scientific seer, using the technology of the time to manipulate and interrogate the events of his present, our past. As we career through the stories, we are no longer participating only in the world of Sir Arthur Conan Doyle's staid detective; we are living life through the lens of the brilliant (and autistic) Holmes in the context of a steampunked twenty-first century. Ritchie's decision to make Sherlock Holmes autistic is not a totally new idea. The symptoms of Holmes's behavior and his observational abilities have prompted several contemporary theorists to come to the same conclusion about Holmes's nature. In a paper presented to the Six Napoleons (a Holmesian meet-up group), A. Michael Maher compares Oliver Sacks's diagnosis of Temple Grandin with the character details provided by Doyle:

> Temple Grandin, according to Sacks, constantly runs "simulations" as she calls them, in her head. . . . Can anyone doubt that during the preliminaries to "The [Adventure of the] Cardboard Box" Sherlock became Dr. Watson, actually entering his mind and discerning his every thought? All autistics, according to Temple, are intensely visual thinkers. They are non-emotional, that is, if they see a beautiful mountain scene they recognize it as beautiful, but the emotional "lift" is missing. . . . An autistic person can appreciate, admire and respect someone—but true love is out of the question. A . . . lonely bachelor's life becomes not only easy, but preferred.[19]

Ritchie's construction of Holmes as almost supernaturally fast, both in body and in mind, presents a Sherlock unaffected by the system of objects. His ability to distance himself from the system of objects makes him uniquely capable of telling the stories he needs to understand clearly, of detecting the cycle of events so as to control and alter them.

Guy Ritchie's Sherlock Holmes is played by Robert Downey Jr., an American actor known for his intertextual exploits and his unexpected comebacks. He is ripped, ferocious, rhetorically savvy, and fast. Each of his interactions with either enemies or allies is marked by speed and speech. The technology of the fast cut, mixed with the use of steampunk objects designed to look old and feel new, create a time-traveling Holmes—the kind of hero steampunks might invent when they are retelling and reimagining the direction of the objective power we seem to have lost after the Industrial Revolution. The movie makes Holmes move faster, think faster, *be* faster in the world. Intermingled with shots of Holmes fast-cut boxing and jump-cut traveling are images of postmodern Victorian tech designed to destroy the world as only great villains can. Another perfect element of the story, of course, is the fact that Watson, Holmes's sidekick, is a medical doctor—as I mentioned earlier in the chapter, the technology of war always outstrips the technology of healing, but the combination of Holmes, the great detective, with a clever and empathetic doctor speaks to a balance between the chaotic forces of evil technology and the steampunked reversion of technological balance.

The character of Holmes matches the fast and furious editing of the film. They are homologous, and well they should be, because in this Victorian postmodernism, the object takes the place of the subject, erasing and substituting the active passivity of an actor (being worked on by the camera) for the passive activity of the object (the camera is the central actor). Discussing the evolutions of nature as a conceptual framework, Baudrillard explores the implications of the object-gone-conscious. He suggests that the ever-faster juggernaut of technology has not destroyed the subject so much as exceeded the line between subjects and objects. We are all subjects. We are all objects. "All of our problems as civilized beings originate here: not in an excess of alienation, but a disappearance of alienation in favour of a maximum transparency between subjects."[20] Sherlock Holmes, our steampunked hero, averts that maximum transparency by making it a subjective focus. His function in the system of objects, his ability to divide himself from both time and space (through the editing processes and the voice-overs), are direct results of the objects used to make him and the technology used to make the film. Likewise, steampunks attending conferences create the world around them with a knowledge of objects and an awareness of the harrowing histories those objects portend. The relationship between the object and the object-user collapses and reasserts itself to reveal a new past, a history corrected—in which the sins of the technology and the motion of the technological creators are rhetorically reconstructed and philosophically re-presented as a whole. Without the advance of the tech, we would not be here, but with the knowledge of the past, we would be somewhere better. The rhetoric of these constructions exists in the replay of historical events, according to contemporary knowledge. Steampunk is a rhetorical do-over.

Conclusion

In a book about writing steampunk, Beth Daniels explains the objective function of steampunk in narrative form: "The story involves steam driven machines, clockwork mechanics, doing things that similar devices were incapable of actually doing in the time period. For Verne and Wells this was science fiction. For the 21st century write of Steampunk, this is Alternative History."[21] Steampunk seeks to rewrite the telos of our contemporary late capitalist society. Essentially, the rhetorical force of steampunk may be seen as a response to post-Marxist concerns that Marx underestimated the power of the object in a system of meaning. The alternative history of Steampunk pushes back at the ills created and maintained by our reliance on technology to help us make our lives "easier." The objects used and created are not designed just for show; they are part of the neo-Victorian story, which, in the language of contemporary historical understanding, is an unavoidable teleological step toward our current technological space.

The faster cuts, the jumpier camera frames all combine in our steampunked Sherlock to create a possible response to this "end." Steampunk, a simulated history, starring an objectified subject named Sherlock Holmes, provides an alternative ending. We are no longer required to balance the tensions between the subject and the object (as impossible as that balance may be) because we have rewritten the past, and the future we created from that past.

Marx predicted that the object would free us from the slavery imposed by ownership and possession. He imagined a world in which the technologies we used would allow us to become the egalitarian employers of a value-laden system. Instead, suggest our post-Marxist friends of the past fifty years, the object has only subsumed those originary imagined freedoms—the use-value has become the symbolic value, the user has become the used, the tech has exceeded meaning in such a way as to erase the very differences between the passive acted-upon and the active object-user. The costs of those missed predictions are high—as we see in the easy, factory-produced deaths of the twentieth century and the coasting twenty-first-century promise of war crimes to come. Into this realization and dismay step our simulated historians. For some simulated histories, the goal is to use objects as an etymological device, a teaching of bodily knowledge that goes beyond reading and writing and lectures. For other simulated histories, however, the goal is to use objects as a re-membering of a different kind. Steampunk is one of these histories.

As we see in the contemporary portrayals of Sherlock Holmes—the fast, furious, tech-savvy science-magician—steampunk performs lenticular logic, a kind of past in which Marx did not underestimate the power of the object. Using the knowledge we have now of what science and technology can do when they don't have a heart beating behind them, steampunkers rewrite and re-vision the history of an industrial revolution, revolving not toward destruction but toward deconstruction and revelation.

Notes

1. The study of objects and their rhetorical-cultural power is a constant theme in most of Baudrillard's works. For an introduction to this theme, see *The System of Objects*, trans. James Benedict (London: Verso, 2005). For a more recent take on it (and to demonstrate the conceptual changes and processes over his career), see *The Perfect Murder* or *The Intelligence of Evil*.
2. Jean Baudrillard spent his entire career—post 1968—exploring this idea. For this chapter, I borrow heavily from his observations. This particular theory is taken from *Passwords*, trans. Chris Turner (London: Verso, 2003).
3. Samantha J. Carroll, "Putting the Neo Back into Neo-Victorian: The Neo-Victorian Novel as Postmodern Revisionist Fiction." *Neo-Victorian Studies* 3, no. 2 (2010): 175.
4. Baudrillard, *The System of Objects*, 213.
5. Baudrillard, *Passwords*, 4.
6. Simulated history is sometimes referred to as living history by theorists. For more information on simulated history, see Jenny Thompson's *War Games: Inside the World of 20th-Century War Reenactors* (Washington, D.C.: Smithsonian Institution Press, 2010), or refer to the Canadian pedagogical project Simulating History at http://simulatinghistory .com/category/about-the-project/. For more about living history, see Jay Anderson's *Time Machines: The World of Living History* (Nashville: American Association for State and Local History, 1984), or "Living History: Simulating Everyday Life in Living Museums," *American Quarterly* 34, no. 3 (1982): 290–306.
7. Randal Allred, "Catharsis, Revision, and Re-Enactment: Negotiating the Meaning of the American Civil War," *Journal of American Culture* 19, no. 4 (1996): 1–13.
8. Kenneth Burke, *A Rhetoric of Motives* (Berkeley: University of California Press, 1969), 22.
9. Jay Clayton, *Charles Dickens in Cyberspace: The Afterlife of the Nineteenth Century in Popular Culture* (Oxford: Oxford University Press, 2003), 7.
10. Burke, *A Rhetoric of Motives*, 22.
11. Baudrillard, *Passwords*, 5.

12. I am borrowing Burke's distinction here, from *A Grammar of Motives* (Berkeley: University of California Press, 1945). In his discussion of dramatism, Burke distinguishes between motion (an oceanic, evolutionary concept, undriven and constant) and action (a kind of motion that has purpose and drive behind it). Action, he says, is a "personal principle, while motion is an impersonal principle" (76–77).

13. Baudrillard, *Passwords*, 5.

14. Tara McPherson, *Reconstructing Dixie: Race, Gender, and Nostalgia in the Imagined South* (Durham: Duke University Press, 2003), 26.

15. Ibid.

16. She is one of the central characters in "A Scandal in Bohemia," although she is mentioned in other stories, and she is admired greatly by Holmes for her ingenuity and imagination.

17. Rob Nixon, "Behind the Camera on *Psycho*," Turner Classic Movies. At http://www.tcm.com/this-month/article/191164%7C0/Behind-the-Camera-Psycho.html, accessed May 14, 2013.

18. Video University, "The Art of Film and Video Editing, part 8: Does Non-Linear Editing Change Style and Art?" At http://www.videouniversity.com/articles/the-art-of-film-and-video-editing-part-8/, accessed May 14, 2013.

19. A. Michael Maher, "Was Sherlock Holmes Autistic?," June 23, 1994. At http://kspot.org/holmes/autism.htm, accessed May 30, 2013. For more on the contemporary debate about Holmes's psychological state, see Jennifer Kennett, "Autism, Empathy, and Moral Agency," *Philosophical Quarterly* 52, no. 208 (July 2002): 340–357; Lorna Wing, "The History of Asperger Syndrome," *Current Issues in Autism* (1998): 11–28; and Lorna Wing and David Potter, "The Epidemiology of Autistic Spectrum Disorders: Is the Prevalence Rising?," *Mental Retardation and Developmental Disabilities Research Review* 8, no. 3 (September 4, 2002): 151–161.

20. Jean Baudrillard, *The Illusion of the End*, trans. Chris Turner (Stanford: Stanford University Press, 1992), 80–81.

21. Beth Daniels, *Writing Steampunk!* (n.p.: 3 Media Press, 2011), Kindle edition.

Works Cited

Allred, Randal. "Catharsis, Revision, and Re-Enactment: Negotiating the Meaning of the American Civil War." *Journal of American Culture* 19, no. 4 (1996): 1–13.

Baudrillard, Jean. *The Illusion of the End*. Translated by Chris Turner. Stanford: Stanford University Press, 1992.

———. *Passwords*. Translated by Chris Turner. London: Verso, 2003.

———. *The System of Objects*. Translated by James Benedict. London: Verso, 2005.

Bourne Identity, The. Directed by Doug Liman. Produced by Doug Liman, Patrick Crowley, and Richard N. Gladstein. Universal Pictures, 2002.

Burke, Kenneth. *A Grammar of Motives*. Berkeley: University of California Press, 1945.

———. *A Rhetoric of Motives*. Berkeley: University of California Press, 1969.

Carroll, Samantha J. "Putting the Neo Back into Neo-Victorian: The Neo-Victorian Novel as Postmodern Revisionist Fiction." *Neo-Victorian Studies* 3, no. 2 (2010): 172–205.

Clayton, Jay. *Charles Dickens in Cyberspace: The Afterlife of the Nineteenth Century in Popular Culture.* Oxford: Oxford University Press, 2003.

Daniels, Beth. *Writing Steampunk!* N.p.: 3 Media Press, 2011. Kindle edition.

Doyle, Sir Arthur Conan, and Christopher Morley. *The Complete Sherlock Holmes.* Garden City, N.Y.: Doubleday, 1988.

Genosko, Gary. *Baudrillard and Signs: Signification Ablaze.* New York: Routledge, 1994.

Maher, A. Michael. "Was Sherlock Holmes Autistic?" June 23, 1994. At http://kspot.org/holmes/autism.htm. Accessed May 30, 2013.

McPherson, Tara. *Reconstructing Dixie: Race, Gender, and Nostalgia in the Imagined South.* Durham: Duke University Press, 2003.

Nixon, Rob. "Behind the Camera on *Psycho*." Turner Classic Movies. At http://www.tcm.com/this-month/article/191164%7C0/Behind-the-Camera-Psycho.html. Accessed May 14, 2013.

Sherlock Holmes. Directed by Guy Ritchie. Produced by Joel Silver, Lionel Wigram, Susan Downey, and Dan Lin. Silver Pictures and Village Roadshow Pictures, 2009.

Sherlock Holmes: A Game of Shadows. Directed by Guy Ritchie. Produced by Joel Silver, Lionel Wigram, Susan Downey, and Dan Lin. Silver Pictures and Village Roadshow Pictures, 2011.

Video University. "The Art of Film and Video Editing, part 8: Does Non-Linear Editing Change Style and Art?" At http://www.videouniversity.com/articles/the-art-of-film-and-video-editing-part-8/. Accessed May 14, 2013.

A RHETORIC
OF STEAMPUNK
NARRATIVE

Kenneth Burke Meets a Time Lord

Steampunk's Grammatical Disruption

JOHN R. THOMPSON

⚙

ACCORDING TO THE *GUINNESS BOOK OF WORLD RECORDS*, THE BBC'S *DOCTOR Who* is the longest-running science fiction TV series in history.[1] A Google search on the terms "Doctor Who steampunk" returns eight million hits. These range from fan blog posts[2] on the steampunk aesthetic found in the show to toys and trinkets in steampunk style that were fashioned lovingly by fans as a demonstration of their devotion to the show.[3] In the nature of Google searches, this one is no more exhaustive than any other pop culture search performed on the Internet. I use it as one bit of evidence of an intersection between a quirky television show about a clever time-traveling alien vagabond and steampunk, the cultural phenomenon that is the subject of this book.

My goal in this chapter is to put steampunk and Kenneth Burke's theory of dramatism into conversation, and I find the BBC's long-running science fiction (or, for purists, science fantasy) program *Doctor Who* a fitting place to study this intersection. Burkean criticism, steampunk, and *Doctor Who* have much to offer one another. One of the central tenets of Burke's theory of dramatism is that any text has a discernible motive force that shapes the text and answers the question, "What is involved, when we say what people are doing and why they are doing it?"[4] In essence, Burke argued that any utterance is a fragment of a philosophy or larger discourse that the rhetor either holds dearly or is drawing on to give a particular text shape. This does not need to be a conscious choice on the rhetor's part. Texts are shaped by human minds and human minds are shaped by societies, so certain patterns of language use can be evidence of one or more discourses or social patterns emerging as a rhetor fashions a text (and "text" here can cover a broad range of communicative forms). Burke established a critical method to excavate those philosophies, or *motivations*, to use his term.

Likewise, Burke developed a critical taxonomy as a means of appreciating the nuances of the answers to his generative question regarding *what people are doing and why they are doing it*. Burke's Pentad, as the taxonomy is known, often suffers in application when critics apply the taxonomy—Scene, Agent, Act, Agency, Purpose—as a whole, assuming that the critical enterprise is to answer the *who, what, when*, and *how* for any text and check off answers in each Pentadic category.[5] Instead, the critical system as Burke articulated it is aimed at discerning the underlying grammar—the motive force—of the text, a motivation that lies in just one category or a specific ratio of two. In essence, the Pentad produces data that the critic can then read for further insights into underlying motivations.

In this light, *Doctor Who* and steampunk offer a unique view of Burkean criticism at work in the twenty-first century. *Doctor Who*'s usage of steampunk changes the obvious scenic grammar[6] inherent in a visual medium attempting to render historical settings in detail through elaborate sets, costumes, and the like. Said differently, steampunk demonstrates a postmodern wrinkle in Burke's Pentad—the grammatical red herring. When Burke articulated the Pentad, his literary and philosophical references were of a modernist cast, from Henry James to Kant and Hegel. In a postmodern world, steampunk purposely messes with the rules of genre in a way that Burke was unlikely to come across in his day, and it is worth stepping back to contemplate what postmodern approaches to literature and rhetoric—the nonlinear narrative, postcolonial identities; the post-9/11 world—might mean to understanding the Pentad in the twenty-first century.

My claim is that steampunk practices a grammatical bait and switch, hooking its audience with what appears to be a scenic grammar calling forth all the static knowledge an audience possesses of a certain historical period—only to shift to an idealistic or agent-based grammar[7] to make rhetorical claims about the past, present, and future. The Victorian Era is one of the most familiar of past eras—or *scenes*, with its cobblestone streets, top hats, and other environmental markers that say "Victorian" to viewers—thanks to various works from Charles Dickens, Arthur Conan Doyle, H. G. Wells, Jules Verne, and even American authors of the equivalent period such as Edgar Allen Poe. Filmmakers and authors pay tremendous attention to detail in rendering the Victorian Era as a familiar scene, making sure to check off all the right boxes in audience expectations. The women's dresses should swish just right and the walking sticks should shine just so. These elements might generally indicate a scenic grammar at work. Exploring the intersection between steampunk literature and Burke's rhetorical theories, this chapter argues that *Doctor Who* troubles that tidy approach to historical drama. When the Doctor travels to the past, the emphasis is on getting the scene *mostly right* at first viewing, but *precisely wrong* in important ways. This is consistent with the grammatical complexity steampunk introduces as an aesthetic; or, as Margaret Rose put it: "[S]teampunk is a fiction that places a premium on minutely accurate historical detail, within flamboyantly wrong imagined pasts, in order to explore the ways in which the conventional historical sensibility sometimes gets it wrong."[8]

Doctor Who is a good example of this anachronistic play, this way of getting things mostly right as part of a strategy to turn things flamboyantly wrong. *Doctor Who*, as the longest-running science fiction TV show in the world, quite fittingly embraces steampunk, given what Steffen Hantke has called steampunk's "primary allegiance to science fiction."[9] The affection is indeed mutual. The control console of the Doctor's time machine is a steampunk creation with hand brakes from the earliest automobiles, an early typewriter, computer screens that look like anything but computer screens, and various knobs and thingamabobs. As Tim Masters wrote for BBC News: "The new console looks like it has been constructed from items out of a junk shop, including an old typewriter, a telephone, pressure gauges and a Morse code machine."[10] The anachronistic technologies that make up the center of the time machine is a staple of the show. The steampunk aesthetic decorates many episodes and often serves a greater purpose than eccentric decoration. Zeppelins often dot the sky over London.[11] The Doctor saves Queen Victoria's life by showing an artifact of the era to be a weapon against interstellar werewolves (an episode critiqued later in this chapter). The Doctor meets Charles Dickens[12] and has a reptilian friend who lives in Victorian London and killed Jack the Ripper.[13] The Doctor also saves the life of Madame de Pompadour, mistress of the eighteenth-century King Louis XV, when she is under attack by clockwork robots with visible gears for brains.[14] The show also has some grounding in steampunk foundational texts such as H. G. Wells's *The Time Machine*. In fact, in one episode the Doctor takes H. G. Wells on a time trip that, within the reality of the show, inspires the Victorian author to write his own story of a Victorian man out of time.[15]

The steampunk aesthetic is a prime mechanism for unsettling the tidy narratives called to mind by the Victorian Era. The Doctor steps in as a god-like agent imposing his will on an unruly scene and exposing some of the hidden truths of the past that shed light on the present. In so doing, he educates the audience and troubles the received wisdom about the past.

The popularity of *Doctor Who* and steampunk are instances of the post-modern reexamination of received wisdom. Here, I want to suggest that a close reading of the Burkean grammar of any historical text is one means of understanding this reexamination. History *should* be a scene, an environment that calls certain things into existence. Yet this grammatical shift emphasizes agents over the scene. The author's position in viewing the scene becomes important and reminds us that that is true of any historical storyteller. By scrambling the scene with steampunk aesthetics, we are reminded that individuals created the scene in question, exposing the workings of history as a human creation in the moment and a story someone created to tell in a later age. Said another way, history tends to sublimate other grammars into a scene that we are conditioned to find familiar. Steampunk is one way to recover the truth of human actions when looking at seemingly familiar scenes. I will proceed by first drawing out the intersections of steampunk as excavated by scholars of the genre and show its parallels in the theories of Burke. From there, I will apply those ideas to *Doctor Who*.

Steampunk Literature and Grammatical Disruption

My claim in this section is that steampunk's aesthetic casts a postmodern light on Burkean grammar, one in which a scenic grammar is used as a subterfuge until an agent-oriented grammar erupts on the scene and extracts some truth out of that scene confounded by anachronistic technology. For the sake of conciseness, I will limit my discussion of the Pentad to the key terms used in this chapter: scene and agent.

In Burke's Pentad, scene is central. It calls other elements into being as the "container" of actions, agents, and acts. "It is a principle of drama that the nature of acts and agents should be consistent with the nature of the scene. And whereas comic and grotesque works may deliberately set these elements at odds with one another, audiences make allowance for such liberty, which reaffirms the same principle of consistency in its very violation."[16]

One might think of a theater stage set for the evening performance. Sofas, stuffed chairs, shag carpeting, and a boxy console television tell you a lot about the performance. You will be watching a play about an American middle-class family of the 1970s. The set—or scene—calls that family onto the stage from the wings. Because we have some sense of the scene from these trappings, we already have some sense of the characters and can call to mind a library of appropriate acts, conflicts, moralities, and the like that are appropriate for that scene; in Burkean terms, they are already *contained* in the scene. Burke argued that the more specific the scenic grammar, the more it embodies a materialistic philosophy rooted in the particulars of a certain scene, the more it reduces "action to motion" where *action* is conscious human agency in the critical/cultural sense and *motion* is simply navigating the scene, obeying its limits.[17] Scenic grammar describes landscapes, environments, or systems that act as both enabler and constraint on anything that happens within their circumferences and anyone who exists there.

In steampunk, the Victorian scene is rendered in detail. The upper-class men wear top hats, the horses drawing the hansom cabs make the appropriate sounds on the cobblestone streets, street urchins have dirty faces, and women wear bustles. This scene is so familiar through its repeated rendition in popular culture and grade-school history classes that, as denizens of the twenty-first century, readers or viewers can take comfort in essentially knowing more about that era than any characters set within the scene. Rose noted that steampunk makes use of scenic cues to root the work in the Victorian Era.[18] It is important to get the Victorian Era right so that it serves as a starting place, consistent with Burke's idea that scenic grammar creates the container. One scenic aspect of the Victorian Era is the importance of certain technologies operating at scale—gas lamps illuminating streets, railroads and telegraph lines spanning continents to compress time and space. Of course, the steam engine powered those trains and industrial enterprises. Steampunk builds a new aesthetic out of this scenic attribute and ultimately disrupts the scene with it.

The ontology—our historical knowledge of the Victorian Era as a scene— cannot call giant steam-powered spiders, submarines, and robotic aliens into existence. What are we to make of this disruption as audience members? We no longer know more about the scene than the characters involved. The library of meanings and understandings we called to mind to deal with the Victorian period are now hanging by a thread or possibly no longer apply. "Obviously, the shaping force behind steampunk is not history but the will of its author to establish and then violate and modify a set of ontological ground rules."[19] The scene is a grammatical red herring. The steampunk author as agent uses scenic grammar to call to mind the ontological history of the Victorian Era and its causal chain to the world we think we know. The disruption of the scene is also a disruption of the ontology called to mind by its detailed representation.

As audience, we are now in the hands of the storyteller. This scenic distortion, rendering the familiar as alien, serves a rhetorical function that goes beyond Burke's nod to the knowing contradictions of scene and characters or acts found in the burlesque or the grotesque forms.[20] This deliberate break with the familiarity of the scenic elements once established calls attention to the act of storytelling and creates a reminder that any representation of the past is actually a story we tell ourselves.[21] We are reminded that the Victorian Era did not spring in full form from the smokestacks of industrial London. It was created by people. We are reminded that powerful people created the scene that reduced others to mere motion. Just as importantly, we are reminded that stories have storytellers, as Hantke writes:

> [Characters in steampunk stories must acknowledge] the truth behind the mask. Since these characters all start out as proponents of the official view of society, the moment of recognition is also one of profound disillusionment. And since the world is more complex than they previously believed, these characters' own role in it is called into question as well. Many of them are forced to abandon the illusion of their own central position.[22]

Hantke argues that steampunk forces everyone to look behind the mask of the received version of history. This act of lifting the mask changes the audience perspective, foregrounding class distinctions and the social complexity that tidy descriptions of the era presented in high school history classes papered over. Through outrageous depictions of machines, cyborgs, and other trappings of a high-tech future, steampunk brings a twenty-first-century sensibility—a more questioning eye—to the Victorian Era. Through this pastiche it is the entire arc of history that is disrupted.

The audience has a new entry point to the history, often an entry point involving some outlandish technology. "Partly due to its close ties to science fiction, steampunk focuses on technology as the crucial factor in its understanding and portrayal of Victorianism. In adopting the name 'steampunk,' that is to say, in choosing the steam engine as the most appropriate icon of the past to describe itself, it makes technology its main focus. Since the contemporary world is highly technological, any past in which it would see itself reflected must share, or rather, must be made to share, its cultural agenda."[23] While technology qualifies as an agency—a tool or means—in Burke's taxonomy, its grammatical impact is scenic disruption rather than imposing an agency grammar. Technology is as much the writer's tool as that of any individual character. By introducing anachronistic technology, the writer asserts his or her presence in the unfolding story and scrambles understandings of the scene. It is the Victorian Era, the author says, but do not flatter yourself that you know this story.

Once this scene is disrupted, agents step forward. Those agents range from the people who created the Victorian Era in factual history, to the characters in the steampunk stories, to the audience members themselves.

Characters reassess themselves through the disruption. Their role in the story is exposed. They also have an opportunity to change the outcomes dictated by the received narrative of history. Obviously, these characters still exist within a fictional framework, yet they are no longer mere parts of a scene the way the smokestacks and top hats and cobblestone streets signal the Victorian Era. They are agents, licensed by the steampunk disruption to do something unexpected. In a moment, I will show how the Doctor comes alive once the scene is disrupted, no longer enjoying the familiarity of a Victorian Era holiday, for instance, but actively working to ferret out criminals and obtain the truth.

Likewise, audience members become more active participants in understanding what is happening in the story rather than just mapping characters and events to the Victorian section of their mental libraries. Steampunk changes the grammar of a work from a scenic grammar to an agent-oriented grammar.

In Burke's taxonomy, agent grammar is not simply a focus on people, although that is part of it. Agent grammar is a matter of idealism in keeping with psychologistic philosophies that focus on the ego, the self, the will, the spirit, and collective manifestations of those individualized terms.[24] Ideals are beliefs and attitudes that people hold and attempt to implement as creators.[25] One might talk of the U.S. Constitution as the source of all rights and use a scenic grammar to do so. However, if one speaks of the Constitution as the product of the wondrous sense of justice first gleaned by the founding fathers, then one speaks of the attitudes of human agents as the creators of a scene. Steampunk emphasizes that the social inequities of a wretchedly polluted London are not simply furniture on a stage framing tonight's show. They were created by people.

Agents are also driven to unify conditions with their ideals.[26] Discussion of finance and technology are especially suited to agent grammar because they create inequalities in conditions, power, and knowledge. Burke notes this relationship when he writes:

> Technology invites idealistic unification on two major counts. First, like money and in conjunction with money, it makes for diversity and unequal rates of change that require as social corrective the unifying function of ideas and ideals "creatively" at odds with conditions as they

look when seen without the idealistic exaltation. And a more technical incentive to idealism derives from the fact that technology, as applied science, invites us to put the major stress upon knowledge. And the problem of knowledge is the epistemological problem, a psychologistic emphasis that falls directly under the head of agent.[27]

So, in Burke's view, technology as the disruptor is an appropriate device to assert the agent grammar. Agents are driven to create a scene that closes the gap between conditions and ideals. The rise of industrial capitalism, with its steam-powered technology and finance on an imperial scale, makes the Victorian Era a prime location for this idealistic agent-oriented grammar. Factual people and events are used to take the audience to the past, and the past survives the eruption of the fantastic—but the story is now something new. It is not the official version of history. Characters are no longer reduced to mere motion. A street urchin might have a steam-powered laser. They can take action in ways that are not necessarily consistent with the received narrative of history. "Steampunk constitutes a special case among alternative histories, a science fiction subgenre that postulates a fictional event of vast consequences in the past and extrapolates from this event a fictional though historically contingent present or future."[28] So, the disruption does not cast aside the Victorian Era in whole cloth. Rather, it explodes the ontology or received wisdom and opens it to new scrutiny. In so doing it shifts the grammar from the scene to agents.

With the ontology in shreds, agents can be featured, including people who might not have featured in the received narrative, as Rose explains:

That is, to look for historical truth in the interconnections between minute events and minor players acting as individuals within, and being shaped by, larger historical forces, especially when such a practice can challenge or revise our existing sense of the grander historical narrative. At the same time, though, this reliance on the extratextual historical record shows that, rather than being irreverent towards the past itself, steampunk fiction puts tremendous value on the practice of engaging with the factual past, especially when that engagement reveals a historical world that differs from the one we expected.[29]

To filter Rose through Burke, Rose is arguing that the only way to engage the Victorian environment—or scene—is through the ideas brought to that scene by all the agents involved: the storyteller, the characters in the story, and the audience members and the perspectives they bring.[30] "The steam engine as the technological icon of certain historic circumstances, on the one hand, and punk as a term vaguely circumscribing a set of attitudes, on the other, each belong to separate cultural spheres. Hence their fusion marks a self-conscious authorial effort at transcending both historical sequence and genre distinctions. The result is a hybrid, a monster."[31] That "attitude" comes from the author reconciling his or her ideals. It is important to get the scene right initially. The hybridity requires an appreciation of the scenic cues that root the story in the Victorian Era, an openness to staying with the story when that scene is disrupted, and a recognition of the remaking of the story by all the agents involved.

It might also help to have a guide. As I turn to applying these ideas to *Doctor Who*, the cleverest person in the universe will do nicely.

Doctor Who and a Steampunk Critic Step into a TARDIS

Doctor Who is a cultural institution in the United Kingdom. It came to the United States via public broadcasting in the late twentieth century and established a cult following with its depiction of the quirky, mad scientist who travels in an anachronistic London police box (about the size of the anachronistic public phone booth in the United States) and the cheesy monsters in rubber suits. Since a well-financed reboot in 2005, the show has been gathering a mainstream audience around the world while maintaining its British sensibilities and the show's lineage back to 1963. As the BBC says on the official *Doctor Who* website, the intention was that:

> Main stars of the show would be a couple of school teachers—the square-jawed Ian Chesterton and the improbably bouffant Barbara Wright. The teen audience could identify with Susan Foreman, one of their pupils. Even if she was an alien. Finally, a mysterious anti-hero in the mould of Conan-Doyle's [*sic*] Professor Challenger would complete the line-up. He would be known only as "The Doctor." Doctor Who? Travelling in their time and space machine, the TARDIS, the Doctor and co. began their adventures on November 23rd 1963 by voyaging 100,000 years into Earth's past to help some slightly dim cavemen discover fire.[32]

The show survived the ill health of its star by inventing the Time Lord ability to regenerate the body and take on a new persona, allowing a succession of twelve actors to play the character.[33] Because of that flexibility, the show survived other existential threats, including cancellation, for much of the 1990s and early 2000s. The show was revived in 2005, and this chapter focuses on the postrevival period. *Doctor Who* celebrated its fiftieth anniversary on television in 2013 and has become a global phenomenon with strong popularity in the United States, France, Australia, and elsewhere.

The show has been studied within the humanities from various perspectives. Priya Dixit studied aliens and alienness.[34] Matt Hills called the show a "dispersable text," a text that is composed of various elements that can be disassembled and used by the audience in various ways and in various media.[35] Lindy Orthia used the show as a place to examine popular culture depictions of scientists.[36] Alec Charles looked at the show through the lens of Freud's concept of the *uncanny*: "This ability to notice things—specifically to notice those inconsistencies which expose the true nature of things—characterises [current head writer Steven] Moffat's depiction of the Doctor."[37]

As Charles implies, the Doctor notices inconsistencies in what should be familiar to anyone with a casual understanding of history, in order to expose the true nature of things. Charles's statement describes the show's rendition of the earthly past. It also describes the use of steampunk in the show.

TV and cinema producers put a lot of effort into getting the scene *right* when producing historical programming. The Victorian Era is a great example of this scenic focus, as the audience is familiar with Victorian trappings from enduring works such as the novels of Dickens and stories about Sherlock Holmes, and from the rise of empire. In what follows, I will critique three specific episodes of the rebooted *Doctor Who* to demonstrate this scene-actor dynamic at work. In each instance, I will begin with as concise an overview of the episode as reasonably possible for my purposes, move to a discussion of some specific steampunk elements and how they disrupt the familiar scene to leave behind the received wisdom of official history, and finish with a Burkean view of the agent-centric grammar at work. The three episodes I have chosen for this deeper critique span the tenth and eleventh iterations of the Doctor. These two iterations encompass two different portrayals of the Doctor and two different production teams, facts that underscore the essential nature of this scenic disruption whenever the character visits the relevant Victorian period.

"Tooth and Claw" (2005)

In "Tooth and Claw," the tenth Doctor and his companion, Rose, not only travel to the Victorian Era—they meet Queen Victoria herself and save her from an interstellar werewolf. The Doctor and Rose meet the queen and her guard by happenstance when damaged railroad tracks disrupt the queen's journey and divert them all to a Scottish estate, where they must spend the night. The estate has been taken over by a band of monks—the train track saboteurs—harboring a human host infected by an outer space virus that transforms the host body into a marauding werewolf at the light of the moon. The monks' plan is to transfer the werewolf-alien consciousness to the queen and thus control the most powerful nation on the planet at that point in history.

The queen apparently harbors her own secret in the form of a large diamond that she carries clutched in a small bag. It was a gift from her husband, Prince Albert, now dead, whom Victoria grieved until her own death in 1901 (more on the historical fact of this diamond and its steampunk treatment in a moment). Eventually, the queen and the Doctor are trapped by the werewolf creature in an observatory with a telescope that does not appear to function because of an overly intricate array of glass lenses throughout its long tube. The Doctor saves the day by puzzling out that the diamond Victoria carries is actually a prism, which—when combined with the lenses in the odd telescope—bends light in a way that destroys the alien organism inhabiting the human host (the human host dies too, but appears grateful for the release). The episode ends with the queen knighting the Doctor and then banishing him from the realm as a potential threat. The Doctor and Rose return to the TARDIS speculating about a potential minor nick of contamination from the werewolf that might explain some behavior in the royal lineage.

The steampunk elements begin with the time travel that opens the episode. The Doctor and Rose are actually not heading to the Victorian Era at all but aiming for 1979 and a famous concert by Ian Dury and the Blockheads, a band prominent in Britain's "new wave" rock and roll period, which was a mainstream outgrowth of the punk rock movement of the 1970s.[38] As often happens in *Doctor Who*, the TARDIS ends up in a place other than where the Doctor is aiming his space-time machine. In this case, he is a century off.

Coaches, castles, costumes, and Queen Victoria all call to mind the Victorian period. But in a Pentadic sense, that familiar scene does not call ninja monks and interstellar werewolves to mind, and we are introduced to them before we get too comfortable with the Victorian trappings. The presence of Queen Victoria and her pursuit by an interstellar werewolf is a strong bending of history consistent with steampunk literature.[39] The monks and the werewolf unsettle the seeming familiarity of the Victorian setting, taking the reader outside the boundaries of any official history lessons from school. Someone needs to make order out of this seeming disorder.

The Doctor steps forward to protect the queen. In so doing, he puzzles out the strangeness of the situation and some of its anomalies. The Doctor and company hide in a library that seems to protect them from the wolf, and he determines that it was constructed to ward off the beast. He unravels the history of how the beast got to earth by imploring his erstwhile team to search through the books of the library—implying to viewers that the truth of the Victorian Era is obtainable for those who choose to seek it. He also saves the day by uncovering the queen's mystery, the Koh-i-Noor diamond, a real artifact of the era.

The Koh-i-Noor diamond was a spoil of the empire, which expanded and consolidated its hold on much of the world during Victoria's reign.[40] For hundreds of years, this large diamond was part of Indian royal culture. It came into the possession of the British East India Company and was passed to Victoria to symbolize her new title as empress of India, as Great Britain took control of this new metaphoric jewel in its imperial crown. In histori- cal reality, Prince Albert believed that such a large diamond would shine as none other before if only it were cut properly. In pursuing this ideal cut, Al- bert reduced the size of this gem of Indian history by more than a third, from 186 carats to its current weight of 108 carats, with no recorded regard for its significance to Indians.

In "Tooth and Claw," Prince Albert's seemingly obsessive cutting and re- cutting of the diamond is explained as an attempt to reshape the diamond to act as a prism that would bend the moonlight to destroy the werewolf. The Doctor brings order back to the Victorian Era by discovering the true pur- pose (within the reality of the episode) of this Victorian artifact.

The Doctor is the chief agent in this story, of course, but other charac- ters are given some rein as agents outside of the conventional history. Queen Victoria and the werewolf are worth considering. We are led to believe at the end of the episode that the wolf did manage to nip or scratch the queen. Here, the author as agent steps forward with a critique of the Victorian in- dustrial era. Before his transformation, the interstellar wolf proudly claims that he will bring about a "world of industrial warfare and commerce" on Earth by infecting Queen Victoria and all her progeny. While the Doctor ostensibly scuttles the plan within the show, this is essentially what happened in reality, as Victorian England claimed an empire and its spoils while other European powers set up their own colonial holdings around the world. In keeping with the steampunk ethos, "Tooth and Claw" sets the Victorian scene, scrambles it, and uses the Doctor to make an argument about how history truly unfolded to create the present. In essence, British history really *was* infected with a version of this interstellar virus.

"The Next Doctor" (2008)

Toward the end of the tenth Doctor's journey it was announced that the beloved actor (David Tennant) playing the role would be leaving the show, making way for the eleventh Doctor. Producers played with this knowledge in an episode provocatively entitled "The Next Doctor." The Doctor returns to the Victorian Era in "the year of our Lord 1851," according to a boy he meets. The Doctor is beginning to relax in an era that strikes him as simple and "a bit dull" when he hears a cry for help, "Doctor!," seemingly aimed specifically at him. The person in distress, a screaming maid, rejects him as the Doctor, however, and waits for another man in sharp Victorian garb who comes up and claims to be the Doctor, "the one, the only." They quickly discover the presence of the Cybermen, who are among *Doctor Who*'s classic foes, a race of humans who have upgraded themselves cybernetically to the point that they have lost their humanity (one sign that *Doctor Who* was steampunk before steampunk existed as a recognized aesthetic). The two men quickly bond as kindred spirits, as one would expect since they are apparently two generations of the same person. The tenth Doctor discovers that this new doctor does not recognize him and that, even though he knows much about the Doctor and his universe—far more than a Victorian man could possibly know—this stranger's memories are incomplete; in fact, the man believes that he has suffered an attack that has impaired his ability to recall details about his life.

Meanwhile, the Cybermen are conspiring with Miss Hartigan, a mysterious lady of the era who dresses in scarlet; she berates a group of men who ogle her lustily but otherwise disapprove of her. Those men are promptly captured by the Cybermen and converted to their purposes, namely kidnapping children and forcing them to work in an industrial sweatshop constructing a massive, clanking monstrosity called the Cyberking. The Cyberking is designed to stride across the landscape and ultimately the globe, converting humanity to Cybermen. The Doctor discovers the plan and in the process pieces together that his would-be successor is actually a local man who was attacked by the Cybermen, his son taken as fodder for the Cyberking; in the process, the man was zapped with an information-storage device that implanted information about the Doctor into his brain but without context. Like Queen Victoria, Miss Hartigan ascends the throne to become the consciousness of the Cyberking as it begins to walk across the globe, first remaking the London landscape. The Doctor eventually defeats the Cyberking with alien technology and a hot air balloon.

When modern fans of the show think of *Doctor Who* and steampunk, this episode is likely to come to mind. The children constructing the Cyberking work in a steamy hell of a sweatshop. It offers some of the most flamboyant steampunk imagery in the series. The sight of the steam-powered Cyberking lurching over London is reminiscent of the giant spider looming over the horizon in the 1999 film *Wild Wild West*, another steampunk touchstone. The Cyberking is not just a large computer but a monstrosity of exposed gears and loud metal-on-metal clanking and scraping. A mix of technologies are deployed in the episode to disrupt the familiar Victorian scene, from the Doctor's trusty sonic screwdriver to the Cybermen's interdimensional transporter to a hot air balloon that the erstwhile *next doctor* considers to be his TARDIS.

The notion that one must first signal the ground rules of the Victorian Era, rooting one's audience in a familiar and predictable environment, is on display from the first moments of the episode. The Doctor steps out of the TARDIS under a bridge and steps into a scene right out of Dickens. He comes up to a street urchin and asks what year it is. The camera moves in a 360-degree arc around the Doctor as he smiles at the familiarity of a land uncomplicated by all that he knows of the universe. The cries for the Doctor that immediately follow shatter the ground rules at the moment the audience is starting to buy into them.

With the familiarity of the historical scene disrupted, agents are once again freed to tell a different story. The Doctor, of course, puzzles all the motivations out and saves the day in the end. Miss Hartigan's ascension of the Cyberking throne solidifies her symbolic connection to Queen Victoria. In the course of the story, she confronts a group of businessmen over their discomfort with her womanhood. This discomfort is resolved by sending them to enslave the children who build the steam-powered industrial beast. The story makes the case that child labor contributed to Britain's industrial might in the Victorian Era and that unscrupulous masters of the all-too-human kind did not necessarily care if those child laborers died in the process, because there were always more waifs in the streets.

As the story's stand-in for Queen Victoria, Miss Hartigan steps forward as an agent who is in full complicity with the businessmen and their treatment of laborers. "What are children ever needed for? They are a workforce," Miss Hartigan says. The Cyberking is an invasion machine striding across the globe much as the British Empire did. "People of the world, hear me," Miss Hartigan says. "Your governments will surrender, and if not, behold my power." The Cyberking then proceeds to deploy energy cannons from its arms and blast the primitive landscape below, much like the superior weapons of the British Empire subdued large swaths of the world.

The Doctor as agent imposes his will on this muddled scene. He saves the children about to die as the Cyberking comes to life, and he eventually opens Miss Hartigan's eyes to the horror she has become as the brain of the Cyberking. In that moment, Miss Hartigan perhaps invites viewers to step forward as agents in their own right to open their eyes to how history actually proceeded, and who were the agents responsible for its current condition.

"The Snowmen" (2012)

The eleventh Doctor is grieving the loss of his former companions and chooses to do so in the Victorian Era. He is cared for by a motley trio of friends: Madame Vastra, a Sherlock Holmes–inspired detective of the era who is actually a warrior from a race of reptilian bipeds who were present on Earth before the advent of humanity; Jenny, Madame Vastra's cockney maid and lesbian lover; and Strax, a disgraced warrior from the potato-headed Sontaran race who serves as Madame Vastra's butler and the episode's comic relief. The Doctor is also joined by a young woman who lives a dual life in Victorian London as a barmaid and an upper-crust governess. She is part of a larger story arc in the series.

It is Christmastime and snowing in London. However, the snow is possessed by a malevolent force that spontaneously creates murderous snowmen. The Doctor is eventually intrigued enough by events to end his funk and battle an old nemesis, the Great Intelligence, and his henchman. The Great Intelligence is manifested through a rotating snow globe in the henchman's lab. The Great Intelligence's plan is to use the DNA of a deceased, ill-tempered governess to remake the human race into an army of zombie-like ice people. The Doctor prevails, but at the loss of his new companion, the governess, an event that sets up the rest of the series.

The scene of Victorian London is disrupted quite soon in the episode. Victorian bars and pretty barmaids are staples of Dickens, but we no sooner meet Clara than we are treated to a malevolent snowman rising up out of the snow accumulated in an alleyway. The snow globe housing the consciousness of the Great Intelligence is also a steampunk contraption cobbled together out of wood, glass, and capacitor towers arcing static electricity.

The phrase "Victorian values" recurs in the episode, telegraphing some of the subtext of the episode as it questions those values and some of the agents who put those values into practice. Madame Vastra, known by the moniker "the great detective" in the episode, is a riff on Sherlock Holmes, a well-known fictional denizen of Victorian London. She appears quite early in the episode, unveiling her scaly face to call to her companions, including Strax, who looks uncomfortable in his butler's uniform that ends where his massive head begins. This is one of the first scenic disruptions in the episode, but it is the first of many, and these disruptions begin unpacking the "Victorian values" and asserting a colorful group of agents who will retell the story of those values.

The idea of a lesbian relationship disrupts the sexual mores of the Victorian Era. The Great Intelligence's henchman suggests that Arthur Conan Doyle was basing his idea of Sherlock Holmes and John Watson on the loving ladies, adjusting it for the time. It is worth noting that, in a prequel to the episode, Madame Vastra explained to a police inspector that she is a warrior from a reptilian race that claims the planet. The inspector seems merely interested. When she explains that she and Jenny are married, he is scandalized—the contrast between the two reactions drawing a comparison to the twenty-first-century view of which would be the greater shock, lesbians in our midst or reptilian warriors.

Likewise, this idea of Victorian values comes into play when the henchman hires poor people to gather snow, ostensibly in exchange for food, but then kills them. This again underscores the disposability of workers in that era and the ultimate power that businesspeople had over them—a power made obvious by constructing the businessperson as an agent who orders the workers eaten alive. The episode also exposes one of the enduring mythological agents of the received wisdom of Victorian history—Mary Poppins. The sinister plot the Doctor foils involves a dead governess feared by two children of a widowed member of the gentry. This governess is reanimated as an ice corpse who hunts the children to force them to do chores, finish their homework, and behave themselves. This is the agent charged by the powerful of the era with instilling Victorian values in the next generation. She is nothing like the scenic image we have of this motif, in which kindly governesses such as Mary Poppins watch out for the children in their care. By turning the governess into an icy agent outside the familiar scene, the author suggests a different view of Victorian values and their transmission.

Conclusion

The Victorian Era is a rich ground for *Doctor Who* and its brand of storytelling. Burkean scholars might be quick to point out that "ground" is a scenic term. There is indeed a great landscape of Victorian depictions, from the works of Dickens and their various permutations to Sherlock Holmes and his periodic revivals. How many of them put their greatest effort into the details of the scene rather than the characters, the story, or even the message they are ultimately trying to convey about the era? Steampunk opens up the black box that the era presents. It troubles what we think we know.

Indeed, *Doctor Who* head writer Steven Moffat is also behind a revival of Sherlock Holmes that places Holmes in the twenty-first century, and there is something of a grammatical steampunk flavor to his reasoning for the update. As Moffat told National Public Radio in an October 15, 2010, interview: "It seemed to somehow make it a bit less reverent and a bit more fun. . . . Much as we love Sherlock Holmes, we love Victoriana. Many of the adaptations become about the period as opposed to about the story." By removing the need to nail down the Victorian Era, Moffat said that he could place the emphasis on everything else: the characters, the story, the action. Essentially, in *Sherlock* he is practicing a different version of this grammatical shift. The audience can now follow the workings of Holmes's mind and his relationship with Watson rather than marvel at the costumes and the sound of horse hooves on cobblestone streets. The *Doctor Who* writer is riffing on steampunk grammar in both his shows.

As technology has become a greater part of our lives in the late twentieth and into the twenty-first century, steampunk is an inevitable postmodern creation. It is a way for those of us trying to critically appraise the received wisdom of history to interrogate the story we have been told. It is academically trite to say that history is the story of great men and great events. Yet that phrase is still a scenic locution (apart from its sexist undertones). History, great men, and great events are part of the same tapestry in that phrase. The phrase is part of history's scenic grammar, sublimating motivations and smaller characters who simply were not deemed great enough to make the cut in the textbooks. Steampunk sucks us in with the scene we think we know—and then disrupts that scene to expose the agents who created the

history, raise the lesser agents back into the limelight, and question the storytellers who compressed it all into an easily digested scene.

Steampunk practices a grammatical subterfuge. It does worry about the
horse hooves, the top hats. It does respect the Victorian Era. It respects it so
much that it wants our understanding of the era to transcend the scene and
see the real forces that called that scene into existence—the agents—and to
extrapolate their impact on our own period.

Notes

1. The particular entry can be found at http://www.guinnessworldrecords.com/world
   -records/4000/longest-running-science-fiction-tv-series.
2. Typical of steampunk fan blogs is Red Rocket Rising (http://redrocketrising
   .com/2013/04/steampunk-j-and-l/). Such sites often ask whether *Doctor Who* is steampunk and then proceed to provide answers that are sometimes worthy of cultural or literary critics. *Jago & Litefoot*, mentioned at Red Rocket Rising, is an offshoot of *Doctor Who*
   that is to *Doctor Who* what Rosencrantz and Guildenstern treatments are to Shakespeare,
   lovingly elaborated stories about minor characters who were never heard from again in
   the canon.
3. For an array of fan products, pictures, and the like, seehttp://www.tumblr.com/tagged/
   steampunk%20doctor%20who.
4. Kenneth Burke, *A Grammar of Motives* (Berkeley: University of California Press, 1945), xv.
5. Ibid.
6. I will address the nature of scenic grammar in greater depth in the next section. Suffice it
   to say here that scenic grammar focuses on landscapes and systems, the environment that
   contains all the elements of a text.
7. Burke, *A Grammar of Motives*, 171–176.
8. Margaret Rose, "Extraordinary Pasts: Steampunk as a Mode of Historical Representation,"
   Journal of the Fantastic in the Arts 20, no. 3 (2009): 319–333. At Academic OneFile, accessed May 23, 2013.
9. Steffen Hantke, "Difference Engines and Other Infernal Devices: History According to
   Steampunk," *Extrapolation* 40, no. 3 (Fall 1999), 244–254.
10. Tim Masters, "New Doctor Who Matt Smith Hopes Series Will 'Thrill,'" BBC News,
    March 19, 2010. At http://news.bbc.co.uk/2/hi/entertainment/8571193.stm, accessed No-
    vember 2, 2013.
11. See "Rise of the Cybermen" and "The Age of Steel" (2007), or "Victory of the Daleks"
    (2010).
12. See "The Unquiet Dead" (2005).
13. See "A Good Man Goes to War" (2011) and "The Snowmen" (2012).
14. See "Girl in the Fireplace" (2006).
15. See "Timelash," *Doctor Who* classic series.
16. Burke, *A Grammar of Motives*, 3.

17. Ibid., 131.

18. Rose, "Extraordinary Pasts," 322.

19. Hantke, "Difference Engines."

20. Burke, *A Grammar of Motives*, 3.

21. Rose, "Extraordinary Pasts," 323.

22. Hantke, "Difference Engines."

23. Ibid.

24. Burke, *A Grammar of Motives*, 171.

25. Ibid., 174–175.

26. Ibid., 175–176.

27. Ibid., 176.

28. Hantke, "Difference Engines," 245.

29. Rose, "Extraordinary Pasts," 325.

30. Burke, *A Grammar of Motives*, 179.

31. Hantke, "Difference Engines."

32. BBC, "A Brief History of a Time Lord: Tea Time Travel." At http://www.bbc.co.uk/doc torwho/classic/news/briefhistory/beginnings.shtml.

33. BBC, "A Brief History of a Time Lord: William Hartnell." At http://www.bbc.co.uk/ doctorwho/classic/news/briefhistory/hartnell.shtml.

34. Priya Dixit, "Relating to Difference: Aliens and Alienness in *Doctor Who* and International Relations," *International Studies Perspectives* 13, no. 3 (2012): 289–306.

35. Matt Hills, "The Dispersible Television Text: Theorising Moments of the New *Doctor Who*," *Science Fiction Film and Television* 1, no. 1 (2008): 25–44. At http://muse.jhu.edu/, accessed May 23, 2013.

36. Lindy A. Orthia, "Antirationalist Critique or Fifth Column of Scientism? Challenges from *Doctor Who* to the Mad Scientist Trope," *Public Understanding of Science* 20, no. 4 (July 2011): 525–542.

37. Alec Charles, "The Crack of Doom: The Uncanny Echoes of Steven Moffat's *Doctor Who*," *Science Fiction Film and Television* 4, no. 1 (2011): 1–23. At http://muse.jhu.edu/, accessed May 23, 2013.

38. See http://www.iandury.co.uk for background.

39. See the episode "Sense and Sensibility and Sea Monsters" (2009) as one example of the insertion of mythical creatures into Victorian settings and classic Victorian literature.

40. See www.kohinoordiamond.org for a brief overview of the diamond's weight and other vital information, along with a brief sketch of its history.

Works Cited

"Age of Steel, The." BBC One, May 20, 2006.

Burke, Kenneth. *A Grammar of Motives*. Berkeley: University of California Press, 1945.

Charles, Alec. "The Crack of Doom: The Uncanny Echoes of Steven Moffat's *Doctor Who*." *Science Fiction Film and Television* 4, no. 1 (2011): 1–23. At http://muse.jhu.edu/. Accessed May 23, 2013.

Dixit, Priya. "Relating to Difference: Aliens and Alienness in *Doctor Who* and International Relations." *International Studies Perspectives* 13, no. 3 (2012): 289–306.

"Girl in the Fireplace." BBC One, May 6, 2006.

"Good Man Goes to War, A." BBC One, June 4, 2011.

Hantke, Steffen. "Difference Engines and Other Infernal Devices: History According to Steampunk." *Extrapolation* 40, no. 3 (Fall 1999): 244–254.

Hills, Matt. "The Dispersible Television Text: Theorising Moments of the New *Doctor Who*." *Science Fiction Film and Television* 1, no. 1 (2008): 25–44. At http://muse.jhu.edu/. Accessed May 23, 2013.

"Next Doctor, The." *Doctor Who*. BBC One, December 25, 2008.

Orthia, Lindy A. "Antirationalist Critique or Fifth Column of Scientism? Challenges from *Doctor Who* to the Mad Scientist Trope." *Public Understanding of Science* 20, no. 4 (July 2011): 525–542.

"Rise of the Cybermen." BBC One, May 13, 2006.

Rose, Margaret. "Extraordinary Pasts: Steampunk as a Mode of Historical Representation." *Journal of the Fantastic in the Arts* 20, no. 3 (2009): 319–333. At Academic OneFile. Accessed May 23, 2013.

"Snowmen, The." *Doctor Who*. BBC One, December 25, 2012.

"Timelash." *Doctor Who*. BBC One, March 9, 1985.

"Tooth and Claw." *Doctor Who*. BBC One, April 22, 2006.

"Unquiet Dead, The." *Doctor Who*. BBC One, April 9, 2005.

"Victory of the Daleks." *Doctor Who*. BBC One, April 17, 2010.

Clockwork Counterfactuals

Allohistory and the Steampunk Rhetoric of Inquiry

JOHN M. McKENZIE

ALLOHISTORY IS THE HISTORY THAT COULD HAVE BEEN, BUT BY HAPPEN-
stance was not. Also known as alternate history, virtual history, or counterfactualism, allohistory revisits "what if" scenarios from our past and posits
new answers. The allohistorical perspective is dependent on a commitment
to exploring historical contingency, what Joel Mokyr describes as the idea
"that the things that really happened in history did not have to happen,
that something else could have happened" (277). Those who consider allohistorical and counterfactual scenarios range from serious academics, to fiction writers, to virtually anyone with an active imagination and an interest
in history. Steampunk can be viewed as a particular strain of allohistory—a
strain offering stories and settings with extraordinary visions of history and
fantasy that turn on the varieties of ways the world could have been different, if only the internal combustion engine had never been invented. Steampunk employs several common allohistorical tropes, and in so doing presents
a coherent rhetoric of science and technology reflective of contemporary
cultural anxieties surrounding technological development. The language
choices, settings, characters, and plots of steampunk stories—as well as the
rhetorical situations from which the authors write—indicate that unresolved
cultural anxieties are being worked through in steampunk's manifestation of
allohistory.

The fundamental conceit of steampunk, I argue, is a world in which ab-
ductive trial and error is more successful than usual in producing pragmatic
(and idiosyncratically stylish) results than sustained, ordered, methodologi-
cally rigorous scientific procedures. This is no large conceit, given the un-
even history of scientific discovery until this period.[1] In short, by returning to this period of scientific uncertainty, steampunk presents a tinkerer's
rhetoric of inquiry. Steampunk uses its allohistorical versions of the scientific

and industrial revolutions of the late nineteenth century as its vehicle. Steampunk's tinkerer ethos splits the continuum between Luddism and technologism by adding a second axis exploring methods of discovery, with the archetypal scientist on one end and the archetypal tinkerer on the other. Steampunk, rather than disavowing technology (Luddism) or universally praising it (technologism), consistently implies that tinkerers create useful or beneficent inventions, whereas scientists—often mad ones—invent technologies of destruction.

In arguing that steampunk presents a tinkerer's rhetoric of inquiry, both the term "tinkerer" and the phrase "rhetoric of inquiry" require some definition before going further.

The common meaning of "tinkerer" is essentially a nonexpert person who experiments with or repairs machines and their parts.[2] A tinkerer is generally a person who has nonspecific mechanical prowess and creates or repairs using primarily the materials that are already on hand. Recognition of the methodological divide between the tinkerer and the engineer or scientist originates from Claude Lévi-Strauss's *La Pensée sauvage* (*The Savage Mind*), in which Lévi-Strauss identifies the characteristics of the *bricoleur*, or tinkerer. He writes:

> [T]he "bricoleur" is still someone who works with his hands and uses devious means compared to those of a craftsman. . . . His universe of instruments is closed and the rules of his game are always to make do with "whatever is at hand," that is to say with a set of tools and materials which is always finite and is also heterogeneous because what it contains bears no relation to the current project, or indeed to any particular project, but is the contingent result of all the occasions there have been to renew or enrich the stock or to maintain it with the remains of previous constructions or destructions. . . . Such elements are specialized up to a point, sufficiently for the "bricoleur" not to need the equipment and knowledge of all trades and professions, but not enough for each of them to have only one definite and determinate use. They each represent a set of actual and possible relations; they are "operators" but they can be used for any operations of the same type. (16–18)

Lévi-Strauss's *bricoleur* matches the model steampunk tinkerer precisely. The tinkerer's machinations are happenstance creations, made with materials that could have served other purposes but unconventionally meet the needs of the moment. The tinkerer is neither an expert nor strictly speaking a crafts-person, but is still more than an unskilled worker.

There is a commonality of experience between the fictional steampunk tinkerer, the real-life steampunk practitioners who tinker to create steam-punk devices and fashions to wear or display, and writers of allohistory and steampunk. All three operate by exploring contingency. For steampunk tin-kerers real and imagined, their craft is defined by a playful relationship with available materials, which could serve this or that aesthetic or functional purpose. For steampunk and allohistorical authors, their available materials are history and their commitment to recognizing its flexibility. Any particu-lar moment can be altered and redeployed in a multitude of indeterminable and indefinite ways, allowing the author to tinker with the contingent possi-bilities of history. For all three, the requisite materials are found objects that have been repurposed, whether they are gears, valves, or moments in time.

The term "rhetoric of inquiry" coincides with a field of study by the same name that focuses on how all modes of inquiry—that is to say scientific dis-covery, quantitative and qualitative research in the social sciences, trial and er-ror, criticism, philosophy, and all other methods of inquiry—are surrounded by discourses that work to both legitimize and delegitimize them. Rhetoric of inquiry could be seen as related to the philosophical field of epistemology. Epistemology is the study of knowledge and how we come to know; the rhet-oric of inquiry is the study of how our constructed discourses of truth, doubt, authority, expertise, and ideology all influence our means of coming to know. John Lyne describes rhetoric of inquiry as "foreground[ing] a concern for the relationship of rhetoric to the epistemological and hermeneutical purposes of academic investigation" ("Rhetorics of Inquiry" 66). As a concept, the rheto-ric of inquiry emerged as a response to certain methodologies that claimed to have a monopoly on the ability to attain "truth" (Lyne, "Social Epistemology" 111). Implied in the methods of the natural sciences and some of the social sciences was the claim that these methods uncovered objective truths about reality. The counterclaim of those advancing the study of the rhetoric of in-quiry was that scientific discovery (whether natural or social) is nonetheless colored by rhetorical influences; as John Nelson and Allan Megill argue, there is always already a "rhetoric *within* inquiry" (33). This approach is not simple relativism—the claim that there is no truth or that the truth is relative—but rather a reminder that there is always a rhetorical component even in sound, legitimate, established, and proven forms of inquiry.

Thus in arguing that steampunk presents a tinkerer's rhetoric of inquiry, what I mean is that it has participated in the larger field of discourse about the nature of inquiry and presented its own analysis and vision of what scientific inquiry means, what its moral valences and social consequences are, and proposes an alternative mode of inquiry in its heralding of the tinkerer over the scientist. Steampunk presents both a rhetoric *of* inquiry and a rhetoric *within* inquiry, insofar as it both philosophizes about existing modes of inquiry and also takes the position that some modes of inquiry are preferable to others. It is a *tinkerer's* rhetoric of inquiry specifically because of how it privileges play, the repurposing of materials, trial-and-error experimentation, and the capabilities of the individual over the specialization, planning, and methodological rigor of the imagined scientist.

This steampunk perspective is critical of the close relationship between science and capitalism that developed during the Industrial Revolution and, given the emergence of the genre in the late-middle twentieth century, also contains echoes of the rise of modern environmentalism and Cold War nuclear panic. Contemporary steampunk continues to use allohistorical motifs to express cultural anxieties—often about the influences of technology on imperialism, the postcolonial world, and environmental devastation. Thus, steampunk's unique allohistorical rhetoric of inquiry serves to highlight and weave together many modern sources of technological, political, and cultural antagonism. I find support for these arguments in analyzing several steampunk texts. In particular, I examine Harry Harrison's *A Transatlantic Tunnel, Hurrah!* and the first book of Cherie Priest's Clockwork Century steampunk series, *Boneshaker*.

These two particular novels were chosen for a reason. Harrison's *A Transatlantic Tunnel, Hurrah!* is an early example of the form that predates the first use of the word "steampunk" by fifteen years (Gross 57). Written in 1972, Harrison's novel contains more of the gallivanting, adventuring style of turn-of-the-century scientific romances like those written by Jules Verne and H. G. Wells. Nonetheless, the story reflects the cultural conditions of its own time, and behind its cheerful demeanor is a serious exegesis on the relationship between technology, capitalism, war, and empire.

On the other hand, Cherie Priest is one of the most popular and widely read steampunk authors writing today, and her work typifies the striations of the modern steampunk genre. A Google Trends search of the term "steampunk" (see figure 1), showing the relative frequency of the use of the term in Google Internet searches over time, indicates that popular interest in steampunk began rising in 2007 and has been steadily growing ever since. In fact, the chart itself is potentially indicative of the extent of Cherie Priest's influence in the genre. On the chart, there are four significant spikes that

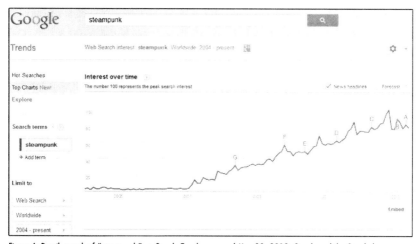

Figure 4: Detail, search of "steampunk" on Google Trends, accessed May 30, 2013. Google and the Google logo are registered trademarks of Google Inc., used with permission. Reprinted in accordance with Google Permissions Guidelines, http://www.google.com/permissions/.

correspond with October 2009, 2010, 2011, and 2012. The first four of Priest's Clockwork Century novels came out in the last week of September of each of these years, suggesting a strong correlation with these spikes in steampunk popularity. Equally telling is that when the sources of the searches are broken down by city, Seattle (Priest's hometown and the setting of *Boneshaker*) leads all other cities in the world by a longshot.[3]

To set up how steampunk functions as allohistory, in the following section I describe the four key tropes used in allohistorical fiction. These four tropes both define the allohistorical form and enable the kinds of reflection and cultural criticism found in allohistory and steampunk.

Four Allohistorical Tropes in Steampunk

A counterfactual historian explores how "history would have unfolded in hypothetical worlds that no one can ever visit or document" (Tetlock and Parker 13–14). Counterfactualism is a serious, if controversial, movement in the academic discipline of history.[4] In the view of counterfactualists, all logical inferences about causality fundamentally rely on assumptions about how outcomes would differ if certain crucial causal factors were altered. Because of this, proponents of historical counterfactualism argue that "like it or not, we are all counterfactual historians" (15).

As a genre, allohistorical fiction depends upon four key tropes to make it work: *reversal of hindsight bias*, establishing a *point of historical divergence*, the *minimal rewrite rule*, and what I call *moment hierarchy*. These tropes are present in nearly all such fiction, steampunk included.

The more-or-less strict reliance on these tropes is the elemental feature of allohistory that leads some critics to oppose the genre as essentially devoid of intellectual value. Whether one comes to that evaluative conclusion or not, and their reasons will be explored shortly, the fact remains that the genre has become a major force in the popular imaginary. An online archive of alternate history records that more than 3,100 novels, short stories, and essays have been published in the genre (Schmunk). The history of the genre extends back to Herodotus, who explored the possibility of the Persians defeating the Greeks at Marathon in 490 BCE (Rosenfeld, *The World Hitler Never Made* 5). It reemerged in the nineteenth century with Louis-Napoleon Geoffroy-Chateau's *Napoleon et la conquete du monde 1812–1832* (published 1836) and Charles Renouvier's *Uchronie* (published 1876), and it has remained a mainstay of the speculative apparatus for Western fiction (Rosenfeld, *The World Hitler Never Made* 5). Regardless of any given work's historical plausibility or academic value, we should consider the cultural significance that the genre not only exists but is thriving. Those who dismiss the genre outright for its "fancy" miss the point: millions of people create, consume, and participate in alternate history and steampunk. In the following pages, I will briefly describe each of these tropes in turn before turning to some specific steampunk texts.

Reversal of hindsight bias. Looking backward, we are plagued by hindsight bias: the illusion that the past was less contingent than the future seems to us now. Emboldened by the knowledge of how things turned out, these alternate histories often appear to us like fantasy rather than possibility. Yet, steampunk and other alternate history writers and scholars reverse this hindsight bias to demonstrate that history is and was as malleable as the future.

Psychologists have noted that most human beings tend to see the future as more contingent and uncertain than the past (Tetlock, Lebow, and Parker 3). This tendency is commonly known as the "hindsight bias." Philip Tetlock, Richard Lebow, and Geoffrey Parker note that the hindsight bias is due to the recognition that "once we know what has happened, it is difficult to recall how unsure we used to be about the future" (3). For the allohistorian, however, the hindsight bias is reversed. Writers and consumers of alternate fiction recognize that history *could have* happened differently, but, for some happenstance, did not. Steampunks look at the late 1800s and explore the possibilities created by what might have been rather than seeing only what was.

Point of divergence. Second, alternate histories commonly operate under a "point of divergence" trope, in which a specific or more general moment of divergence from historical record is indicated. Gavriel Rosenfeld considers this the primary difference between historical fiction and allohistory:

> What links such "analytical" and "fictional" alternate histories is their exploration of how the alteration of some variable in the historical record would have changed the overall course of historical events. The inclusion of this element—often called a "point of divergence"—is what distinguishes alternate history from other related genres, such as historical fiction. . . . Alternate histories are essentially defined by an "estranging" rather than a mimetic relationship to historical reality. (*The World Hitler Never Made* 4–5)

In other words, works of alternate history tend to make explicit a point of divergence from "true" historical records. For example, one could claim that if Britain had surrendered after the Battle of Britain in 1940, the Nazis would have eventually won World War II. The point of divergence from historical record is made clear, and stories could be written exploring alternate series of events that follow.

Steampunk's historical point of divergence is, significantly, the golden period of technological enlightenment and discovery immediately prior to the arrival of atmosphere-polluting coal-powered power plants and factories, the wide adoption of environmentally destructive diesel and coal combustion engines, and the dangerous and polarizing experiments in atomic physics that followed them. Thus steampunk returns to and preserves a moment in technological history in which the destructive potential of science was still largely unrealized, when inventors were imagined to be journeyman tinkerers like Tesla, Edison, or da Vinci rather than scientists like Oppenheimer. In some grittier steampunk stories, some of these technologies have recently been discovered and contribute to the core antagonism of the plot by threatening to unravel the utopic steampunk societies.

Minimal rewrite rule. Following from this second trope is the third, the "minimal rewrite rule," which suggests that works of alternate history should favor "causes that require little tampering with the actual historical record" (Tetlock, Lebow, and Parker 10). This trope follows the rationale that, despite the speculative nature of allohistorical works, they should strive nonetheless for plausibility. Thus, alternate histories become more plausible the smaller or more incidental the deviance from actual history. Alternate histories relying on a complex series of deviations tend toward the realm of the fantastic rather than the allohistorical, and lose their anchor to reality.

At the opposite end of the minimal rewrite standard lies the need to avoid the "Cleopatra's nose" fallacy. The argument, first made by Blaise Pascal, is that Cleopatra's nose is responsible for the fall of Rome: "thus Anthony's passion for her proboscis determines the fate of Rome" (Ferguson 12–13). Ferguson notes that this is, of course, a fallacious argument: "Now, while there is no logical reason why trivial things should *not* have momentous consequences, it is important to beware of the reductive inference that therefore a trivial thing is *the* cause of a great event" (12).[5] Thus, despite the initial entertainment value of scenarios like Pascal's account of the "probiscuous" affair that led to the fall of Rome, the minimal rewrite rule must be held in dialectic opposition to the problem of making too reductive a claim and still failing to meet the plausibility standard.

Of the four allohistorical tropes, the minimal rewrite rule is the one that steampunk plays with most loosely, while adhering closely to the other three. The gadgets and contraptions of steampunk worlds are often fantastical, implausible, or even impossible. This no doubt stems from characteristics of the steampunk subgenre that distinguish it from alternate history in general. While a work like Philip K. Dick's *The Man in the High Castle*, an alternate history of World War II in which the Axis powers win the war, strives for historical accuracy and plausibility in all aspects but its core divergence, works of steampunk often embrace the fantastic with a sense of liberation. Nonetheless, steampunk does not shed the rule entirely; the more complicated the historical divergence that leads to the ascendancy of steam power, the less plausible the story probably feels. Cherie Priest defines steampunk's ideal historical ethos as "the science fiction of the future that never happened" (Carrott and Johnson 73). Thus the fantastical elements of steampunk—idiosyncratic gadgets and the like—are often best approached as devices that may have been actually created if only the circumstances of technological history had differed.

Moment hierarchy. Finally, a fourth trope is identified by Benedetto Croce. Croce falls into the camp of professional historians who staunchly oppose counterfactual fiction and who see allohistory as, in E. P. Thompson's words, "*Geschichtswissenschlopff,* unhistorical shit" (Ferguson 5). Croce argues, and I believe correctly so, that allohistory constructs an arbitrary distinction between types of historical facts. Croce writes:

What is forbidden is . . . the anti-historical and illogical "if." Such an "if" arbitrarily divides the course of history into necessary facts and accidental facts. . . . Under the sign of this "if," one fact in a narrative is graded as necessary and another one as accidental, and the second is mentally eliminated in order to espy how the first would have developed along its own lines if it had not been disturbed by the second. (Ferguson 6)

In short, Croce argues that a central feature of allohistories is the tendency to find a historical moment that deterministically must have been as it was, and then alter a secondary moment or series of secondary moments so as to allow the ripple of the first moment to continue. I call this common trope "moment hierarchy." These moments are different from the point of divergence; rather, moment hierarchy is an exploration of which moments are changed and which remain the same in the wake of the initial change. For example, in counterfactual Hitler tales, the war itself is often the immovable historical object, while specific battles or smaller circumstances within the war are those deemed contingent and changeable. In steampunk, the era of scientific discovery coinciding with the Industrial Revolution still occurs without the discovery, deemed less crucial, of the combustion engine. In steampunk stories that are set in later periods or the present, as we will see in Harrison's novel, readers and viewers discover which aspects of the history they are familiar with remains mostly the same and which have been dramatically altered or erased by the initial tweak of the timeline. By Croce's account, these decisions to privilege some historical moments over others are made largely arbitrarily and for the sake of "fancy." While Croce may be right that these choices are not always historically or academically sound, in the case of steampunk the choice is clearly not at all arbitrary. There are complex reasons that this particular allohistorical moment has had an entire subculture form around it.

When analyzing the rhetorical meanings of both allohistory and steampunk, it is important to recognize that alternate visions of the past are not only about those past moments, but are also reflections of the periods in which they are written or created. For example, if one were to today begin writing an allohistorical account of the Roman Empire in which its collapse never happens, one almost certainly could not help but blend themes and concerns arising from contemporary contexts in with the exploration of that historical period—this new alternate Rome would inevitably take on characteristics of the present. Even if an author consciously sought to avoid doing so as much as possible, audiences would still interpret the piece through the lens established by the present.

Some of the best evidence for the argument that allohistorical reimagining is an expression of contemporary cultural anxieties comes from the work of allohistorical scholar Gavriel Rosenfeld. In his study of changes from 1940 to the present in film and fiction depicting alternate versions of World War II and Nazism, he found that the moral valences attributed to Nazism continually shifted over time in such ways as to address concerns emerging from the events of each decade ("Why Do We Ask 'What If?'"). The allohistories of Nazism made in the early 1940s were primarily oriented toward motivating American audiences to support American intervention in the war (95). This was accomplished by depicting the possibility of Nazi victory as unambiguously bleak and nightmarish. There was a clear contemporary exigency for this kind of narrative; there was widespread anxiety over the growing influence and military might of German Nazism, and only tales that reflected Nazism as an uncomplicated evil could push popular opinion toward American intervention. This anxiety is unsurprising, and the moral tone of the narratives is untroubled and straightforward.

More interesting and remarkable is how the themes changed in allohistorical narratives in the years after Nazism was already solidly defeated. In the 1950s and early 1960s, allohistories of Nazism and World War II experienced a resurgence in popularity due to the rise of neo-Nazism in West Germany and the well-publicized trials of Nazi war criminals like Adolf Eichmann (Rosenfeld, "Why Do We Ask 'What If?'" 96). Rosenfeld notes that while the moralistic imagery of Nazism as supreme evil remains unchanged during this period, within the narrative accounts this tone no longer served as a call to arms (which it could have easily been, given the standoff with Soviet Russia) but as a "didactic function of preserving the Germans' crimes in memory and of triumphalistically vindicating America's historic decision to intervene against them" (96). By the 1970s, however, the tone had significantly changed from an expression of the "nightmare" of a Nazi-ruled world into a fantasy of normalization, wherein Nazi rule was not significantly better or worse than the world as it was. Rosenfeld attributes this shift to the building anxiety of Americans over their perceived national decline (97). America could no longer legitimately be seen as a force of unwavering justice in the world in the wake of the Vietnam War, the civil rights struggles of the 1960s, the Watergate scandal, and the escalation of the Cold War. Stories of this period wavered in terms of "how" to be dissatisfied with history as it actually unfolded, but the trend of national self-consciousness and pessimistic self-critique was nearly universal. Many stories emerging from both the political right and the left concluded that American neutrality in World War II would have led to a more moderate postwar Nazism and a defeat of Soviet communism.[6] The attitudinal shift from the allohistorical stories of the war period and early postwar period is clearly indicative of the impact of shifting cultural anxieties in allohistory and counterfactualism.

Whether we reimagine Rome, the Second World War, or the Industrial Revolution, in our allohistories the past will always be revisited in the terms of the present. In the remainder of this chapter, I explore how steampunk's allohistorical reimagining of the past wrestles with some specific topics of common contemporary unease. Concerns about environmental destruction, overdependence on technology and the fast pace of technological growth, and imperialism run through both Harrison's and Priest's novels.

Steampunk, Technology, Empire, and Inquiry

Detailed descriptions and depictions of technology play a significant role in steampunk. In visual media such as film and television, gears, cogs, tubes, and various apparatuses feature prominently as indicators of the genre. In maker fairs and cosplay conventions, costumes display these same features and often, as Barry Brummett describes in this volume, "jump scale." In steampunk literature, the descriptions are equally vivid and effusive, sparing few details for the reader. Vital in each case is that these devices do not actually exist; it is their nonexistence that enables the comparison to the technologies with which we actually live.

Steampunk gadgets range from those that sound as though they could almost plausibly work to others that remind one of impossibly complex, overengineered, but nonetheless functional Rube Goldberg devices. On the more plausible side, take James Blaylock's description of a diving bell in his 1984 novel *The Digging Leviathan* for example:

> The diving bell itself, borrowed by Professor Latzarel from the Gaviota Oceanographic Laboratory, was round as a ball. It was almost an antique. Hoses led away out of it into great coils, and in a ring around the bell, within the upper one third or so, were a line of portholes riveted shut. There was a hatch at the top, screwed down with what looked like

an immense brass valve. The whole thing was etched with corrosion and flaked with blue-green verdigris. It looked to Jim like something out of Jules Verne. (55)

The reference to Jules Verne is more than a throwaway line; it clues the reader in to an aesthetic current that runs through steampunk. Verne's speculative fiction of the late 1800s is a key influence for the modern steampunk genre. The elaborately described contraptions of Verne's stories such as the *Nautilus* submarine in *Twenty Thousand Leagues under the Sea* find their counterparts in today's steampunk. In fact, the concept of the tunnel in Harrison's proto-steampunk novel *A Transatlantic Tunnel, Hurrah!* is itself the subject of the Verne short story "An Express of the Future," published in the *Strand Magazine* in 1895. In Verne's story, a train connecting Liverpool to Boston turns out to only be a dream, but in a sense Harrison's novel is also a kind of dreaming. For Verne, the dream was about the future; for Harrison, an examination of possible futures that have already been passed. For Harrison's audience, the dreaming is a means of contrasting what might have been with that which is.

This high attention to detail in gadgets is prevalent throughout Harrison's *Transatlantic Tunnel*. Take, for example, Harrison's description of a steam-powered car:

> As it began to close behind them, there was an imperious blast of a steam whistle from the street beyond, and it hurriedly opened again to admit the extended form of a Skoda Steamer, a vehicle much favored by European royalty. It had six wheels, the rear driving pair almost twice the size of the two others, as well as a cabin to the rear that housed the engine and the stoker. It emitted a plume of steam again as its whistle sounded and it eased silently by. (55)

Also published under the title *Tunnel through the Deeps*, Harrison's novel is set in an alternate version of 1973. This alternate world diverges from ours in 1212 with the Moors defeating Christian Spain in the Battle of Las Navas de Tolosa (47–48). As a consequence of the Moors' victory, Columbus's voyage west was never financed by Spanish royalty, and John Cabot discovered America instead. There was still an attempted American revolution, but it failed when George Washington lost the Battle of Lexington and was executed as a traitor. In present-day 1973, the British Empire is intact, still in control of its colonies, and still governed by monarchy. In an odd expression of moment hierarchy, Elizabeth II is still queen in this alternate world (51). The plot follows the hero, Augustine Washington, and the construction of a transatlantic tunnel connecting Britain to America. Augustine's hope is that success in the construction of the tunnel will at last "erase the family shame" brought on by his ancestor George.

Throughout the novel, Harrison uses its setting to comment on a variety of social problems. Harrison tackles the nature of empire, militarism, modern technology, and even Keynesian economics. In a surreal passage for the reader, Harrison describes how Lord Keynes is at fault for the tunnel's financial problems:

[I]t was Lord Keynes who had his way, the queen's adviser, author of I don't know how many books on economics, ninety years if he is a day and still spry enough to take on all comers. He had us all convinced; it sounded so good when he told us how well it would work. Money in circulation, capital on the move, healthy profits for investors, businesses expanding to meet the needs for building the tunnel, employment all around, pay packets going out to the small merchants, a healthy economy. (36)

Harrison's criticism is somewhat prescient for 1972, given the economic recession in the Western world that began in 1973. The rhetorical use of a fictional transatlantic tunnel as a reason to critique Keynes is either deft or silly, but in any case is remarkable. Allohistories set in the present day often create a sudden sense of the uncanny by introducing unexpected details about what has *not* changed. Reading a critique of Keynes in the context of a fictional world that nonetheless holds validity for our own is jarring when we have read about a series of fantastical steam-powered devices only moments earlier. In a very Burkean moment, the sudden presentation of incongruity summons new evaluations of the relationships and contrasts between our world and the fantasy world (Burke 90).

Another noteworthy passage comes near the conclusion of the novel, when a psychic character has a vision of *our* reality: "I see London, I see Paris, I see New York, I see Moscow, I see strange things. I see armies, warfare, killing, tons, tons, tons, tons of bombs from the air on cities and people below, hate him, kill him, poison gas, germ warfare, napalm, bomb, big bombs, atom bombs, hydrogen bombs, bombs dropping, men fighting killing dying, hating it is it is . . . ARRRRRRGH!" (221). This moment most clearly indicates the progressive potential of the (literally) utopic vision of alternate, allohistorical worlds. Harrison was himself staunchly antiwar, having been drafted into the army during World War II (Martin). His speculative fiction became his vehicle for expressing his views against war, typified well by the horror of the psychic's vision in this scene. Although it is obviously possible to express distaste for war without resorting to the creation of alternate universes, the comparison between two worlds creates a unique poignancy. Another character reacts to the psychic's vision: "Perhaps this world does not exist after all, for it sounds terrible and we cannot possibly imagine how it could have become like that" (222).

The contrast between Harrison's upbeat descriptions of steam-powered technologies—cars, tunnels, trains, airships, and the like—and the bleak technologies of destruction we know to actually exist is stark. What is made explicit in this scene is the logical counterpart to the optimistic tone of much of the novel: if Harrison's alternate world is so exciting—*hurrah!*—ours is bleaker. Harrison illustrates that visions of utopia are not only about nonexistent places, but ultimately also reflect concerns about the places we inhabit.

Harrison was a fan of Voltaire and used him as inspiration for his own work (Martin). *A Transatlantic Tunnel, Hurrah!* is in some ways a turn on the satire of unrelenting optimism in Voltaire's *Candide*. In Voltaire's novel, the character Candide is repeatedly exposed to the most painful hardships while espousing the philosophy of his mentor, Pangloss, that "all is for the best in the best of all possible worlds." In the end, Candide finally and abruptly rejects Pangloss's philosophy and says simply: "[W]e must cultivate our garden" (Voltaire lo. 1499).[7] Harrison's utopic steampunk fantasy world, brought into sheer relief against our own by the psychic's vision and other moments interspersed throughout the novel, tells the reader that we must tend to our world.

In recognizing the contrasts between reality and Harrison's steampunk world, the reader infers how this tending should happen. The most obvious difference lies in the changes to the historical timeline. Harrison's allohistorical world preserves an imperfect British Empire and thwarts American independence. For American readers, this invites reflection on America's role in the world in a period dominated by the conflict in Vietnam, the conflicts over civil rights for African Americans and women, the free speech movement, and other situations that taxed notions of American exceptionalism and greatness. The reader must contend with notions of empire—British or American. The second key difference lies in the technologies of the two worlds. Harrison's gadgets and devices are objects of celebration and awe, and are explicitly contrasted with atom bombs, germ warfare, and cars run by anything other than steam. Which set of scientific discoveries is to be preferred is not in doubt.

The revelation that Harrison's novel is actually dark satire is made apparent in the final chapter, titled "The Wonderful Day," with its utterly over-the-top description of the day of the ceremony celebrating completion of the transatlantic tunnel. Here again, the rhetorical effect is made by comparing our own world to that depicted by Harrison:

What a day, what a glorious day to be alive! Children present on this day would grow old with memories they would never forget, to sit by the fire some future evening and tell other wide-eyed children, yet unborn, about the wonder of this day. A cheerful sun shone brightly on City Hall Park in New York City; a cooling breeze rustled the leaves upon the trees while children rolled hoops and ran merrily about among the slowly promenading adults. What a microcosm of the new world this little park had become as people flocked in for this wonderful occasion, a slice of history revealed with the original owners there, the Lenni-Lenape Indians, a few Dutchmen—for they had been intrepid enough to attempt a colony here before the English overwhelmed them—Scotch and Irish who then came to settle, as well as immigrants from all the countries of Europe. And Indians and more Indians, Algonquin of all the five nations in their ceremonial finery of tall-feathered headdresses; Blackfeet and Crow from the west, Pueblo and Pima from even farther west, Aztec and Inca from the south, resplendent in their multicolored feather cloaks and ceremonial axes and war clubs—black rubber inserts replacing the deadly volcanic glass blades, Maya as well and members of the hundreds of other tribes and nations of South America. They strolled about, all of them, talking about pointing and enjoying the scene, buying ice cream, tortillas, hot dogs, tacos, and hot chillies from the vendors, balloons and toys, fireworks and flags galore. Here a dog ran barking chased by enthusiastic boys, there the first inebriate of the date was seized by one of the blue-clad New York's Finest and ushered into the waiting paddy wagon. All was as it should be and the world seemed a wonderful place. (224–225)

Embedded in this moment is a criticism of U.S. imperialism. Contrasting with the real-life celebration of the end of British colonialism after World War II, Harrison creates a vision of wonderful things that have *not* happened because of America's independence. Most significant among them in this scene is the presence of Native Americans who display indicators of their culture while clearly not having been victimized by American and Spanish genocides. Harrison's point seems to be that, while Americans can relatively easily identify many of the problems created by British colonialism and be comfortably critical of Great Britain, the ways the United States has been equally imperialistic and colonizing are not as transparent. When, on the final page of the novel, the reader learns that America has gained its independence at last, the effect is a feeling that American independence may not be a good thing after all.

Steampunk's generic connection to the Victorian Era has necessarily prompted some entanglement with the notion of empire. Some, such as occasionally steampunk-inspired author China Miéville, criticize the genre for uncritically "rehabilitating" British and American empire. Miéville notes: "There is no such thing as Victorian Britain without the fucking Raj for example, this is obvious. But in steampunk you don't have that, it is just not there" (Carrott and Johnson 184). James Carrott even added a text box in the middle of his printed interview with Miéville to address the issue: "Since many of you reading this book are Americans, this may call for a little explanation. The United States tends to have a problem admitting to empire, though we've been working hard on ours at least since the Mexican-American War" (185). Miéville and Carrott thus indicate a shortcoming in Harrison's vision. To critique American imperialism, Harrison depicts an uninterrupted British Empire as utopia.

The Victorianism that many see as inseparable from steampunk is a topic taken up by Priest in her Clockwork Century novels. In an interview with Carrott, Priest described how she first got into steampunk, specifically as an American, while browsing online forums:

> There were a number of teenagers who were complaining about Americans pretending to be steampunks. They were getting all riled up because, obviously, you can't have steampunk set in America. Steampunk has to be about Victorian England. And I got thinking about it, reading their list of reasons. Well, we had colonialism, check. We had all this technological revolution, this industrial uprising, check. We had wars, check. We had the socioeconomic disparity, check. . . . So, when people said that steampunk had to be only about Victorian England, I thought they were being ridiculous. (Carrott and Johnson 73)

Priest's American setting allows her to escape some of the criticism steampunk faces for its nostalgia for British imperialism, although one could argue that she only swaps it for a romanticized vision of the American West. Priest is one of steampunk's foremost authors writing today. The CC series currently comprises five novels with a sixth planned for release in late 2013. *Boneshaker*, the first in the series, was nominated for Hugo and Nebula Awards for Best Novel.

Boneshaker is set in Seattle in 1880. Starting in 1850, the promise of gold in the Klondike region brought prospectors to the Pacific Northwest.[8] Russian investors offered a 100,000 ruble prize to anyone who could invent a device capable of mining through the thick Alaskan ice. As Priest writes:

> Across the Pacific Northwest, big machines and small machines were tinkered into existence. They were tricky affairs designed to withstand bitter cold and tear through turf that was frozen diamond-hard. They were powered by steam and coal, and lubricated with special solutions that protected their mechanisms from the elements. These machines were made for men to drive like stagecoaches, or designed to dig on their own, controlled by clockwork and ingenious guiding devices. (lo. 65)

After these devices fail to break through the ice, a man named Leviticus Blue convinces the Russians to advance him funds for parts and labor to build "Dr. Blue's Incredible Bone-Shaking Drill Engine." This device

> would be the greatest mining vehicle ever constructed: fifty feet long and fully mechanized, powered by compressed steam. It would boast three primary drilling and cutting heads, positioned at the front of the craft; and a system of shoveling devices mounted along the back and sides would scoop the bored-through ice, rocks, or earth back out of the drilling path. Carefully weighted and meticulously reinforced, this machine could drill in an almost perfect vertical or horizontal path, depending on the whims of the man in the driver's seat. Its precision would be unprecedented, and its power would set the standard for all such devices to come. (lo. 65)

However, in the process of building the machine Blue inadvertently destroys the population of downtown Seattle, releasing "blight gas," which kills all who breathe it and turns them into living dead "rotters." Blue disappears and is presumed dead. In the aftermath of the disaster, walls are erected to protect the rest of the city from the Blight. The story follows Briar and Zeke Wilkes, wife and son of Leviticus Blue. Zeke, now adolescent, wants to clear his father's name of the accident and sneaks into the closed-off area still affected by the Blight. Briar decides that she must find and rescue him, and both use a variety of steampunk gadgets to protect themselves from the blight gas, the rotters, and the people who still live in the affected zone.

Boneshaker's story serves as an environmental warning about the negligent abuse of scientific knowledge. Priest sees a connection between the recent resurgence of interest in steampunk and the recent resurgence of environmentalism, commenting that "reduce, reuse, recycle" works as a philosophy for either (Carrott and Johnson 79). In *Boneshaker*, the devastation of Seattle is caused by a noxious gas, released by excessive drilling, that never goes away. A character in the novel, Lucy, says the following about the Blight gas:

> I mean, these walls are just a bowl—and a bowl can only hold so much. The Blight is coming up from underground, ain't it? Pouring more and more into this sealed-up shape. The gas is heavy, and for now, it stays down here like soup. But one day it's going to be too much. One day, it's going to overflow, right out there to the Outskirts. Maybe it'll overflow and poison the whole world, if you give it enough time. (lo. 4051)

Priest's Blight gas manages to combine the environmental concerns raised by excessive oil drilling with the dangers of ever rising levels of carbon dioxide in the atmosphere into a single entity. Both oil and carbon dioxide are notable for their intrinsic connection with combustion engines, the looming technology that threatens to end our fantasies of a steam-powered world.

While writing *Boneshaker*, Priest researched late-nineteenth-century patent applications at the University of Tennessee's archives for inspiration. In her interview with Carrott, she described her discoveries:

> You can go through the old patent archives there, and find crazy, crazy patent submissions for machines that people wanted to make. These crazy war machines . . . would they have worked, who knows? Probably not. But they were very interesting. And they were the most steampunk things I had ever seen and I thought, I would love to use these. Except they never happened, because they ran out of war. (Carrott and Johnson 75)

Priest's steampunk Seattle has airships controlled by complex systems of pulleys and levers, makeshift gas masks that require the user to frequently change out filters, and an invention known as "Daisy" that emits loud piercing noises that stun the rotters but requires fifteen minutes to build its charge, among many others. All of these devices serve beneficial purposes, and all are the results of tinkering. The only threatening device in the entire story is the Boneshaker drill itself, the only one that we are told required more than one individual's own ingenuity and grit to create.

There is significance in the descriptive and contextual differences between the various tinkerers' machines and the Boneshaker. The tinkerers' devices are tricky and haphazard, and must be manually controlled rather than automated. By contrast, the Boneshaker is described as "carefully weighted," "meticulously reinforced," and "fully mechanized," with unprecedented precision and power. While the tinkerers' devices ultimately don't solve the mining problem, they also don't destroy the city and environment like the Boneshaker does. *Boneshaker* reminds us of the distinctions made in steampunk about *how* its technologies and gadgets come to be created, and these distinctions carry with them certain moral warnings. When scientific reach exceeds scientific grasp but remains nonetheless propped up by external forces (e.g., capital, investors, corporations, governments), calamity follows.

These messages may impact the reader in a variety of ways. For those sympathetic to Priest's perspectives on technology and environmentalism, the impact may come in the form of feelings of catharsis, relief, or escape. For those struggling to identify "the moment it all went wrong," it may be cathartic to identify a specific point of divergence between the worlds. Likewise, there is affective relief in temporarily countering one's hindsight bias with the recognition that the history which led to our current difficulties could have been different. As creator of this allohistorical world that is critical of the present, Priest also becomes a spokeswoman for those who have grown uneasy with the complex relationship between science and capitalism, and feel that it has contributed to environmental degradation. For those who are less sympathetic or who feel apathetic about such matters, the setting nonetheless summons reflection and reconsideration. These effects are enhanced by the rhetorical distance between contemporary reality and the allohistorical fantasy that Priest has woven. It is less controversial and safer for a skeptic to consider critique in the context of fantasy, or a setting that does not exist. This has both advantages and disadvantages, if Priest intends her work to be not only entertaining but also persuasive to this audience. On the one hand, any opportunity to encourage reflection and critique is welcome. On the other, by couching that criticism in fantasy, it may make it easier to dismiss. Regardless, Priest's primary audience is clearly made up of steampunk enthusiasts who, in part in virtue of that enthusiasm, identify with these critiques.

Priest's world is not utopic in the same manner as Harrison's, but there is still celebration in surviving its grit and grime. When reading Harrison's novel, one almost has the sense that the world is sparkling clean. When reading Priest's, the grime is ubiquitous but is primarily caused by the one device—the Boneshaker, created through the alliance of science and capitalism—that nearly ends the world.

Neo-Victorian and material cultural scholar Rebecca Onion writes: "A large component of the steampunk project of human reintegration with the machine lies in the ability of the bystander or self-taught tinkerer to master important pieces of machinery that, in the current technological landscape, would be the exclusive province of specialists" (151). This is a point about steampunk's appeal that Cherie Priest has herself made in interviews: "I think that part of that appeal—the analog appeal and the hands-on tech, I want to do it myself appeal—is this idea that, well like I said, if my iPhone broke, I couldn't fix it, not in a million years, but if a giant death ray killing machine broke, I could probably fix it with a wrench and a couple of rivets. There's something very reassuring about that" (Carrott and Johnson 85). Priest's prose often evokes this lived-in world where technology works through simple mechanical processes and physics of the sort an individual agent/tinkerer could reasonably be expected to master, rather than the many modern technologies that require the expertise of whole teams of scientists and engineers backed by large organizations with opaque processes driven by complex financial incentives. Steampunk finds its path to this hands-on tinkerer's society through its allohistorical divergence from reality. The innovative spirit of the late 1800s takes a different turn without the combustion engine and the factory-driven industrialism it created.

Kenneth Pomeranz, in a counterfactual study of the Industrial Revolution, takes up the question of how long a tinkerer society could reasonably keep up with modern science. He writes:

> While I never shared the position that industrialization was bound to follow from any particular set of economic arrangements, I was inclined to minimize the importance of science in the early stages of the process, while emphasizing "tinkering." But if one assumes that "sustained" growth would have eventually required exploiting electricity and the chemical processes that allowed coal and petroleum

by-products to be turned into substitutes for so many vegetable and mineral products, the importance of science becomes undeniable. (261)

Thus, we return to what I earlier called the fundamental conceit of steampunk: a world in which Pomeranz's conclusion doesn't stand, and tinkerers are able to sustain technological growth through more successful processes of trial and error.

Joel Mokyr speaks to this divergence in describing counterfactual approaches to the history of technology as about identifying transitions between *potential* and *feasible* techniques. Naturally, steampunk techniques usually differ from actual historical techniques. He writes:

> There should, however, be a fair amount of interest in techniques that could have emerged but did not or in techniques that could have emerged much earlier than they did. Counterfactual history here is handicapped by hindsight bias: that is, we know which techniques occurred historically, and for that reason they seem more plausible than others. Techniques that were imagined but did not occur are written off as science fiction. . . . The dirigible and the electric car, to pick two obvious examples, are frequently dismissed not only as "never were" but also as "never could have been," though such inferences were often unwarranted. (289)

Steampunk revels in precisely what Mokyr finds lacking in academic counterfactualism. Steampunk is able to embrace those "techniques that were imagined but did not occur" that strict counterfactualism often overlooks.

• • •

Ultimately, steampunk is significant not just because it imagines an allohistorical society of technological tinkerers but because of what it indicates by preferring such a society. It offers a complex analysis of how scientific inquiry has been transformed in the twentieth and twenty-first centuries. Steampunk's rhetoric of inquiry, its claims of what it means to *find out* about the world, identifies the anxieties of a time in which an individual can no longer attain the tinkerer's advanced competence across multiple areas of current scientific knowledge—especially without years of focused study and training—that was still possible in the nineteenth century and earlier. As Priest says, "as our technology has become so terribly, terribly powerful and we've become so dependent on it, there's simultaneously something very fragile about it" (79). In such a world as ours, steampunk's settings suggest, the alienation of the individual knower from the products of her knowledge leads to technologies of war, to environmental crisis, to imbalances in economic power and empire. Expressed in steampunk is the hope that we can find the means to save ourselves from our own creations. Steampunk's allohistorical worlds depend on steam power, but they nonetheless combust, sparking critical reflection about the state of our own.

Notes

1. As many have noted, until the scientific and industrial revolutions of the late 1800s, scientific discovery often came in spurts interrupting long periods of stagnation. Industrialization, alongside myriad social and economic changes that have brought better education and new incentives for scientific inquiry, has been a significant factor in the rapid growth of scientific knowledge we have experienced since that time.

2. The *Oxford English Dictionary*, *Merriam-Webster Dictionary*, and *Free Dictionary* each offer definitions that closely approximate this description.

3. Following Seattle, the next cities indicated are (in order) San Francisco, Los Angeles, Chicago, New York, Sydney, and London.

4. As an example of the kind of opposition counterfactualists sometimes face from other historians, I offer the following line from Allan Megill's 2004 article "The New Counterfactualists" in the journal *Historically Speaking*: "When professional historians write virtual history we ought to treat their claims as to 'what might have been' with about the same distanced skepticism that we would treat the playing out of World War II by a group of fifteen-year-olds" (17).

5. One could make the same criticism of the nearly proverbial butterfly flapping its wings and causing a hurricane, commonly used to explain chaos theory.

6. For three examples, see John Lukacs, "What if Hitler Had Won the Second World War?," in *The People's Almanac #2*, ed. David Wallechinsky and Irving Wallace (New York: William Morrow, 1978), 396–398; Brad Linaweaver, *Moon of Ice* (New York: Tor Books, 1993); and Bruce M. Russett, *No Clear and Present Danger: A Skeptical View of the United States Entry into World War II* (New York: Harper & Row, 1972).

7. I use the abbreviation "lo." to designate the location marked within the Kindle e-book edition.

8. Note that Priest deliberately accelerates the timing of the Klondike gold rush, indicating a kind of moment hierarchy in which the rush itself is inevitable, but *when* it happens is contingent and flexible.

Works Cited

Blaylock, James P. *The Digging Leviathan*. New York: Ace Science Fiction Books, 1984.

Burke, Kenneth. *Permanence and Change: An Anatomy of Purpose*. 3rd ed. Berkeley: University of California Press, 1984.

Carrott, James, and Brian David Johnson. *Vintage Tomorrows: A Historian and a Futurist Journey through Steampunk into the Future of Technology*. Sebastopol, Calif.: Maker Media, 2013.

Ferguson, Niall. "Virtual History: Towards a 'Chaotic' Theory of the Past." In *Virtual History*, edited by Niall Ferguson, 1–90. New York: Basic Books, 1999.

Gross, Cory. "A History of Misapplied Technology: Exploring the History of the Steampunk Genre." *SteamPunk Magazine*, no. 2 (2007): 54–61.

Harrison, Harry. *A Transatlantic Tunnel, Hurrah!* 1972; reprint, New York: Tor Books, 2011.

Lévi-Strauss, Claude. *The Savage Mind*. Translated by George Weidenfeld and Nicolson Ltd. Chicago: University of Chicago Press, 1966.

Lyne, John. "Rhetorics of Inquiry." *Quarterly Journal of Speech* 71, no. 1 (1985): 65–73.

———. "Social Epistemology as a Rhetoric of Inquiry." *Argumentation* 8, no. 2 (1994): 111–124.

Martin, Douglas. "Harry Harrison, a Prolific Writer of Satiric Science Fiction, Dies at 87." *New York Times*, August 17, 2012. At http://www.nytimes.com/2012/08/18/books/harry-harrison-a-prolific-writer-of-satiric-science-fiction-dies-at-87.html?_r=0. Accessed May 30, 2013.

Megill, Allan. "The New Counterfactualists." *Historically Speaking* 5, no. 4 (2004): 17–18.

Mokyr, Joel. "King Kong and Cold Fusion: Counterfactual Analysis and the History of Technology." In *Unmaking the West: "What-If?" Scenarios That Rewrite World History*, edited by Philip Tetlock, Richard Lebow, and Geoffrey Parker, 277–322. Ann Arbor: University of Michigan Press, 2006.

Nelson, John S., and Allan Megill. "Rhetoric of Inquiry: Projects and Prospects." *Quarterly Journal of Speech* 72, no. 1 (1986): 20–37.

Onion, Rebecca. "Reclaiming the Machine: An Introductory Look at Steampunk in Everyday Practice." *Neo-Victorian Studies* 1, no. 1 (2008): 138–163.

Parker, Geoffrey, and Philip Tetlock. "Counterfactual History: Its Advocates, Its Critics, and Its Uses." In *Unmaking the West: "What-If?" Scenarios That Rewrite World History*, edited by Philip Tetlock, Richard Lebow, and Geoffrey Parker, 363–392. Ann Arbor: University of Michigan Press, 2006.

Pomeranz, Kenneth. "Without Coal? Colonies? Calculus? Counterfactuals and Industrialization in Europe and China." In *Unmaking the West: "What-If?" Scenarios That Rewrite World History*, edited by Philip Tetlock, Richard Lebow, and Geoffrey Parker, 241–276. Ann Arbor: University of Michigan Press, 2006.

Priest, Cherie. *Boneshaker*. New York: Tor Books, 2009. Kindle edition.

Rosenfeld, Gavriel D. "Why Do We Ask 'What If?' Reflections on the Function of Alternate History." *History and Theory* 41, no. 4 (2002): 90–104.

———. *The World Hitler Never Made*. Cambridge: Cambridge University Press, 2005.

Schmunk, Robert. *Uchronia: The Alternative History List.* 1991–2013. At http://www.uchro
nia.net/. Accessed May 30, 2013.

Tetlock, Philip, Richard Lebow, and Geoffrey Parker. "Unmaking the Middle Kingdom." In
Unmaking the West: "What-If?" Scenarios That Rewrite World History, edited by Philip
Tetlock, Richard Lebow, and Geoffrey Parker, 1–13. Ann Arbor: University of Michigan
Press, 2006.

Tetlock, Philip, and Geoffrey Parker. "Counterfactual Thought Experiments: Why We Can't
Live without Them and How We Must Learn to Live with Them." In *Unmaking the West:
"What-If?" Scenarios That Rewrite World History*, edited by Philip Tetlock, Richard Leb-
ow, and Geoffrey Parker, 14–44. Ann Arbor: University of Michigan Press, 2006.

Verne, Jules. "An Express of the Future." In *Science Fiction by Gaslight: A History and Anthology of Science Fiction in the Popular Magazines, 1891–1911*, edited by Sam Moskowitz,
115–119. Westport, Conn.: Hyperion Press, 1968.

Voltaire. *Candide.* New York: Boni and Liveright, 1918. Kindle edition.

Steampunk's Identity Horizon and Contested Memory

ANDREW MARA

STEAMPUNK, A PORTMANTEAU COMPOSED OF TWO WILDLY DIVERGENT SUB-
terms—a backward-looking and conservative "steam" and a forward-looking
chaotic "punk"—invokes an inherent tension between historical fidelity and
aesthetic transgression. It is at this paradoxical junction between backward
glances and redemptive destruction that Steampunk constitutes its primary
creative tension. An aesthetic that couches itself in memory yet depends on
bending that kind of memory risks undoing its own legitimacy, but in so
doing sets up the engine of its creative possibility. At a historical moment
when people document their quotidian life details with hundreds of Face-
book friends and when factual claims can be checked through smartphone
Internet searches, any aesthetic movement that builds upon a shared sense of
a past that no members of the movement actually experienced seems tenuous. Furthermore, when this shared historical sense serves as not only a compass but also the departure point for speculative creativity, violent artistic
turbulence seems inevitable. The contradictions embodied by Steampunk
artists, artisans, and fan crafters who festoon their bodies and fill their lives
with speculative period pieces demand more attention from both practitioners and critics. The critics of Steampunk note how the nostalgic aesthetic
gestures inflect the genre's historical sensibility, but the way that aesthetics,
medium, and memory interrelate to create possible public subjectivities remains to be explored.

Victorian England, the staging ground of the British Empire, provides a
complicated backdrop for exploring the boundaries of what it means to be a
man or a woman, a citizen of a nation-state or a racialized and subaltern self
in a postnational and global present. Rhetorical relationships open up a range
of gendered, racialized, and denationalized public subjectivities through
the aesthetics of empire that Steampunk creates, circulates, and disrupts.
Through its juxtaposition of historical memory and aesthetic transgression

of implied boundaries, Steampunk creates an agonistic set of relations and rhetorically situates agents who participate. Re-creating the past in nostalgic gestures, Steampunk creates claims about the past that invite identification, both in the nostalgia and the destruction involved in reformulating that nostalgia. In examining how Steampunk and related aesthetics of Nazipunk, cowboypunk, and spacepunk play with the classed and raced signifiers of the Victorian British Empire, this chapter will question how performed memory provides a denationalized and resistant aesthetic identity horizon for individuals to form articulable, and therefore changeable, public selves. The performed memory of Steampunk lays down stringent historical and artistic rules of rhetorical engagement to help practitioners reconstitute identity markers that have been gradually dissolved by an always-on cultural commons.

To people who even have a passing familiarity with Steampunk, it is not surprising that this subculture defines itself through backward glances to earlier historical moments and signals allegiance through particular aesthetic gestures. Steampunk enthusiasts obsess about the aesthetic fidelity and plausibility of their depictions of alternate Victorian scenarios. Steampunk artifacts, costumes, and fan art deploy the textures and the details of the era—the brass, the wood, the clothing, and the steam technology; moreover, Steampunk culture typically embodies these stylistic gestures in depictions of particular Victorian technologies—the typewriter, the monocle, the zeppelin, the steamship. The haunting presence of now-antiquated techniques and vestigial approaches to contemporarily championed technologies opens a two-way door to the past. Precursors of word processors, cars, contact lenses, jet aircraft, and speedboats provide speculative and diachronic artistic explorations of what might have occurred if we had maintained an allegiance to the aesthetic and technical characteristics of the Age of Steam. Steampunk provokes, repulses, and ultimately creates new affective scenes for people to work out who they are, what they believe in, and where they belong. In short, it is a topos for rhetorical work.

What remains murky, however, are the limits that fans impose upon this speculative genre. After all, the very premise of Steampunk is the unrealized potential of the era. Absolute fidelity to the Victorian Era could only result in period pieces. Steampunkers seem decidedly uninterested in yet another Dickens re-creation, a dusty Masterpiece Theater staging of a George Eliot story, or a mere rehashing of the glories of early industrialism and the rise of the modern city. Instead, Steampunk's restless fans weigh a particular historical sensibility against their creative drive and desire to create alternative worlds. It is in defining what counts for Steampunk (and what does not) that an analyst can discern some of the networks that fans use to build a different relationship to each other and relate them to an increasingly connected world. By locating the ever-shifting edges of what counts for Steampunk, the analyst can discover the horizon against which participants create their alternative public identities, an identity horizon constructed by an increasingly obvious relationship between border-erasing technologies and the agents who depend upon them.

Steampunk and other historicized punks (Nazipunk, cowboypunk, cyberpunk) inhabit a set of technologies that have been aesthetically fetishized to reflect a particular era, locale, and set of sensibilities. The worlds that these aesthetic gestures inhabit have historical origins, but they have aesthetically superseded these historical origins with a visual vocabulary created in several modalities (most famously, graphic novels and films). Cowboypunk depends heavily upon images and gestures established in John Ford movies and later developed in the existentially barren spaghetti westerns; similarly, Nazipunk depends heavily on the post–World War II depictions of Nazis, especially the antihuman technologies and technocratic ethos built into filmic Nazi villains. Steampunk enjoys a somewhat different relationship to the historical precedent it references. Instead of merely pointing to an aesthetically intensified fetish of the period, it can instead pick and choose from more direct references. The prevalence of the English novel in the Victorian period—and the persistent popularity of these novels—allows contemporary cultural remixers to mine their samples from a much more direct source with greater fidelity. In *The League of Extraordinary Gentlemen*, for example, graphic novelists Alan Moore and Kevin O'Neill could choose from widely remembered historical events and a range of nineteenth-century fictional characters to drive the plot. Bram Stoker's Wilhelmina "Mina" Harker, Mark Twain's Tom Sawyer, Jules Verne's Captain Nemo, H. Rider Haggard's Allan Quatermain, Robert Louis Stevenson's Dr. Jekyll, and H. G. Wells's Invisible Man (among many others) make appearances. Outside of fictionalized versions of Adolf Hitler and Joseph Goebbels, Nazipunk artists have few well-known characters to borrow. Cowboypunk similarly borrows from a post–frontier period pantheon of characters and borrows aesthetic gestures created in the mid-twentieth century. At the edges of these different punks reside a number of conflicts that vie to replace the nation-state as the definer of postnational identity. The conflicts that arise as a result of the difference between our values and the values that our technological choices forward enable agents to create versions of a public self that either adhere to or resist embodied ideologies presented by technology. Today's global citizens cannot escape the ubiquity of the cell phone, the computer, and the car, but they can pledge allegiance to these kinds of technologies and the ideology they manifest, or declare their citizenship to alternative states of mind through the public performance of alternative aesthetics. Because Steampunk is currently the preeminent "punk" in film and literary culture, it makes sense to look there to see how its alternative sense of empire informs the retoggling of a public subjectivity. Steampunk occupies an empire state of mind and shows how other historical punks help people create alternative public subjectivities in a time of rapid global flows.

Performing the Experiment

My exploration of Steampunk identity began with a serendipitous experiment. In order to populate the performance stream of the 2011 Computers and Writing conference at the University of Michigan, the organizers of the conference asked to repurpose a fairly routine panel presentation proposal on Steampunk aesthetics into something a bit more theatrical. In the spirit of experimentation, I created an interactive game to collect informal data on how colleagues from my particular subdiscipline of computers and writing would react to different aesthetic interpretations of historical punking. As a subdiscipline of English studies, computers and writing is populated with some the more technologically inclined and geeky practitioners of English studies. We blog. We MOOC. We read and watch science fiction. Still, I had no idea how many people in my subfield participate in Steampunk culture (or, for that matter, even read or watch Steampunk). In the hopes of provoking some sort of response that I could then write about, I modified my more staid panel proposal to include a staging of a mock game show that asked people to publicly perform what they thought about portrayals of various historical punks. I wanted to know if my colleagues would own up to their knowledge of the ins and outs of Steampunk.

During my performance, I enjoined conference goers to fire up their laptops and join a game I called "Too Steam, Too Punk, or Just Right?" In order to see if my colleagues would play along and/or resist particular constructions of aesthetic/historical punking in real time, and in front of their friends, I dared my fellow computers and writing professionals to throw down their votes publicly on Twitter. Participants would expose their avatars as well as be able to creatively use 140 characters to project and defend aesthetic choices in a social media space I was displaying at the front of the auditorium. I enlisted, cajoled, and urged a crowd of people in a University of Michigan auditorium to tweet their votes for a reel of eleven film clips, photos, and artifacts I had captured on a QuickTime video as either "Too Steam," "Too Punk," or "Just Right." While this survey was intended to be more performative than scientific and was in no way designed to comprehensively represent broader social attitudes toward Steampunk, I hoped to gather reactions that would either dispel or reinforce my suspicion that my colleagues harbored an interest in Steampunk. I imagined that having to publicly identify what they thought about the eleven clips I selected would split this decidedly academic crowd into two camps—people who openly care about Steampunk and those who treat it as an occasion to be a bit more subversive. This process of projection and defense was engineered to reveal the presence of possible multiple selves—the fan, the expert, the outsider—who would be exposed during the play of affective stances.

At the beginning of my fifteen-minute game show performance, the crowd received the simple rules (which I also handed out in a flyer): (1) Open your Twitter account; (2) Watch each clip; (3) Identify the clip/photo/artifact you are voting for; (4) Vote "Too Steam," "Too Punk," or "Just Right"; and (5) append the #2s2p hashtag so that I can project the results in real time on a split screen using the search function in Twitter. Participants were treated to what I called eleven tableaux: a trailer for the crowd-funded movie *Iron Sky*, a photograph of young adults dressed in Steampunk clothes, the trailer for the film *Wild Wild West*, the trailer for the film *The Golden Compass*, the trailer for the film *The League of Extraordinary Gentlemen*, a clip from "The Train Job" episode of the *Firefly* television show, a trailer for the Robert Downey Jr.–acted *Sherlock Holmes*, an extended look at a *Steam Wars* T-shirt, the trailer for film *Suckerpunch*, a clip from the video game *Bioshock*, and the trailer for the *Firefly*-based film *Serenity*.[1] While not everyone in the crowd participated (not everyone brought wireless-enabled laptops), roughly one-quarter of the attendees (out of about 120 people) participated in the livetweet section of the performative experiment. About half of the livetweeters took a more sarcastic/subversive bent (commenting on the soundtrack, or declaring a movie trailer "Too Awesome," for instance), and the other half took it more seriously. Of the section of the crowd that took it seriously, there was a pattern of agreement of what constitutes the center of Steampunk, but a wider divergence on where the definition ends. For example, the livetweeters generally agreed that *The League of Extraordinary Gentlemen* was "Just Right" (at least in terms of representing the aesthetics of Steampunk—there was not a lot of enthusiasm for endorsing the quality of the plot). The divergence happened with outliers like Nazipunk and spacepunk. For example, people voted for all three of the descriptors for the movie *Iron Sky*, a crowd-funded Nazipunk movie that came out in 2012. Despite the fact that the villains use post-Victorian technology evocative of World War II, some people voted it as something that was either "Just Right" or even "Too Steam." I had explained "Too Steam" as being too historically faithful when queried by the crowd, which indicates that most of the participants in this hypereducated crowd had not thought about the provenance, etymology, or implications of the term "Steampunk." Obviously, the depiction of Nazis creating a moon base and coming back to attack the Earth in the present should not strike anyone as either alternative Victoriana or something that was historically faithful.

Firefly and *Serenity*, the television and filmic versions of Joss Whedon's spacepunk ensemble adventure drama with a cowboypunk aesthetic, both were considered wide of the "Just Right" mark (although the clips I showed were alternately tweeted as "Too Steam" and "Too Punk"). Much of the technology depicted in both *Firefly* and *Serenity* evokes the Victorian period by modeling the ethos of time on the postbellum period of the United States. The main conflict pits protagonists who act as a band of outlaw smugglers roughly resembling Confederate soldiers against a government trying to "reconstruct" an interstellar union. Ostensibly, the aesthetics from this spacepunk fiction could fall under the auspices of Steampunk. Joss Whedon's characters walk around shooting six-shooters; the spaceships have a mechanical physicality that resembles the devices created by Steampunk enthusiasts; the cast of characters hold positions commonly portrayed in Victorian novels (the soldier, the outlaw, the prostitute, the doctor, the muscles, and the mysterious stranger); and even the speech mannerisms of the main characters mimic the affect and speech patterns of nineteenth-century Americans (at least filmic ones). Interestingly, the scene I projected during the game was set in a western town and centered on a train robbery, and it was considered too true to historical fidelity by the crowd. Alternatively, the preview to the film *Serenity*, which contained a lot of footage that showed space flight, was consequently considered too punk.

As might one might expect with a group of geeky academics in an Ann Arbor museum, there was some sarcastic pushback in the Twitterstream. About half of the participants appended snarky comments with meticulously correct hashtags. While it would be tempting to dismiss many of the votes as being merely sarcastic, or as people pushing back on a game they found overly tedious, the fact that resisting participants came up with ever more elaborate snark, combined with the low cost of opting out (there was no tracking of nonparticipation), forced me to look for alternative explanations for votes like theirs. Many of the participants may have been unaware of Steampunk conventions, yet the snark of the subversive participants played off cultural stereotypes of Steampunk enthusiasts as nerds and perhaps a bit introverted or unaware of social norms. Combine these more oppositional stances with the fact that more serious players were willing to broaden their notion of what Steampunk would be, and I had to complicate my more straightforward notions of why people embrace particular aesthetics. Identification isn't enough to explain why Nazipunk as portrayed in *Iron Sky* was acknowledged to be somewhere in the ballpark of *The League of Extraordinary Gentlemen*. It is at that intersection of Nazipunk and Steampunk, of cowboypunk and spacepunk, and other juxtapositions of aesthetic punking where I found kinds of resonances that might explain why contemporary audiences seem to crave speculative fictions steeped in historical stylizations. People revealed their roles in a rhetorical process of sorting out identities through this game.

The Aesthetic Memory of Public Subjectivity

In order to understand how Steampunk creates an identity horizon, I first wanted to understand how memory orients people in their public subjectivities. Rhetoric postulates that memory creates a topography in which individuals can create a public subjectivity, and can thus enable particular kinds of agency. Generation Xers, for example, can choose to embrace or reject the imagery associated with the late 80s–early 90s; embrace, reject, or opt out of the image of the disaffected slacker; and so on. Jenny Rice, in *Distant Publics: Development Rhetoric and the Subject of Crisis*, gives contemporary detail to the ancient rhetorical canon of memory when she identifies public subjectivity as "the role(s) we inhabit when we speak and act about matters that put us into relation with others."[2] Rice extends Robert Asen's notion of subjectivity as a kind of invitation to encounter and interact with others.[3] Rice's project on how performed memory circulates claims interrelates agency and affect: "[T]he subject of true feeling renders all emotions and affective experiences as primary orientation devices between self and the world."[4] How we feel about the signifiers of our experiences orients us to our opportunities to meet, interact with, and possibly change other agents. We are who we feel we are, and others array themselves in these affective fields because of what we claim to remember, and how we relate to those claimed memories. Memory, whether speculative or realistic, allows people to participate in rhetorical fields that may seem otherwise closed. Memory creates opportunity for change.

In order to create particular kinds of invitation to action and interaction, an individual needs to locate where agents are and how they can move across particular topoi, or rhetorical spaces; "we can think of memory claims and their horizons as rhetorical orientation devices. . . . Public memory is not a vertical line that attaches its memorializers to the authentic point of origina- tions."[5] To return to the Gen X example, just because one wears neon green does not mean that one did so during the 1980s, or that one was a Cyndi Lauper or Wham! fan. In fact, many people who currently wear bright neon clothes, as part of a 2013 minirevival of 1980s neon clothing, were not alive during the 1980s. Steampunk functions in much the same way. As David Beard notes in the introduction to this volume, Steampunk's memory ho- rizon is formulated against the imagined historical signifiers of the Age of Steam. The aesthetic gestures of Victoriana and its difference with contem- porary manifestations of postmodernity, postindustrialism, and posthuman- ism create the space for individuals to craft aesthetic invitations and repul- sions. Public subjectivity, finally, creates a new set of creative possibility, through the repetition of aesthetic gestures and their inevitable changes and bending. Toward this end, Rice echoes Bradford Vivian's postulation that public memory's "sheer repetition across changing contexts, in response to new exigencies, transforms its character and brings about new iterations, new desires."[6] Steampunk allows readers, viewers, fans, and producers to ex- press allegiance, rejection, and exception in a particularly situated identity horizon that is connected to articulations of the Age of Steam. In, out, or indifferent—invitations can be issued, accepted, rejected, or ignored based on a created and shared memory. In short, people can negotiate their world rhetorically through a shared aesthetic that gives them both a set of rules and the means to recast those rules.

Global Articulations of Steampunk Identity

Arjun Appadurai's and Saskia Sassen's notions of scapes and denationaliza- tion can help an analyst better understand how sideshadowing an alterna- tive Victoriana might cast particular doubts on what it means to live in the present. Appadurai, in *Modernity at Large*, describes a number of connected chains of signification that connect heterogeneous networks semiotically despite their spanning borders and landscapes that might imply semiotic discontinuity. Appadurai's scapes describe how globalism supersedes the boundary-setting conditions of nationhood. His scapes each inflect the network-centric view of nationalism with a particular flavor. These scapes—which include mediascapes, ethnoscapes, technoscapes, ideoscapes, and financescapes—aggregate distinct agencies across borders and view them as entities that are linked through identity. Each of these scapes contain their own motivation for spanning national boundaries, but they all traverse the global pathways that international travel and communication technologies enable. The most obvious place to start in explaining how these scapes can help an analyst describe how remixing Victorian England can provide a creative outlet in a twenty-first-century international milieu would be with ethnoscapes, because of the way that Steampunk can inflect what has been heretofore normalized in the white, male body of the Victorian gentleman genius. Appadurai, who defines ethnoscapes as "the landscape of persons who constitute the shifting world in which we live: tourists, immigrants, refugees, exiles, guest workers, and other moving groups and individuals constitute an essential feature of the world,"[7] paints the picture of a heterogeneous yet connected mass of people. Seeing Steampunk as the glue for sticking particular gestures into a scape can provide a pathway for the artist, fan, and consumer to participate in the creation of coherent speculative nostalgia. Specifically, the connective power of technology, media practices, and ideology can help reintegrate the separate strands of identity that the perforation of national boundaries threatens to permanently sunder. We are all part of some sort of empire, even if it is only a malleable and imagined empire.

Although Appadurai assumes that identity endures the perforation of national boundaries and the dissolution of national identity, Saskia Sassen points toward why this is even possible. In her article "The Repositioning of Citizenship and Alienage: Emergent Subjects and Spaces for Politics," Sassen presents the critic with a set of possibilities for understanding how affective bonds between subjects can persist despite the apparent dissolution of national bonds. A denationalized subject contrasts with, but does not contradict, the postnational subject: "[P]ostnational citizenship is located partly outside the confines of the national. In considering denationalization, the focus moves on to the transformation of the national, including the national in its condition as foundational for citizenship."[8] Sassen notes that the unfulfilled promise of equality that citizenship has not fully bestowed legally and economically upon its subjects (especially gendered, racialized, and sexualized subjects) creates an unresolved tension.[9] She defines the process of denationalization as the transformation of a subjectivity based upon the nation-state for the purposes of political discussion, and opens up the possibility for aesthetic identification as a way to map what might resolve the tension. While being a citizen of the United States might not get us to equality (something that representative democracies promise), people will find other ways to identify like-minded individuals working toward the world they desire. Considering that the nation-state has not lived up to its billing, exploring mash-ups derived from the height of the nation-state (which Sassen notes as spanning the eighteenth, nineteenth, and early twentieth centuries) seems like fertile ground for finding the citizens of an imagined DIY Steam nation. Find the signifiers that you care about (and the ones you avoid), and you may find a better crowd to build the world you desire.

Gothic Steam, Global Film, and Denationalized Supermen

Van Helsing, the 2004 Gothic action-adventure film, helps illustrate how the film industry—itself a globalist enterprise—depends on the willingness of audiences to suspend notions of historical fidelity, sometimes joyfully tearing the webs of history using the tools of historical feeling, in service to building a denationalized public subjectivity. *Van Helsing* in many ways is an utterly pedestrian global entertainment vehicle. It was neither spectacularly successful nor singularly unsuccessful. This poorly reviewed film did moderately well financially—costing $160 million to make, and earning $300 million (at least according to publicly available studio estimates). That the leading man, Hugh Jackman, a New Zealander, could easily find work after this film attests to the fact that he did nothing out of the ordinary to threaten his career. The film was widely released during its film run and to this day is broadcast both domestically and internationally. During my unrelated three-month research trip to Kenya in 2012, this movie was still playing over global film networks catering to international travelers.

The directorial and filmographic choices in *Van Helsing* appear conservative by contemporary action film standards. The film made a number of nostalgic, Steampunk-related aesthetic choices—including setting the story in nineteenth-century Europe and using a number of Victorian villains. The film also heavily depended on a number of Steampunk speculative innovations, including alternate technologies (like a Gatling gun crossbow), contemporary notions of choreography, an electronically altered soundtrack, and CGI exaggerations of the features of a Victorian menagerie to create a decidedly übermasculine aesthetic vernacular. Fight sequences use Matrix-like "bullet time" slow-motion sequences, and costuming and CGI feature exaggerated secondary gender characteristics (disproportionately large male pectoral muscles and biceps as well as voluptuous female breasts) in addition to exaggerated teeth and nails on the monsters. A. O. Scott, in his review of the film, notes the promise of breadth in detail matched with a mushy historical narrative; "despite the rococo obsessiveness of its special effects and its voracious sampling of past horror movies, *Van Helsing* is mostly content to offer warmed-over allusions and secondhand thrills."[10]

Van Helsing, a film that follows in an artistic vein foregrounded by *The League of Extraordinary Gentlemen*, pits the Archangel Gabriel against a historical cross section of Victorian/Romantic monsters. Bram Stoker's Dracula, Mary Shelley's Frankenstein's Monster, Victor Hugo's Hunchback of Notre Dame, and the Wolf Man (a character made famous in twentieth-century film but who has roots in nineteenth-century fiction) all make an appearance. *Van Helsing* was noted for a particularly sloppy knitting together of storylines (A. O. Scott, in the film review cited above, also noted that "neither originality nor efficient storytelling is really the point of this sloppy, sometimes amusing exercise"). The eponymous protagonist seems to run from European castle to castle to keep the plot going, when he isn't being drawn by a horse and carriage. This archangel's use of neo-Victorian weapons—including his Gatling crossbow—elevates this supposedly supernatural being above the backward Eastern European populace terrorized by Gothic monstrosities. His almost quaint technology is invested with an impressive power through a combination of a backwardly projected Steam Age authenticity and a postmodern sensibility. The contemporary filmic practices of bullet-time filming and slow-motion fight sequences only heighten the importance of attending to the details of these historical mergings. The impressiveness of the Gatling crossbow is emphasized as the viewer gets to see every bolt shot skyward toward succubi who fly through a Romanian town, kidnapping the townsfolk and rustling their livestock. Similarly, the audience is given the chance to see every Hugh Jackman punch land against the CGI wolfman as the fight continues above, below, and inside a burning horse-drawn carriage. International audiences get to see every pixel in slow motion, and every punch landed on a CGI-rendered beastie, all the while wondering what the hell this all has to do with them.

Punking Identity through Play

Despite the messy plot and choreographic anachronisms, movies like *Van Helsing* find their audience. People watch, and like, these kinds of films (at least enough for the film to net $300 million worldwide). Despite the critics' protestations about plot blandness and CGI exaggeration, audiences continue to stream into movies in which New Zealanders happily slay Victorian antagonists, literary characters like Sherlock Holmes battle progressively more muscular villains, and historical figures like Abraham Lincoln do battle with vampires. Stuart Hall's articulation theory can provide additional theoretical insight to explain how Steampunk's rhetoric unfolds as an agonistic contest between historical memory and aesthetic imperative for the sake of novelty. Hall's theory, a kind of soft Marxism that frames the material struggle apart from a more teleological narrative of the proletariat versus capitalists, maintains that there are pressures that exert shape over the ideological landscape even when the larger narratives about revolution and change no longer hold. As Johndan Johnson-Eilola describes in *Datacloud*, articulation theory "builds on the work of several key social theorists, which Hall brings together—articulates—to construct a workable social theory for postmodernist cultures. Working with trajectories from Gramsci, Althusser, Foucault, Laclau, and others, Hall constructs a neomarxist theory of cultural production that understands class as well as postmodernism, without sliding completely in one or the other. Subjects are constructed in cultural contexts, including class belongingness, but not without some ability to intervene in that construction."[11] The postmodern difficulty of finding meaning in what can seem like an eternally flexible set of semiotic relations is at least partially solved when we consider that locations and relations are neither fixed and permanent, nor infinitely flexible. People can use aesthetic gestures in Steampunk to map their positions in relation to a dominant ideology (in this case, one marked by global transportation, rapid telecommunication, and ubiquitous Internet access), but they are not entirely trapped by their counterpublic rhetorical stance. The revolution may not be televised, and it may not even happen; however, what is *on* television may lead to its own minirevolution of sorts.

The ability to intervene in processes of power and oppression that neither originate with the person nor are fully controlled by the subject illustrates how an aesthetic drawn from the once-beating heart of the British Empire might be used to create new and enabling subjectivities across a range of cultural contexts. The Victorian period, a time when India was fighting for independence, connects the romanticized images of the British Empire at the height of its power with the historical resonances associated with technologies that helped countries fight for and win their independence from Great Britain. Memory and identity provide the primary means by which audiences engage in locating and measuring distances. Nostalgia's etymology provides one clue to the bifurcation between memory and identity. Nostalgia, a word coined by Johann Keyssler in his *Travels through Germany, Bohemia, Hungary, Switzerland, Italy, and Lorrain*, derives from the Greek *nostos* and *algos* as a way of designating extreme and debilitating homesickness.[12] Despite the softening of the term that emerged in the 1920s to designate a much gentler wistfulness, the gesture still mixes both memory and pain— even if that pain results in some form of pleasure. Steampunk's gesture toward a past that never existed signals a desire that plays out against a chronological axis. The object of desire, in this case, involves the loss of the British Empire, along with the signifiers of the philosophies and technologies that had vaulted Britain to the top of the world order.

Terry Gilliam Punks Empire

To illustrate this tension between a homesickness invoking the British Empire and the contemporary denationalization and variegated ethnoscapes that give this nostalgic glance its creative power, we turn toward an American expatriate, Terry Gilliam, and his movies *Brazil* and *Twelve Monkeys*, which both invoke nostalgia against the political and ideological backdrop of a remix culture. Even though *Brazil* and *Twelve Monkeys* are not customarily discussed as Steampunk works, they rely on the same tension between nostalgia and punk to enact their satiric critique. Not coincidentally, these movies play with memory and sequence. The protagonists in both of these movies struggle with notions of identity and memory through the plot devices of dreams and imagined memories. We meet the protagonist in *Brazil*, Sam Lowry, as a bureaucrat who gets caught in the gears of the police state where he lives because of an actual bug (a housefly caught in a printer ends up changing a police warrant to include Lowry). The movie is set in a world that is characterized by a mishmash of both contemporary and older technologies spliced together. The use of a retrograde aesthetic in the service of technology critique offers the opportunity to see how this rhetoric of identity operates both aesthetically and culturally. The information technology that confuses Sam Lowry's identity with that of a criminal appears much like an electronic typewriter. The technology in Sam's home, ducts and pipes, is decidedly industrial, as is the technology in Sam's workplace. In a particularly comic scene, Sam fights with a neighboring employee over use of the same desk, which protrudes into both their offices but which is inadequate for sharing. Sam and his office neighbor pull the desk back and forth through the wall. The comic effect is heightened by the absurdity of a company that would provide such obviously inadequate equipment—conversely, this absurdity highlights the darker possibility that companies design purposefully inadequate work environments.

Sam's dream world more beautifully welds the future and the past through magic. The dream Sam can fly by using a mechanical metal suit with wings. His ability to wind between buildings and escape from perils does not carry over into his waking life, however; in reality, he is doomed to always be subverted by the technology that promises to help. Instead of gaining any sort of assistance from his dream suit, Sam feels only frustration and inadequacy in his waking life. Sam's home life is no less absurd. His heating and air conditioning are nonfunctional and he is not allowed to fix them by edict of the state. The ductwork is externalized, industrial, and seemingly easy to repair, which makes the edict to not repair it all the more absurd. Robert De Niro's terrorist/repairman character weds this absurdity with Marxist critique. Although this critique seems pointed metaphorically at late capitalism, the aesthetic takes a painful backward glance. The World War II aesthetic and technologies evoke fascist Italy and Nazi Germany just as easily. The technocratic fantasies of tyrants provide no relief for the critic who thinks that a simple reversal of the main character's ideology is all that is needed. A historical U-turn is neither desirable nor possible. The technoscape that the viewer lives in marks Sam's world as distinctively different, and definitively retro. What makes it dystopian is a function of the technology-hinged plot. The technology we see in Gilliam's films is too simple and too visibly clunky to create the kinds of simulacra and the kinds of surveillance that we attribute to contemporary computer-enabled technology.

This conundrum of yearning for a more obvious technology while holding off the possibility of historical backtracking provides the central plot pivot for Terry Gilliam's later movie *Twelve Monkeys*. The film's protagonist lives in a world that combines futuristic technology (time travel) and retrograde aesthetics. The gears, hoses, and mechanical underpinnings of both of Gilliam's futuristic worlds hearken back to early-twentieth-century industrial Britain. In *Twelve Monkeys*, Gilliam uses chronological confusion and perceptual ambiguity to heighten the tension between a yearned-for tactile technology and the nefarious ideologies and motivations that have historically taken advantage of them. James Cole, the protagonist of Gilliam's postapocalyptic psychological thriller, has to discern whether or not the official story about biological terrorism has caused the dissolution of society. Underpinning James's confusion is the presence of a disorienting pastiche of technologies that resemble the pneumatic tubes, lenses, and assorted laboratory equipment ubiquitous in Steampunk. Never afforded a clear view of the allegations against the man he is being sent to kill, James has to trust that he is being sent back in time to stop the apocalypse that presumably causes his incarceration. As with Sam, the technology James is surrounded by, ocular and scientific in nature, holds out the possibility of distillation of the truth while working in exactly the opposite direction. The tools of science have been used to perpetuate the terrorism and psychological warfare that they were supposed to prevent. This nostalgic tension offers the viewer the chance to imagine a simpler and more understandable time while thwarting that possibility with the interfering ideologies associated with that technology.

Terry Gilliam, formerly a collage artist in the Monty Python's Flying Circus comedy series, creates an aesthetic nostalgia and vertigo using a distinctively Steampunk pastiche and bricolage. By using the assumptions of futuristic speculative fiction (time travel, posthuman body modification, etc.) and by undermining the assumptions about the technology that allows it (that such technology is invisible, clean, harmless), a director can harness the multiple emotional valences of nostalgia and the ambivalent possibilities of futurism. As the protagonists struggle to understand who they are, they walk through landscapes that simultaneously attest to miraculous possibility and clunky artificiality. In both movies, this artificiality enables a fascistic power structure to take control of the populace and provides the opportunity for the protagonists, if only briefly, to jam the machinery that enables that near-total power.

In articulation theory, this simultaneous assertion of power and the means to subvert it at the margins provides the paradoxical means to resist. Steampunk aesthetic, seen from this perspective, frames the world as a place still hurtling along a particular trajectory (time travel, space travel, superhero intercession, supernatural threats, etc.), but with a more delicate machinery that puts the seemingly inevitable destination in question. The memory of a past that is both familiar and askew puts a dependent future in doubt. The fondness for the brass, the valves, the knobs, and the less-threatening steam power of the past also gives the viewer a reason to root for failure. We know that the machine can be broken, and in spectacular fashion. After all, if the protagonists succeed in their endeavors, the fetishized and embodied memory might fade. Audiences know what happens after the Age of Steam and do not necessarily want to go there, even in an alternative history. The protagonists of Gilliam's movies—Sam and James—seem comfortable enough with the quotidian affordances of their technology, but they cannot seem to wrap their minds around the way that the state seems both limited by the technology and enabled to abuse power through that limitation. We want them to smash their world but keep it frozen in its quaintness, so that we can avoid the historical and moral corruption that we associate with advances in technology.

Conclusion

Steampunk's backward glance allows every participant—whether a fan, an onlooker, a critic, or an outsider—to turn a critical eye toward the past in service to an altered future. The passive viewers of *Van Helsing*, the hipsters who snarked at my "Too Steam, Too Punk, or Just Right" game show, and the intellectuals who celebrate another Terry Gilliam production all put themselves back on Queen Victoria's map, even if that map is tenuous, temporary, and devoid of the queen herself. Instead, we are all left to navigate the networks that empire traversed while trying to fix the problems that this period of industrial and national arbitrage created. The inequalities that the nation-state initially exacerbated abroad continue even in the seats of Western power. The trade routes that brought the riches of the African, Asian, and Pacific cultures to the Western world continue to carry cargoes of capital and labor across national boundaries and threaten to erase the very boundaries that inscribe difference. Ultimately, my experiment in aesthetic provocation only uncovered deep-seated ambivalence toward the signification of network persistence. More than the gratification that Beard claims in his introduction, people are claiming a shape for how they want to relate in our postnational identity horizon. Any response to Steampunk, even a shrug, is a response to how individuals envision their ideoscape, technoscape, and ethnoscape. Beyond the new allegiance to always-already-old Victoriana, the ordinariness of Steampunk signals a greater affective awareness that we have not moved past the past and that we are all somehow connected to an aestheticized memory that Beard notes is set "against a backdrop of imperialism, manifest destiny, and slavery." Who we are depends on how we connect in our affect-saturated, historically aestheticized moment. Who we are depends on whether or not we want to be more steam or more punk.

Notes

1. Andrew Mara, "Too Steam, Too Punk, or Just Right," June 1, 2011. At http://www.you tube.com/watch?v=Yun18OuQcGk&list=UUo-PkPcvrRtK9SnnKkgYq_w&index=10, accessed April 10, 2013. Andrew Mara, "Too Steam, Too Punk, or Just Right Trailer," April 21, 2011. At http://www.youtube.com/watch?v=eGp4u9jGzrw, accessed April 15, 2013.
2. Jenny Rice, *Distant Publics: Development Rhetoric and the Subject of Crisis* (Pittsburgh: University of Pittsburgh Press, 2012), 45.
3. Ibid, 193.
4. Ibid., 55.
5. Ibid, 125.
6. Bradford Vivian, "Jefferson's Other," *Quarterly Journal of Speech* 88 (2002): 299.
7. Arjun Appadurai, *Modernity at Large: Cultural Dimensions of Globalization* (Minneapolis: University of Minnesota Press, 2006), 33.
8. Saskia Sassen, "The Repositioning of Citizenship and Alienage: Emergent Subjects and Spaces for Politics," *Globalizations* 2, no.1 (2005): 88.
9. Ibid, 85.
10. A. O. Scott, "Full Moon, Romance and a Demon Rustler: Review of *Van Helsing*," *New York Times*, May 7, 2004.
11. Larry Grossberg, "On Postmodernism and Articulation: An Interview with Stuart Hall," in *Stuart Hall: Critical Dialogues in Cultural Studies*, ed. David Morley and Kuan-Hsing Chen (New York: Routledge, 1986), 25.
12. *Oxford English Dictionary*, online edition.

Works Cited

Appadurai, Arjun. *Modernity at Large: Cultural Dimensions of Globalization*. Minneapolis: University of Minnesota Press, 2006.

Asen, Robert. "A Discourse Theory of Citizenship." *Quarterly Journal of Speech* 90, no. 2 (2004): 189–211.

Brazil. Directed by Terry Gilliam. Universal Films, 1985.

Grossberg, Larry. "On Postmodernism and Articulation: An Interview with Stuart Hall." In *Stuart Hall: Critical Dialogues in Cultural Studies*, edited by David Morley and Kuan-Hsing Chen, 45–60. New York: Routledge, 1986.

Johnson-Eilola, Johndan. *Datacloud: Toward a New Theory of Online Work*. Cresskill, N.J.: Hampton Press, 2005.

Mara, Andrew. "Too Steam, Too Punk, or Just Right." June 1, 2011. At http://www.youtube .com/watch?v=Yun18OuQcGk&list=UUo-PkPcvrRtK9SnnKkgYq_w&index=10.

———. "Too Steam, Too Punk, or Just Right Trailer." April 21, 2011. At http://www.youtube .com/watch?v=eGp4u9jGzrw.

Rice, Jenny. *Distant Publics: Development Rhetoric and the Subject of Crisis*. Pittsburgh: University of Pittsburgh Press, 2012.

Sassen, Saskia. "The Repositioning of Citizenship and Alienage: Emergent Subjects and Spaces for Politics." *Globalizations* 2, no. 1 (2005): 79–94.

Scott, A. O. "Full Moon, Romance and a Demon Rustler: Review of *Van Helsing*." *New York Times*, May 7, 2004.

Twelve Monkeys. Directed by Terry Gilliam. Universal Films, 1985.

Vivian, Bradford. "Jefferson's Other." *Quarterly Journal of Speech* 88 (2002): 284–302.

Guy Ritchie's *Sherlock Holmes*

Steampunk Superhero?

LISA HORTON

⚙

THE RECEPTION HISTORY OF SHERLOCK HOLMES, THE MOST FAMOUS CRE-
ation of Sir Arthur Conan Doyle, and the renewal and re-creation of the
character through film and television have varied enormously with the wax-
ing and waning popularity and shifting interpretation of the Victorian period.[1] Although portrayals of Holmes have proliferated on the small screen,
since the death of Basil Rathbone in 1967 only three feature films have attempted seriously to represent the character as Doyle drew him within the
period in which he was created.[2] On Christmas Day of 2009, a feature film
again brought the characters of Sherlock Holmes and Dr. John Watson as
well as the soot-stained but industrious world of their Victorian London
back to the forefront of popular culture with an unprecedented splash of
notoriety. The film *Sherlock Holmes* achieved a wild success, realizing a box
office gross exceeding $209 million in U.S. ticket sales alone (from a produc-
tion budget of $90 million).[3] Doubtless, there were many contributing fac-
tors to such popularity, such as the recent reemergence of Robert Downey
Jr. as a Hollywood superstar after *Iron Man* in 2008, the heartthrob status of
Jude Law,[4] and the previous successes of Guy Ritchie as a director. Certainly
there had never been a portrayal of Sherlock Holmes like this one, and the
public, especially the American public, stated its vociferous approval. At the
same time, the groundswell of interest in the period driven by the Steampunk movement prepared the public to accept and appreciate a superhero of
the Victorian age, as this Holmes was presented.

Despite approval both from the public at large and from Steampunk fans,
there was less support for the film from the select but active international
subculture of dedicated Sherlock Holmes aficionados, self-identified in the
United States as "Sherlockians." The two best-known organizations dedicated to the topic are the Sherlock Holmes Society of London, founded in 1951,[5]

177

and the Baker Street Irregulars, founded on January 6, 1934. The BSI is an international society, although their annual meetings have always taken place in New York. Both of these organizations, their memberships, and the Sherlockian community at large have an acute sense of institutional history and a strong inclination toward more traditionalist interpretations of the characters of Sherlock Holmes and Doctor Watson. In the realm of film, the BSI has been courted by, and has consulted with, producers, directors, and actors alike. Several, including Basil Rathbone, Nigel Bruce, and director Nicholas Meyer, have been invited guests at the BSI's annual Birthday Weekend celebrations. BSI member and editor of the *New Annotated Sherlock Holmes*, Leslie Klinger, was asked to consult on the Guy Ritchie movies—he also appears in the special features on the Blu-ray edition of the first film.[6] The response of these organizations, particularly the Baker Street Irregulars, has therefore had significant impact on the reception history of the characters and the stories. Nevertheless, among Sherlockians, the reception of Ritchie's 2009 film was not unreservedly positive.

There is a nexus point here at which fan studies, the rhetoric of popular culture, and postmodernist critical theory intersect. Any time an interpretation of a beloved character, book, or series departs substantially from its original, the specialized audience of dedicated fans who have learned to value that original are disappointed. At the same time, most kinds of speculative fiction, into which category literary reinterpretations often fall, are reliant on the questions "what if?" and "what then?" The whole Steampunk movement is also predicated on this concept: what if human technological advancement had never discovered the internal combustion engine—how would that have changed human history? Sherlock Holmes "pastiches" follow precisely the same process.[7] These "what if" and "what then" questions address variables, often related to the concept of free will and the relative probabilities of human behavior. However, occasionally speculative fiction changes not only the variables but the constants, such as the inherent character of an individual or the nature of the known universe. The degree to which an audience is prepared to suspend their disbelief equates to the commercial success of the text[8]—the larger the target audience, the greater the commercial impact. Willing suspension of disbelief is generally dependent on individual personality or on normative group dynamics. For example, a group of *Star Trek* fans might be willing to accept that Ambassador Spock's accidental journey through a wormhole in time and space could change the course of the narrative continuity of the show's history,[9] but at the same time would resist the reversal of personalities between the two protagonists.[10] This same factor, which could be termed the pastiche reception phenomenon, is like-wise true of traditionalist Sherlockians. Such an audience might, as many do, accept the chronological relocation of the stories to contemporary London, which necessitates a shift in almost all of the possible variables.[11] However, the same specialized audience resists changes to constants like Sherlock Holmes's height or Watson's gender.[12] As a result of this phenomenon, which arises from the group's quotidian-level privileging of the literary over any other media and the original over any and all interpretations of it, every production, portrayal, and pastiche of Sherlock Holmes has garnered its share of outraged disaffection.[13]

A partial explanation of this reaction lies in the definition of "pastiche." Fredric Jameson, in his 1982 lecture "Postmodernism and Consumer Society," characterizes it thus: "Pastiche is, like parody, the imitation of a peculiar or unique style, the wearing of a stylistic mask, speech in a dead language; but it is a neutral practice of such mimicry."[14] He later laments: "In a world in which stylistic innovation is no longer possible, all that is left is to imitate dead styles, to speak through the masks and with the voices of the styles in the imaginary museum."[15] If this summarizes the capabilities of pastiche, then small wonder that any produced text so categorized would meet with disapprobation. However, there is much more happening in these interpretations than mere mimicry; for an adequate explanation, pastiche theory is insufficient. Shifts in the media of popular culture have given rise to new definitions and new theories. One theory more appropriate to this crisis between Sherlockian subculture and the popular reinterpretation enthusiastically embraced by Steampunks is what Eduardo Navas defines in 2006 as "remix."[16] As pastiche comes to postmodernist critical theory by way of painting and other studio art, remix also comes through another medium—hip-hop music. Navas explains further:

> To understand Remix as a cultural phenomenon, we must first define it in music. A music remix, in general, is a reinterpretation of a pre-existing song, meaning that the "aura" of the original will be dominant in the remixed version. Of course some of the most challenging remixes can question this generalization. But based on its history, it can be stated that there are three kinds of basic remixes, which extend in culture as a fourth type, which I refer to as Regenerative.[17]

The heart of what is at stake for Sherlockians and Steampunks, and via this same cultural phenomenon all fan cultures, is subcultural self-awareness and a better understanding of how the rhetorical process of remix adapts original material and how it fundamentally differs from the postmodern definition and process of pastiche. Remix does not merely imitate a dead style or original in the manner of traditional pastiche; it revitalizes it, imbuing it with new creative vitality.

The end result of Ritchie's *Sherlock Holmes* films was to attract thousands of new fans to the characters and stories, and to encourage the development of two successful television series that have attracted even more fans.[18] As of May 24, 2013, according to official lists compiled by Peter Blau, there were 901 Sherlock Holmes fan groups in existence worldwide, with as many as 419 listed as "active." These numbers are higher even than the last census taken in February 2013.[19] Among fans both old and new, the potential of an alliance between Sherlockians and followers of the Steampunk movement seems like a fruitful direction for a continued conversation begun as early as 1999 when Alan Moore and Kevin O'Neill called up three famous characters from Sir Arthur Conan Doyle's fiction to thicken the plot of *The League of Extraordinary Gentlemen*.[20] It seems both inevitable and desirable that Sherlockians and Steampunk fans should find common cause. The impulse among Steampunk fans to engage their fandom from within, to create, to immerse themselves, and actively to participate in cosplay, echoes the phenomenon in Sherlockian subculture known as "playing the game." Discussion of the stories and the characters are cast in the historic past; the characters really lived, or in Holmes's case live;[21] there is no fiction involved beyond discretionary name changing; and Sir Arthur Conan Doyle is not author but literary agent for Dr. Watson, who is himself not merely narrative voice but author. At the same time, and perhaps surprisingly, few traditional Sherlockians are enthusiasts of cosplay; the occasional deerstalker cap or pipe may appear in a gathering of fans,[22] but the full Victorian costume with frock coat and starched shirt is a rarity. Steampunk fans, at the other extreme of fandom, seem to be driven by a unifying aesthetic rather than a particular story, character, or even particular historical moment. There is more agreement in what the fandom "looks like" than what the fandom is "about."

A lifetime's study of literature, and concomitant obsession with the Sherlock Holmes stories, has made it clear that no two interpretations of any text will entirely agree, whether that "text" is a single character, a whole series of stories, or an entire historical period.[23] However, the plentitude of variety in the Steampunk universe has expanded to a nearly infinite extent.[24] As Jeff VanderMeer acknowledges:

Over the past fifteen years, Steampunk has gone from being a literary movement to a way of life and a part of pop culture. A Steampunk aesthetic now permeates movies, comics, fashion, art, and music, and has given a distinct flavor to iconic events such as Maker Faire and the Burning Man Festival. At this point, too, the term "Victorian" has become so malleable that its use no longer corresponds to its historical boundaries: the period of Queen Victoria's reign (1837–1901). For a Steampunk, it may encompass the succeeding Edwardian era (1901–10) or serve as a catchall to evoke the Industrial Revolution. At the extreme of Steampunk artifice, the term can be a received idea of "Victorian" as popularized in movies and elsewhere that has no historical basis.[25]

The engagement of such fans in the consideration of a single pivot point, a character through which the Victorian period may constructively be viewed and by which it might be judged, may reinvigorate or provide a sense of solidarity for a fandom whose disparate threads are perhaps unraveling into a disorganized chaos. Again, the potentially unifying factor here is remix, and the stakes for mutual endeavor are the revitalization of organized Sherlockian fandom and the reorganization of the Steampunk movement. Ultimately, the greatest lure of the neo-Victorian or Steampunk movement is the compelling notion of re-creating history and the figures of historical literary periods in our own image.[26] As has been mentioned, Alan Moore and Kevin O'Neill's comics series *The League of Extraordinary Gentlemen* is very nearly a case history in the co-opting of Victorian literature to twenty-first-century repurposing. An underexploited archvillain, perhaps the quintessential archvillain of all popular fiction, squares off against underexploited heroes in an apocalyptic vision of the military industrial complex and the hopelessly corrupted bureaucracies of an ineffectual imperial government. Social commentary abounds. In a much lighter vein but undergoing a similar process, the early Victorian fiction of Jane Austen, whose novels encapsulate both period and genre in the canon of British literature, is lampooned hilariously in the novel *Pride and Prejudice and Zombies*, in which Elizabeth Bennett and her sisters, trained abroad by Chinese martial arts masters, do battle against reanimated hordes in a peculiar mash-up of *Dawn of the Dead*, *Kill Bill*, and *Masterpiece Theater*.[27] Reexamining the fiction of the past through the lens of the present is hardly a new practice; neither is rebuilding or rewriting the stories of the past to speak significantly to the themes of the present. While

Steampunks engage in such remix with enthusiasm, the hesitation among traditionalist Sherlockians to embrace this remixing process arises from a fear of anachronistic contamination creeping in and jeopardizing what is unique about Sherlock Holmes and Dr. John Watson for the sake of an explosion of popular exposure and renewed popular interest.

As the above examples demonstrate, the kind of reinvention inherent in the process of remixing other characters from Victorian literature with fully operational neo-Victorian entities necessitates adding recognizably twenty-first-century attitudes and characteristics to these characters. To a fan subculture that privileges the literary original over all subsequent interpretations, although this process arguably makes them more relatable for a twenty-first-century audience, it inevitably destroys their uniquely Victorian nature and, thus, a significant aspect of their appeal. Many examples of this insidious process exist in the *Sherlock Holmes* films of Guy Ritchie. One jarring anachronism that is understated in the first film is Watson's cohabitation with Mary Morstan, their engagement unannounced and no proposal yet given. Such "irregularity" in a doctor's household would have been unthinkable; it would have been the irredeemable ruin of his clinical practice among the upper middle class of London, whose scandalized reaction would have at best pilloried Watson in the gossip columns and at worst cost him his medical license. The scene in which this anachronism comes up is the very first scene in the Baker Street apartments, as though the filmmakers wanted to be clear from the beginning that this was definitely an interpretation of the Holmes stories not for their own time but for ours.[28] For a twenty-first-century film audience, of course, such a practical solution to Watson's frustration with Holmes's eccentricities and the need to adapt to a new domestic partnership before the legal responsibility of marriage is so commonplace that it warrants barely a glance. One example not of anachronism but of fatal inconsistency in characterization is the very appearance of Sherlock Holmes. Holmes in this film perpetually exhibits what the habitually neat Watson terms a "general lack of hygiene,"[29] with hair forever uncombed, face perpetually unshaven, and clothes often slept in or simply filthy. Such habits are common enough in a twenty-first-century bachelor and are doubtless intended to give the modern audience a point of fellow-feeling either with Holmes or with the exasperated Watson. However, this behavior would have been utter anathema to a character whose precision and correctness of personal appearance was maintained even when living rough on a case. Watson remarks in *The Hound of the Baskervilles* that "[i]n his tweed suit and cloth cap he looked like any other tourist upon the moor, and he had contrived, with that catlike love of personal cleanliness which was one of his characteristics, that his chin should be as smooth and his linen as perfect as if he were in Baker Street."[30] Such changes not of variables but of constants in the characterization of Holmes epitomizes the difference between the limitations of stylistic mimicry available to pastiche and the breadth available to remix. Within Sherlockian fan culture, unassisted by the potentially liberating influence of a Steampunk alliance, this process of reinvention is at least awkward and, at most, insufferable. One Sherlockian quipped in an interview that followed her first viewing of the film: "My first reaction was, 'Who was that scruffy guy and why does he keep quoting Sherlock Holmes?'"[31]

Of course, this kind of remixing has been done to Holmes and Watson before, just not in quite the same way or for so innocuous a reason as entertainment. The most obvious example was created before the remix phenomenon was popularized—the Universal film series with Basil Rathbone and Nigel Bruce, already mentioned, in which a long-haired, fedora-wearing Holmes does battle with the Nazis. Despite the success of their first two period pieces for Twentieth Century Fox, Rathbone and Bruce's remaining films did not merely update themes and allusions but fully modernized the look of the characters and their surroundings. In the 1940s, the world was in dire need of rescue and called upon Sherlock Holmes to raise the spirits of a society embroiled in a conflict with human evil on a massive scale and to solve not the commonplace mysteries of criminal endeavor but the global problems of a world at war. After all, Holmes had played a role in foiling an espionage plot at the outset of the First World War; in the story "His Last Bow," chronologically the last Holmes story published by Doyle, a disguised Holmes dupes an otherwise effective German imperial agent out from under his cover as an international playboy on the eve of the war.[32] The successful employment of a strong Steampunk aesthetic in the *Sherlock Holmes* films of Guy Ritchie, while perhaps not addressing as urgent a societal need as those of the 1940s, nevertheless illuminates these somewhat remote characters of Victorian fiction for the edification of a broader public. Moreover, it draws together the two very specialized subcultures of Sherlockians and Steampunks into a potential mutually beneficial alliance of interest as they observe Guy Ritchie's singular vision of the adventures of Steampunk Sherlock.

Ritchie's first film, *Sherlock Holmes* (2009), makes bold choices in art direction—costumes, props, and sets—remixing the erstwhile monochromatic Holmes and our perceptions of his Victorian world with more colorful comic book heroics of today. The first character to be updated is Dr. John Watson; as mentioned earlier, his proposed living arrangements signal to the viewer that this Watson is not simply a Baker Street bachelor as he is presented in most film and television depictions.[33] Even in such subtle ways as his wardrobe, this is a very different Watson. He appears in military uniform when he takes Mary Morstan to meet Holmes. In the Doyle stories, there is no indication that Watson, as a former army doctor, ever wore military dress after his retirement; even in the illustrations of the stories, the only drawing of Watson in uniform is for the discussion of his backstory in *A Study in Scarlet*.[34] When the Watson of the film is not in uniform, his apparently mundane and meticulously respectable Harris tweed suit carries a subtle but distinct plaid that stands out only in certain scenes and in certain light, as in his ascent of the stairs into Baker Street.[35] When this Watson is neither at a formal public occasion nor working with patients, he relaxes in the Baker Street sitting room in shirtsleeves and braces[36] with the eccentric addition of his jauntily angled hat. In the public street and under normal conditions, Watson wears his hat in the usual formal manner; however, when he is preparing to do battle he sets it somewhat askew, presumably the better to keep it on his head when he isn't using it as a projectile.[37] These minor adjustments to accepted Victorian costume and practice nevertheless represent an important contemporary remix of the more conservative of the two protagonists.

Another character in the film who undergoes a thorough overhaul of her prose-based image is Holmes's investigative sparring partner, Irene Adler. In the Doyle stories, Adler appears in exactly one installment, the first short story published, "A Scandal in Bohemia." Her status as the only woman to best Holmes in a case sets her apart from other female characters in the series, so it is not surprising that film and television interpretations have been fascinated by Adler. In Guy Ritchie's *Sherlock Holmes*, the operatic prima donna from New Jersey is even more colorful than the character described by Doyle. The choice to put her in a sensationally pink frock with a blue brocade overcoat and cutaway tails to show off the bustle displays a direct and provocative design that borders, in conservative Victorian London, on the outrageous.[38] However, when she is not in the dress, she is even more controversial. Adler's lack of body consciousness, or her choice to use her sexuality as a weapon in her sparring with Holmes, is evident when she admits the detective into her room at the Grand Hotel while she is wearing only a towel; when she removes the towel before stepping around a screen to change, she wins a brief moment of distraction from Holmes, which she exploits to strategic advantage later in the scene.[39] However, neither her provocative color and design choices nor her shock-value immodesty, which are the invention of the film, quite measure up to her canonically accurate cross-dressing. In "A Scandal in Bohemia," Adler herself in a personal note to Holmes vouchsafes that as an operatic contralto, "male costume is nothing new to me."[40] In her case at least, Doyle's original is at least as culturally daring as the film's remix.

Holmes himself, of course, receives an update in color and texture commensurate with his new twenty-first-century filmic image. While the clothing he wears in the first scene of *Sherlock Holmes* is subdued, as befits the working and fighting conditions of the outing, Holmes's costuming elsewhere in the movie is striking. While Doyle's Holmes is usually drawn in either the gabardine black frock coat, waistcoat, and pinstripe trousers of traditional city wear or the tweed suit of traditional country wear, the default look of Holmes in the Guy Ritchie film features a frock coat in dark blue corduroy.[41] Both its color and its texture would have seemed out of place in upper-middle-class Victorian London, but in the world of this film, which does not sport the monochrome or sepia tones of old daguerreotypes but the glorious Technicolor of Hollywood, such a costume befits the colorful character of this Steampunk Sherlock Holmes. The dressing gown he wears in the first Baker Street scene is not just a garish color, as was fairly characteristic of the Holmes of the stories, who did occasionally wear a purple dressing gown.[42] This article of clothing is also egregiously threadbare, consistent with the habits of dubious hygiene previously mentioned as characteristic of this screen Holmes.[43] The disguises of Sherlock Holmes are almost as ubiquitous to his legend as the pipe, the magnifying glass, and the deerstalker cap. In the film *Sherlock Holmes*, the audience experiences two such disguises. The first is the garb of a street person selected and assumed spontaneously as the need arises. Holmes hastily applies a false nose, steals Watson's overcoat on his way out a second-story window, then acquires a hat, two scarves, and an eye patch from a street circus in the back alley as he follows Irene Adler to her rendezvous with her mysterious associate. His other disguise is much more deliberate; he puts on the white coat, neat goatee, slicked-down hair, and precise suit of a German medical doctor in order to gain access to the hospital where the injured Watson has been taken for treatment. These two disguises serve to contrast the two modes of Holmes's working methodology—one a brilliantly effective spontaneity, the other a meticulously strategized deliberation.[44] The colorful garishness of the circus performers visible as Holmes sprints by, elements of their world adhering, as it were, to his slightly more normal persona, might almost serve as a metaphor for the larger remix as elements from the twenty-first-century world affix themselves perforce to his character in this film.

A second aspect of the art direction that exhibits Steampunk or at least neo-Victorian elements in this first Guy Ritchie film is the set design. Here, axiomatically garish Victorian tastes in both interior and exterior design are reexamined and re-created, sometimes with noticeably Steampunk effect. This is the fantastical familiar—the transformation of recognizably modern London into its neo-Victorian counterpart—a London that does not quite exist and probably never quite did. Certain sets and location choices demonstrate a particular emphasis on the localizations of power in the Victorian society of the film. From the first long establishing shot in the movie showing the relative position of the action within the City of London, the great dome of Saint Paul's Cathedral dominates the skyline and implies that the crypt where the first action scene takes place is actually the crypt of Saint Paul's.[45] This problematizes the situation even further than Holmes's investigation of kidnapping, murder, and black magic suggests. It means that this Victorian society of London as represented by this familiar landmark is literally being undermined by criminal enterprise in the person of Lord Blackwood.[46]

A less recognizable landmark, and in the world of the film an important part of the cultural establishment threatened by Blackwood, is the Temple of the Four Orders. Apparently modeled on the Freemasons, whose influence in Victorian society has often been the subject of conspiracy theories,[47] this organization's headquarters has the glamour and pomposity of Victorian patriarchal high society and the mystique of magic use. This hybrid is one familiar to Doyle and to Steampunk fiction. One of the masters of the Order, wishing to enlist Holmes in their struggle to resist Blackwood, attempts to quell Holmes's cynicism about the efficacy of supernatural evocation, saying: "Be as skeptical as you like, but our secret systems have steered the world towards a greater good for centuries." Certainly, their premises feature much gilt furniture and a smattering of the specious Victorian orientalism that tends to creep into some variations on the Steampunk aesthetic.[48]

Another London landmark that localizes Victorian societal power in the film is the Café Royal. Holmes calls it "my favorite," and indeed several of Doyle's stories feature a visit by Holmes and Watson to this renowned eatery.[49] As a gathering place for the highest society and the powerbrokers of the age, the Royal offers the ideal public setting for the Holmes of the film to notice many things out of balance in this proper picture: a socially high-ranking couple arguing in public, a liveried waiter stealing the silver, and the maître d' adjusting the necktie of a male subordinate in an inappropriately familiar and possibly flirtatious manner. All completely unacceptable to

Victorian society but perhaps ghosts of our own, these behaviors bombard Holmes almost against his will until Watson appears, snapping him out of a fugue state of intensifying misery.[50]

The greatest localization of societal power, at least the place where such power should have been localized, is Parliament—the House of Lords and the House of Commons occupy a building that is perhaps the most instantly evocative of London even in the twenty-first century. In the film, it is because the entire government of Great Britain is gathered into one room that it is collectively vulnerable. The endgame of Lord Blackwood's nefarious machinations involves a direct attack on those gathered in this famous building. The great and powerful leaders of the empire devolve into a chaotic mass of panicked, shouting humanity that only Holmes can rescue.[51] Again, the film uses familiar images and places to make the kinds of societal commentary reminiscent of the dystopian visions of Steampunk alternate history.

One of the most direct instances of this process appears in the film's re-creation or rebuilding of London's Tower Bridge. As they pass by, Holmes takes a moment to make a brief commentary on this Victorian landmark and, by extension, on Victorian society as a whole: "Look at those towering structures. It's the first combination of bascule and suspension bridge ever attempted—most innovative. What an industrious Empire."[52] Note that in the effects shot in the drive-by, there are recognizable portions of the Tower of London visible, although neither the instantly identifiable White Tower nor the section of the complex nearest the actual bridge approach can be seen. Again, this is a re-creation of period—neither grossly inaccurate nor gratuitously exact. Of course, as such a dramatic location, this partially constructed Tower Bridge is irresistible for the filmmakers, who choose it as the setting for the climactic confrontation between hero and villain.[53]

There are many details within the Baker Street set itself demonstrating how Guy Ritchie's art department made the uneasy alliance between Victorian historical period realism and the twenty-first-century accessibility that seems to be at the heart of the Steampunk aesthetic. The Baker Street sitting room functions almost as an independent character in Doyle's Sherlock Holmes stories. Sherlockians through the ages have venerated this fictional space, have produced precise scale models of it,[54] and have created meticulous and comfortably habitable reconstructions of it.[55] Indeed, when Doyle determined to kill off Holmes in 1893,[56] the story he wrote ominously foreshadowed coming events when Holmes admits to Watson that "they set fire to our rooms last night."[57] That attack on the room, beyond Watson's sobering introductory narration or even beyond Holmes's own report of assault and injury, signals to the reader that something very serious is happening. This space defines daily reality for the characters, the relationship between them, and significant aspects of their personalities. The room in the film echoes the familiar bachelor squalor already noted in the personal habits of the film Holmes himself; however, what borders on inexcusable mischaracterization in Holmes's "scruffiness" is entirely accurate for the condition of the sitting room. As Watson himself admits in one of the stories:

> Our chambers were always full of chemicals and of criminal relics which had a way of wandering into unlikely positions, and of turning up in the butter-dish or in even less desirable places. But his papers were my great crux. He had a horror of destroying documents.... Thus month after month his papers accumulated until every corner of the room was stacked with bundles of manuscript which were on no account to be burned, and which could not be put away save by their owner.[58]

Holmes, then, is as unlikely to pick up after himself as any untidy reader or viewer of today might be. By contrast, and in keeping with his precise personal appearance, the film Watson's own space in the suite is tidy, organized, and professional. He sees patients in a small, neatly arranged consulting room just next door to the chaos of Holmes's personal space.

The quality of the general furnishings of the suite is good, but perhaps on account of the mess or because of Holmes's perpetual smoking, everything we see in the film set is wreathed in smoke and somewhat drab. It is not all shiny new brass, leather-bound books, richly overstuffed chairs, and opulent wall hangings. This is a suite shared by two middle-class bachelors with more interest in utility and comfort than in appearance. Walls, carpets, and draperies are all smoke darkened or damaged, while the furniture looks as though three generations of tenants have been using it. Also, as Watson complains in the above passage, the debris of Holmes's profession litters the room. However, a notable difference stands next to one of the bookcases. This strange object proves upon closer inspection to be Holmes's Victorian equivalent of hanging a punching bag next to the sofa—his martial arts training target—demonstrating that this bachelor, like many film viewers, combines gymnasium and living space. Here again is the filmmakers' compromise. Untidy the Holmes of the stories might be, but he does not work out in his living room. Watson, indeed, is unsure how he maintains his physical preparedness:

Sherlock Holmes was a man who seldom took exercise for exercise's sake. Few men were capable of greater muscular effort, and he was undoubtedly one of the finest boxers of his weight that I have ever seen; but he looked upon aimless bodily exertion as a waste of energy, and he seldom bestirred himself save where there was some professional object to be served. Then he was absolutely untiring and indefatigable. That he should have kept himself in training under such circumstances is remarkable.[59]

Holmes manages to keep himself fit somehow, but his martial arts training, if he trains as such, happens somewhere else in the stories. Beyond the boxing and fencing that Watson mentions in the stories, Holmes also knows a strange mixed martial art he calls "baritsu," which saves his life and which the filmmakers apparently have taken to mean that he practices it right there at Baker Street.[60]

The clearest indication of Steampunk aesthetics in the art direction of the *Sherlock Holmes* film is the design and construction of the props, gadgets, and gimmicks—the technological gizmos of Guy Ritchie's idealization of the Victorian world of Holmes and Watson. The lab of Reordan, "the ginger midget," is filled with technological gadgets adapted to the science and magic hybrid discussed above. This eccentric scientist who works for the villain Blackwood, and whom Holmes is hired to find, conducts experiments of many kinds, keeps meticulous notes on pages, tables, and walls, and does enough inventing to keep any Steampunk tinker happy. Among these inventions is an item resembling a large serving fork that apparently stores static electricity and functions as a Taser or cattle-prod-like weapon. Holmes picks this up in curiosity during their investigation of the lab and then uses it effectively against the gigantic opponent called Dredger.[61]

Holmes is also an inventor of practical professional gadgets. He demonstrates the use of his utility-belt-mounted mobile forensics laboratory in his examination of Reordan's body when the kit unrolls nearly to his knees and he selects various instruments from it in a way that suggests that he and Watson have relied on its use in their mutual professional cases for some time.[62] Irene Adler's shadowy ally uses a more lethal kind of Steampunk tinker's invention; when Holmes in his street beggar disguise tries to peer into the closed carriage that Adler has entered, Moriarty, who the film eventually reveals him to be, produces what appears to be a single-shot pistol from a spring-loaded mount on his forearm.[63] Near the end of the film, it transpires that he has used this weapon to dispatch the only witness likely to connect him with the scene of Blackwood's unsuccessful crime.

Blackwood's own device, a bafflingly complex design of gears, cogwheels, springs, electrical elements, and a chemistry set, epitomizes Steampunk weaponry. Indeed, in the sense that Steampunk gadgets are marvels of reverse engineering designed to use the components of yesterday to accomplish technological tasks of today, Blackwood has created a clockwork yet remote-controlled weapon of mass destruction. Furthermore, while Adler absconds with one component of this device, to the chagrin of Holmes, who gives chase, Moriarty removes the minuscule portion of the device that acts as the remote receiver. Holmes suddenly realizes, too late, that "the wire-free invention was the game all along" and that the real enemy was never the politically ambitious Blackwood but the ruthless and elusive Professor Moriarty.[64]

In all parts of its conception, Guy Ritchie's *Sherlock Holmes* is a foray into a world driven by the Steampunk aesthetic. From the compromises of its interpretation of story and characters to its strongly drawn art direction, this film explores what a Steampunk superhero might look like. Ritchie and his team successfully demonstrate that for the purposes of Victorian period fiction, he looks like Sherlock Holmes.

When the same team ventured into a second film with an option on a third, they were not to be merely "The Further Adventures of Steampunk Sherlock." Now that Sherlockians were familiar with director, actors, and franchise, the second film created substantially less critical alarm among the traditionalists, but it still defied expectations to the disappointment of some. This movie, called *Sherlock Holmes: A Game of Shadows*, appeared in 2011 and represented a significant advancement in both design and themes. One criticism of the film suggests that the visible and well-defined villain that Moriarty becomes seems less menacing than his more nebulous threat in the first film. Moriarty's invisible presence in the first film hints throughout that there are even greater stakes to the game than Lord Blackwood's ambitious, empire-seizing coup. A top hat and a chalk-dusted opera cape (and his spring-loaded sidearm) are all that is seen of him, but his presence is formidable. In his first appearance in the second film, Moriarty literally emerges from behind the curtain. When Adler and by extension we the viewers first perceive him, his disembodied hands are busily jotting equations while he awaits her recognition.[65] There is far more difference here than just the level of engagement of the adversary.

The solemnity of the beginning the film with Watson at his typewriter tells the viewer several things. First, we are not in medias res as we were in the first film. Watson here, as in the stories, is giving us an account of a settled history—complete and irreversible. It also evokes that most solemn of his narrative introductions: "It is with a heavy heart that I take up my pen to write these the last words in which I shall ever record those singular gifts by which my friend Mr. Sherlock Holmes was distinguished."[66] Indeed, in the voiceover, Watson uses the exact words: "my friend Sherlock Holmes."[67] While film one was a thrilling, gleeful, and fantastical romp through a re-imagined, re-created London on an adventure with two immortal characters of popular Victorian fiction, and as such the ideal carrier for the Steampunk aesthetic, film two promises from its first scene to carry a different and darker tone entirely. Rather than opening with film one's nefarious scheme foiled by our heroes, film two begins with an anonymous and successful act of terror perpetrated in faraway Austria, well outside Sherlock Holmes's usual jurisdiction and completely beyond his sphere of influence.

From these first moments, film two promises a broader canvas. Evil prowls in Europe and, although they might start, as always, in London, our heroes must leave their usually comfortable surroundings behind them. The plot also involves encounters with known history. The Europe of the 1890s was fraught with political intrigue as expansionist empires began to run out of unclaimed or uncontested territories abroad and turned to squabbling more directly with their neighbors at home. Unlike the backdrop of many a revisionist historical Steampunk novel, featuring fleets of rival airships both military and freelance, the twitchy and earthbound Europe of *Sherlock Holmes: Game of Shadows* is all too terribly familiar. Here, grim reality presents adequately insurmountable challenges to our heroes without resorting to fantasy.

Yet there are more subtle indications. The first recognizable character whom we meet in the film is Irene Adler, but there are subtle alterations here too. This is not the colorful adventuress of the first film.[68] She emerges from the London crowd in an ensemble even more subdued than the one she used in her film one flight scene—blue-on-blue but with a midnight velvet over jacket rather than the lively brocade of the first film. It further transpires that the parcel she unsuccessfully tries to keep from a playfully determined Holmes hides another "anarchist's" bomb. No more simply in over her head, this Irene Adler is an active terrorist for hire, grim, herself terrified, and ultimately doomed. Fun and fantasy no longer obtain in this new Sherlockian world; likewise, the Ritchie-verse appears to be straying from the comfortable setting of the Steampunk aesthetic.

Nevertheless, vestiges of Steampunk remain. There is still a tendency within this film to apply the expectations and assumptions of a twenty-first-century perspective to a nineteenth-century setting and to view the realities of a very unromantic past through the lens of Victorian Romanticism. One example is the film's treatment of the France-based gypsy community that Holmes and Watson encounter. The society alluded to during the "chance" encounter with the gypsy fortune-teller Flora in film one[69] is fleshed out in thoroughly enjoyable terms in film two. Madame Simza first appears in the Shush Club scene as an investigator in her own right operating under the cover of her fortune-telling profession while searching for her brother. Travelers or gypsies as a group were, especially in that period, ostracized, reviled, and vilified. However, in this film their way of life is characterized in a variant of European orientalism as quaintly picturesque, colorful, and festive—they represent a place for our heroes to escape to, despite Holmes's expressed cynicism. Also, from a practical standpoint, to Holmes Simza represents "a comrade who knows their way around borders"; in that capacity she and her community can provide cover for Holmes's movements through Europe and can help him bypass the official channels of travel that would alert or alarm his enemy. However, at one point, Watson hints at the more standard Victorian reception of gypsy culture: "I smell like a fantastic gypsy." The depiction of this community, despite their usefulness and quaintness to the principal characters in the story, still reinforces stereotypes of thieving, vagrancy, drunkenness, and other negative assumptions with which Victorian society labeled them.

Also participating in a Steampunk depiction of Victorian reality is Her Majesty's Secret Service. The Secret Service is mentioned in passing in the final scene of film one as the recipient of Blackwood's device, entrusted with wrapping up the case of the threat to Parliament. Personified in film two by the person hinted to be its head, Mycroft Holmes, the service and its international reach is just starting to come into its own. In Doyle's stories, Mycroft Holmes's official position is never clearly explained, although Watson does get some broad hints during the second case they handle, which involves contact with the elder Holmes. Sherlock Holmes tells Watson in response to his inquiry: "You would also be right in a sense if you said that occasionally [Mycroft] is the British government. . . . Mycroft draws four hundred and fifty pounds a year [in salary],[70] remains a subordinate, has no ambitions of any kind, will receive neither honour nor title, but remains the most indispensable man in the country."[71] The interpretation of this by the filmmakers carries strong echoes of *The League of Extraordinary Gentlemen*.

Additional pieces of the Steampunk aesthetic remain in the art direction of the film, particularly in the construction of props, although, as Colonel

Moran points out to Holmes: "Now put your gun down, it's a bit old-fashioned."[72] In this film, the characters have certainly moved beyond simple revolvers of the kind Holmes carries; Irene Adler is the first to demonstrate this with a clockwork infernal device of her own, courtesy of some anarchists for hire.[73] Likewise, the team of soldiers paid to assassinate the Watsons carry a heavy suitcase onto a train from which they deploy a frighteningly effective machine gun.[74] Moran himself, who Watson describes as the deadliest shot in the British forces during the Second Afghan War, carries a silenced sniper rifle concealed in a briefcase.[75] Of course, the ultimate Steampunk accessory in the film has to be the car that is "so overt it's covert," according to Holmes; but is it steam or an internal combustion engine? It stands on the very technological crossroads where Steampunk diverts from the modern world. Since the first car was patented in 1886 and steam-powered buggies were also in use at the time, Holmes's car in *A Game of Shadows* could be either. Whichever technology powers their vehicle, both Watson and Holmes avail themselves of the perfect opportunity to don the goggles that are virtually synonymous with, or at least a cliché of, Steampunk fashion. Holmes also evokes the other ubiquitous Steampunk vehicle type when, in his completely uncharacteristic dismay at the necessity of riding a horse, he remarks in disgust: "It's 1891, we could have hired a balloon."[76]

Although these vestiges of the Steampunk aesthetic persist into the second movie, the clearest indication that the world of the films is a world in flux is the Meinhardt factory sequence. This first iteration of the modern military industrial complex sells the same destruction to all its European clients regardless of the dire result.[77] As Moran succinctly summarizes: "That's what you get, Mr. Holmes, when industry marries arms." It is this movement that, as the film suggests, would put a final end to the Victorian world. Through the agency of the First World War, all the picturesque old-world empires with their colorful outfits, ridiculous titles, and outlandish facial hair, as celebrated by the neo-Victorian side of Steampunk, would destroy themselves beyond recovery. Holmes himself says to Watson in the story titled "His Last Bow," which takes place on August 2, 1914, the day of the declaration of war: "Stand with me here upon the terrace, for it may be the last quiet talk that we shall ever have. . . . There's an east wind coming, . . . such a wind as never blew on England yet. It will be cold and bitter, Watson, and a good many of us may wither before its blast."[78] The rare third-person omniscient narrator of that story (perhaps Doyle's own voice rather than Watson's) begins by saying: "It was nine o'clock at night upon the second of August—the most terrible August in the history of the world. One would have thought already that God's curse hung heavy over a degenerate world."[79] Sir Arthur Conan Doyle might be considered the perfect representative of the Victorian age; he saw that age end on that day. The shot of the factory warehouse as the lights come up on the arsenal evokes a similar shot in the film version of *The League of Extraordinary Gentlemen*—a suggestion that Guy Ritchie's Steampunk-infused world is aware of the specter of history in similar ways that other Steampunk visions have been. That the arsenal in *League* is also the work of Moriarty indicates the level of respect that this subgenre has for Moriarty's ruthlessly single-minded villainy.

While Holmes successfully triumphs over his nemesis in film two despite their "mutual assured destruction" in the plunge over the Reichenbach Falls, the sequel is unclear. In the world of the films, Holmes has returned to London in disguise, this time in what he had described to Watson as "urban camouflage."[80] Watson is given a clue to Holmes's survival, a particularly useful example of Steampunk tinkering, but their meeting has not yet taken place. In the world of the filmmakers, writer, director, and actors are all under contract to produce a third film, but when it will be produced and what its content will consist of, as of November 2013, is unknown. Just after the release of *A Game of Shadows*, Robert Downey Jr. was quoted as saying that he would be perfectly happy alternating between *Iron Man*'s Tony Stark and Sherlock Holmes for the rest of his career. However, in a recent interview, he expressed broader interests. Indeed, all of the cast and crew of the first two films are busily engaged in other projects, partially as a result of their resounding success in bringing Sherlock Holmes back to the big screen, so future installments are temporarily on hold. Nevertheless, this film universe is indeed changing, evolving beyond even the spacious confines of Steampunk, and the effective interpretation of a Steampunk Sherlock Holmes established in the first film is no longer a stable "reading" of the character.

Still, a connection has been made; two subcultures, heretofore operating independently of each other, have realized that they have potential common cause. Steampunks and Sherlockians recognize in each other the desire on some visceral level to idealize and rewrite the past. While traditionalist Sherlockians have been plagued by the label of "pastiche" as the only way to describe this process, they have resisted the revitalizing potential of "remix"; whereas Steampunks, whose subculture thrives on a contemporary remix of the past, lend the tinkers' and costumers' passions of cosplay and technological innovation to the Sherlockians' fascination with "one fixed point in a changing age."[81]

From a rhetorical perspective, remix theory is poised to completely eclipse pastiche theory, as its relevance for engaging varying types of media demonstrates. Henry Jenkins suggests as much when he explains that fan-culture-created video remix has saturated mainstream culture: "Such creative reworkings of science fiction film and television are no longer, and perhaps never were, restricted to fan culture, but have become increasingly central to how contemporary popular culture operates."[82] Jenkins does not associate blockbuster commercial film productions with the principles of remix, but the many examples from the two films examined here demonstrate that even such a production can partake of this theoretical methodology. In her 2012 article "The Rhetoric of Remix," Virginia Kuhn worries that there remain "some obstacles that prevent us from seeing remix as discourse, and I believe that they are encoded in the values and assumptions of a print-literate culture."[83] The implication of applying this theory to the reading of such texts as the Guy Ritchie *Sherlock Holmes* films is that the "print-literate culture" need no longer be the fundamental framework of rhetorical inquiry, even when the original source material for the remix derives directly from the literary tradition.

From the fan studies perspective to the traditionalist Sherlockian, the most important consideration in the examination of these films and their success is that such interpretations of Sherlock Holmes, Doctor Watson, their Victorian world, and the stories themselves should draw the interest of more and more new fans.[84] As the Guy Ritchie *Sherlock Holmes* films have introduced the characters, the world, and the stories to a hitherto unprecedented number of potential new readers through this hip new remix of Victorian fiction, Steampunk aesthetics, and contemporary attitudes, Sherlockians everywhere rejoice. If such readers are inspired to seek out the further adventures of this Steampunk superhero through the Arthur Conan Doyle stories, then the television series, radio production, pastiche novel, and feature film have done their part in keeping green the memory.

Notes

1. Portrayals of Holmes on stage and on the radio abound and have contributed significantly to the reception of the character and the period. Some notable or notorious examples are William Gillette's stage hit *Sherlock Holmes*, which premiered in 1899 with Doyle's collaboration during the character's infamous print hiatus; the American radio series starring Basil Rathbone and Nigel Bruce, which was a spinoff from their film series; a 1953 Broadway failure starring Rathbone, which ran exactly three performances; a two-handed

stage production called *The Secret of Sherlock Holmes* starring Jeremy Brett and Edward Hardwicke, which enjoyed a successful run in London's West End; and a monumental BBC radio series that began in 1989 starring Clive Merrison and Michael Williams, which produced all sixty stories and then continued after Williams's death with Andrew Sachs to produce pastiche stories until 2009. Basil Rathbone, *In and Out of Character* (1962; reprint, New York: Limelight, 1989), 212.

2. Rathbone may be said to have defined the character for twentieth-century film; although of the thirteen films in which he portrayed Holmes, eleven were themselves set in the twentieth century, the first two films that were made for Twentieth Century Fox, *The Hound of the Baskervilles* and *The Adventures of Sherlock Holmes* (1939), were both Victorian period pieces, and they firmly established his characterization. All three films since Rathbone's death were made in the 1970s: *The Private Life of Sherlock Holmes* (1970), *The Seven-Per-Cent Solution* (1976), and *Murder by Decree* (1979). Several other films appeared during this period that either presented the character outside of Doyle's timeline, such as the 1985 Steven Spielberg feature *Young Sherlock Holmes*, or did not seriously represent the character or period, such as the 1971 George C. Scott psychological drama *They Might Be Giants*, Gene Wilder's 1975 swashbuckling farce *The Adventures of Sherlock Holmes' Smarter Brother*, and the 1988 Michael Caine and Ben Kingsley role-swapping comedy *Without a Clue*. The other definitive twentieth-century portrayal of Holmes was produced by Granada Television in the United Kingdom; Jeremy Brett appeared more than forty times as the great detective between 1984 and his death in 1995, since which no feature-film Holmes has been attempted for the big screen. Alan Barnes, "Chronology," *Sherlock Holmes on Screen: The Complete Film and TV History*, 2nd ed. (London: Titan Books, 2011), 316–320.

3. *Sherlock Holmes* (2009), The Internet Movie Database, last modified March 10, 2012. At http://www.imdb.com/ title/tt0988045/?ref_=sr_2.

4. Law was the subject of *People* magazine's yearly feature "The Sexiest Man Alive" in 2004. Michelle Tauber, K. C. Baker, Amy Longsdorf, Tom Cunneff, and Courtney Rubin, "Jude Law," *People* 62, no. 44 (November 29, 2004): n.p. At http://www.people.com/people/ archive/article/0,,20146138,00.html, accessed May 15, 2013.

5. This page of their website describes their origins and history: http://www.sherlock -holmes.org.uk/society/ society.php. I myself entered this community by becoming a member of a Sherlockian Scion Society (considered an offshoot or scion of the Baker Street Irregulars), the Norwegian Explorers of Minnesota, in 1995. The Norwegian Explorers, another long-lived if regional Sherlockian community, was founded by a group of University of Minnesota professors in 1948. More information about the group and their history is on their website at http://www.norwegianexplorers.org/history.html.

6. Nicholas Meyer directed the film *The Seven-Per-Cent Solution* (1976); he also wrote a novel version of the script and two sequel novels, *The West End Horror* and *The Notorious Canary Trainer*. Despite the traditionalist Sherlockian dismay at the time over his portrayal of Holmes as a drug-addled delusional, he was awarded a BSI investiture in 2004 ("A Fine Morocco Case").

7. Sherlock Holmes pastiches are a wildly popular subgenre of detective or mystery fiction; see note 12 below. There are, therefore, many novels and related questions. Loren D.

Estleman's 1978 novel *Sherlock Holmes vs. Dracula* poses a fairly obvious "what if" question. Edward B. Hanna's 1993 novel *The Whitechapel Horrors* asks the question "what if Sherlock Holmes were tasked with bringing down Jack the Ripper?"

8. Here and elsewhere in this chapter, "text" is not just a published literary work but any commercial publication, including film, television, or radio production.

9. This is the basic plot of the first film in the J. J. Abrams *Star Trek* reboot.

10. This is the general direction taken by the second film in the same series.

11. This acceptance is demonstrated by their overwhelmingly favorable reception of the newest BBC television series, *Sherlock*. In this series, most of the variables are different—settings, styles, and mannerisms are updated—but the constants remain the same.

12. The height problem is one of the complaints against the Guy Ritchie films. While Watson states in the very first novel, *A Study in Scarlet*, "In height he was rather over six feet, and so excessively lean that he seemed to be considerably taller," Robert Downey Jr. reaches only five feet, nine inches. Arthur Conan Doyle, *A Study in Scarlet*, in *The Complete Sherlock Holmes* (New York: Doubleday, 1930), 20. In the CBS series *Elementary*, Watson's first name is "Joan" and she is portrayed by Lucy Liu.

13. Since the early 1990s, the principal online presence of Sherlockians has been an email Listserv called the Hounds of the Internet. In 1994, when I was an active member of that online community, one of the most hotly debated topics of discussion, among other regular subjects for conversation and commentary, was the relative merits of Rathbone's portrayal against the complete Brett oeuvre. As the Rathbone films of the 1940s, after the first two period pieces, were not only anachronistic but also so heavily coded that they could qualify under some definitions as war propaganda, it was interesting to observe how many traditionalist Sherlockians still preferred them to Brett's more stylistically frenetic but period-accurate interpretations. As for pastiches, those published Sherlock Holmes stories that are created in honor of, in imitation of, or in exploitation of Doyle's own, the degree and variety of outrage is matched only by the innumerable varieties of publications. Authors down the ages have taken to heart a telegraphic exchange attributed to Doyle and William Gillette during a rewrite of the stage script. When asked by Gillette, "May I marry Holmes [off]?," Doyle replied, "You may marry him, or murder him, or do what you like with him." Many publications do one or the other; several do all three. The last printed reference work to compile information on all such pastiches was published in 1994; however, the exhaustive online database now lists over 10,140 pastiches, parodies, and related fiction in various media. Philip K. Jones, "Sherlock.xls," Sherlocktron, last updated April 20, 2013. At http://www.sherlocktron.com/, accessed May 20, 2013.

14. Fredric Jameson, "Postmodernism and Consumer Society," in *The Critical Tradition: Classic Texts and Contemporary Trends*, 3rd ed., ed. David H. Richter (Boston: Bedford/St. Martin's, 2007), 1958.

15. Ibid., 1959.

16. "Generally speaking, remix culture can be defined as the global activity consisting of the creative and efficient exchange of information made possible by digital technologies that is supported by the practice of cut/copy and paste. The concept of Remix often referenced in popular culture derives from the model of music remixes. . . . Today, Remix (the activity of taking samples from pre-existing materials to combine them into new forms according

to personal taste) has been extended to other areas of culture, including the visual arts; it plays a vital role in mass communication, especially on the Internet." Eduardo Navas, "Remix Defined," Remix Theory. At http://remixtheory.net/.

17. Ibid.

18. Although neither the BBC's *Sherlock* (2010–) nor CBS's *Elementary* (2012–) are period pieces, they have also swelled the ranks, to the frank elation of even the most cynical of Sherlockians.

19. Societies are listed as "active" in this compilation if their contact person responded in a timely manner to the census questionnaire. Peter Blau, "Information on the Listings," Sherlocktron, last updated May 24, 2013. At http://www. sherlocktron.com/, accessed May 31, 2013.

20. The eponymous "gentlemen" act under the orders of a shadowy superior referred to as M who relays instructions through an intermediary. They speculate that this is the notorious Mycroft Holmes, older brother of Sherlock. While the supervisory role is eventually assumed by Mycroft Holmes at the end of their first assignment, the true hand at the helm meanwhile is another Doylean "M" entirely. Alan Moore and Kevin O'Neill, "Some Deep Organizing Power," *The League of Extraordinary Gentlemen*, vol. 1, part 5 (La Jolla, Calif.: America's Best Comics, 2000).

21. As the final published Sherlock Holmes story, "The Retired Colourman," featured Holmes in active practice, and the final chronological story, "His Last Bow," includes a discussion between Holmes and Watson about the former's retirement to a bee farm on the Sussex Downs near Eastbourne, the character's perpetual longevity remains part of the ethos.

22. Both cap and pipe appear in the illustrations for the original serialized stories in the *Strand Magazine* as drawn by Sidney Paget. William Gillette's stage play etched this image of Holmes permanently onto the public imagination, and it persists to this day.

23. The ingenious team of Steven Moffat and Mark Gatiss seem poised to provide the exception that proves this rule. Their vision for the BBC's *Sherlock*, now filming its third series, seems to be almost preternaturally unified, but as self-professed fan boys themselves, perhaps this is not so surprising. Moffat's forward to the second edition of Alan Barnes's *Sherlock Holmes on Screen* expresses their unified vision succinctly. Barnes, *Sherlock Holmes on Screen*, 6–7.

24. To take a single medium as an example, films in the Steampunk vein range wildly. It was inevitable that there should be a film version of so foundational a Steampunk cornerstone as *The League of Extraordinary Gentlemen* (2003); the fact that the film thoroughly understates the grimness of the original's social commentary and simultaneously overstates the bloodthirstiness of characters who were strangely demure in the original speaks again to the unpredictability of interpretation. From a reception history perspective, the image of an arthritic, age-racked James Bond (Sean Connery) resurrected to lead a crack team of misfit superfriends against the Napoleon of Crime (as portrayed by the same actor who had essayed Sherlock Holmes on television the previous year) is both mind bending and nostalgically satisfying. On the flip side of nostalgia, the disappointing film version of the *Wild Wild West* (1999) turned a much-beloved, gadget-filled 1960s vision of the nineteenth-century American West into a Michael Bay–style action movie with some great character moments but a completely dysfunctional plot. The adaptation of three

novels into the single film *Lemony Snicket's A Series of Unfortunate Events* (2004) had a surprisingly clear plot, and the unifying Steampunk aesthetic of the art direction in the film helped orient the audience for what was in the novels a chronology-resistant setting. The evocatively neo-Victorian art direction for *The Golden Compass* (2007) reinforced the otherwise elusive parallel-universe subplot of the film, while similar aesthetic themes in *The Prestige* (2006) served to emphasize the fantastical darkness of a real historical backdrop in a story haunted by the specters of scientific achievement.

25. Jeff VanderMeer, "It's a Clockwork Universe, Victoria: Measuring the Critical Mass of Steampunk," in *The Steampunk Bible: An Illustrated Guide to the World of Imaginary Airships, Corsets and Goggles, Mad Scientists, and Strange Literature*, ed. Jeff VanderMeer and S. J. Chambers (New York: Harry N. Abrams, 2011), 9.

26. Strangely, or perhaps inevitably, this process by which postmodern culture reimagines and rewrites the Victorian mirrors a similar process by which Victorian culture reimagined and rewrote the medieval. The study of that movement and its contemporary equivalents is termed "medievalism"—a fascinating branch of interdisciplinary academia whose methodologies may provide useful parallels for the study of the rhetoric of Steampunk.

27. There is to be, yes indeed, a film adaptation.

28. *Sherlock Holmes*, dir. Guy Ritchie, starring Robert Downey Jr. and Jude Law, Silver Pictures and Village Roadshow Pictures, 2009; DVD release, Warner Home Video, 2010.

29. All such specific incidents from the Guy Ritchie films are given a time index reference. *Sherlock Holmes*, 00:56:17.

30. Arthur Conan Doyle, *The Hound of the Baskervilles*, in *The Complete Sherlock Holmes* (New York: Doubleday, 1930), 740.

31. Tim Reich, "Norwegian Explorers at the Movies," *Explorations*, no. 60 (Winter/Spring 2010): 7.

32. Because the second of Guy Ritchie's Sherlock Holmes films also alludes to this story, it is discussed in more detail later in this chapter.

33. Nigel Bruce's Watson of the 1940s films was the perpetual bachelor roommate; even in the more up-to-date Granada Television series of the 1980s, David Burke and Edward Hardwicke's Watsons did not live anywhere but Baker Street.

34. It is perhaps important to note that Watson's retirement was a result of being wounded in action, although the stories are somewhat ambiguous on the nature and location of his injuries, which are the subject of perennial and even proverbial Sherlockian debate.

35. See time index 00:31:07.

36. In American English these are suspenders, but since the costume is Victorian I will use the British terminology.

37. In the penultimate fight in the sewers, Watson throws his hat into the face of his first opponent, the better to fell him quickly and move on to the next.

38. See time index 00:31:16.

39. See time index 01:03:38–43.

40. Doyle, *The Complete Sherlock Holmes*, 174–175.

41. The texture of this coat is most easily observable at time index 00:37:54.

42. This vividly colored bathrobe, to use the American expression, appears first in "The Adventure of the Blue Carbuncle." Doyle, *The Complete Sherlock Holmes*, 244.

43. See time index 01:58:18.

44. In what is perhaps the most challenging apparel-related situation in this film from the standpoint of a traditionalist Sherlockian, Holmes is wearing, basically, handcuffs and a strategically positioned pillow. However, as the title of Samuel Rosenberg's controversial 1975 critical analysis of the Holmes stories suggests, "naked is the best disguise." Samuel Rosenberg, *Naked Is the Best Disguise: The Death and Resurrection of Sherlock Holmes* (New York: Penguin, 1975).

45. The ubiquitous association of Saint Paul's with Steampunk Victorian London is demonstrated by a photograph in an illustrated history of Steampunk featuring a dirigible in close proximity to the great cathedral. Brian J. Robb, *Steampunk: An Illustrated History of Fantastical Fiction, Fanciful Film and Other Victorian Visions* (Minneapolis: Voyageur Press, 2012), 54.

46. An interesting interpretive discovery is that the name of the villain in the film, Lord Blackwood, is a fair translation of the name of the antagonist in one of Doyle's own Holmes stories, Count Negretto Sylvius. Doyle, "The Mazarin Stone," *The Complete Sherlock Holmes*, 1013.

47. Indeed, this particular conspiracy theory forms a key subplot for one of the three post-Rathbone Holmes films. *Murder by Decree*, dir. Bob Clark, starring Christopher Plummer and James Mason, Canadian Film Development Corporation, 1979.

48. For a good view of the premises, see the wide shot at time index 01:12:43.

49. In one notable incident in the canonical Doyle stories that takes place just outside the Café Royal, Holmes is attacked and seriously injured by several paid assassins. Watson learns of this assault when the newspaper boys announce it as a banner headline the next morning—Doyle's fictional London was outraged that such violence should intrude on such a prestigious locale. Doyle, "The Adventure of the Illustrious Client," *The Complete Sherlock Holmes*, 993. In a note of Sherlockian history, I attended a memorial luncheon held at the Café Royal in honor of Jeremy Brett by members of several societies including the Sherlock Holmes Society of London in March 1996.

50. See time index 00:12:00.

51. The height of the attack takes place at time index 01:42:33.

52. See time index 00:21:28.

53. For this final and picturesque fight scene, see time index 01:48:03.

54. One of the most complete scale models of the Baker Street premises was constructed by Dorothy Shaw, wife of celebrated collector John Bennett Shaw. The model now forms part of the premier collection of Sherlock Holmes memorabilia (or "Sherlockiana") in the world; it resides in the Anderson Special Collections Library at the University of Minnesota and can be viewed by appointment.

55. For many years, arguably the most complete life-size reproduction of the sitting room belonged to the Northumberland Hotel in London and could be visited in the rooms above the Sherlock Holmes Pub at the street level of the hotel. The installation has now been relocated to the Sherlock Holmes Museum, which occupies the building at 221 Baker Street, London NW. It receives thousands of visitors each year, who each pay a nominal fee to visit the room.

56. Leslie S. Klinger, *The New Annotated Sherlock Holmes: The Novels* (New York: W. W. Norton, 2006), 385.

57. Doyle, "The Final Problem," *The Complete Sherlock Holmes*, 475.

58. Doyle, "The Musgrave Ritual," *The Complete Sherlock Holmes*, 386.

59. Doyle, "The Yellow Face," *The Complete Sherlock Holmes*, 351.

60. In the story called "The Adventure of the Empty House," Holmes explains that this "system of wrestling" gave him the advantage he needed in a fight to the death with a desperate adversary.

61. See this item in action at time index 00:49:54.

62. See time index 00:44:46.

63. He deploys this weapon, although he does not fire it, at time index 00:31:57.

64. See time index 01:59:57.

65. *Sherlock Holmes: A Game of Shadows*, dir. Guy Ritchie, starring Robert Downey Jr. and Jude Law, Silver Pictures and Village Roadshow Pictures, 2011; DVD release, Warner Home Video, 2012.

66. Doyle, "The Final Problem," *The Complete Sherlock Holmes*, 469.

67. *A Game of Shadows*, time index 00:00:58.

68. The term "adventuress" was applied to Irene Adler by the king of Bohemia in the first Sherlock Holmes short story, the only story in which she appears. The epithet had been in use since 1707, according to the *Oxford English Dictionary*, and usually carries a negative connotation, as it certainly did in this instance. Doyle, "A Scandal in Bohemia," *The Complete Sherlock Holmes*, 165.

69. See *Sherlock Holmes*, time index 00:42:35.

70. By comparison, Watson's salary as a middle-class doctor was around 250 pounds a year, yet Mycroft's salary is not extravagant. A senior government clerk, which most accurately describes his general position, would have received up to 500 pounds a year.

71. Doyle, "The Bruce-Partington Plans," *The Complete Sherlock Holmes*, 914.

72. For this exchange, see *Game of Shadows*, time index 01:19:31.

73. See *Game of Shadows*, time index 00:06:24.

74. See *Game of Shadows*, time index 00:47:15.

75. See *Game of Shadows*, time index 01:09:26.

76. See *Game of Shadows*, time index 01:14:05.

77. See the selling and shipping chart on the wall at *Game of Shadows*, time index 01:18:29.

78. Doyle, "His Last Bow," *The Complete Sherlock Holmes*, 980.

79. William S. Baring-Gould, *The Annotated Sherlock Holmes*, vol. 2 (New York: Clarkson N. Potter: 1967), 792–793.

80. The choice of camouflage adds piquancy to the mystery subgenre descriptor "armchair detective."

81. This is how Holmes describes Watson on the brink of the destruction of their age and everything, positive and negative, that it stood for. Arguably, Holmes himself as a character with remarkable generational resilience represents an even more stable "fixed point." Doyle, "His Last Bow," *The Complete Sherlock Holmes*, 980.

82. Henry Jenkins, "Digital Cinema, Media Convergence, and Participatory Culture," in *Rethinking Media Change: The Aesthetics of Transition*, ed. Brad Seawell, Henry Jenkins, and David Thorburn (Cambridge: MIT Press, 2003), 282.

83. Virginia Kuhn, "The Rhetoric of Remix," in "Fan/Remix Video," ed. Francesca Coppa and Julie Levin Russo, special issue, *Transformative Works and Cultures* 9 (2012).

84. The two well-attended sessions on Sherlock Holmes at CONvergence 2012, a large science fiction convention held annually in Minneapolis since 2001, suggest that this might be the case. How else and when before would straight Victorian literature not by H. G. Wells or Jules Verne draw crowds of science fiction fans? "Panels and Programming," *CONvergence 2012 Souvenir Program Guide* (Convergence Events, 2012), 70–71. The two sessions slated on the online schedule for the 2013 convention indicate ongoing, enthusiastic interest. The schedule can be found at the convention's website: http://convergence-con.org/at-the-con/schedule/.

CONTRIBUTORS

DAVID BEARD is an associate professor of rhetoric in the Department of Writing Studies at the University of Minnesota Duluth. He has published in the *International Journal of Listening, Archival Science, Philosophy and Rhetoric* (for which he won the Rohrer Award with his coauthor, William Keith), *Southern Journal of Communication*, and *Enculturation*, among other venues. Additionally, he has placed essays in anthologies including *Engaging Audience: Writing in an Age of New Literacies* (NCTE) and the *SAGE Handbook of Rhetorical Studies*. With Richard Enos, he edited *Advances in the History of Rhetoric* (Parlor Press), and, on his lighter side, he has written for the *Comics Journal* and the *International Journal of Comic Art*.

ELIZABETH BIRMINGHAM teaches and writes about anime, antimodernism, and gender at North Dakota State University, where she is associate professor of English.

BARRY BRUMMETT is the Charles Sapp Centennial Professor of Communication and chair, Department of Communication Studies, at the University of Texas at Austin. Brummett's most recent ongoing interests are in the rhetoric of popular culture. Brummett has published a textbook, *Techniques of Close Reading*, and a third edition of his popular textbook, *Rhetoric in Popular Culture*. Brummett is the author of the scholarly book monographs *A Rhetoric of Style, Rhetorical Dimensions of Popular Culture, Contemporary Apocalyptic Rhetoric, Rhetoric of Machine Aesthetics, The World and How We Describe It*, and *Rhetorical Homologies*. He has edited *Landmark Essays on Kenneth Burke, Uncovering Hidden Rhetorics, Sporting Rhetoric, Reading Rhetorical Theory*, and *The Politics of Style and the Style of Politics*. Brummett is the author or coauthor of numerous scholarly essays and chapters.

JOSHUA GUNN is an associate professor of communication studies at the University of Texas at Austin, where he teaches and researches at the intersection of rhetoric and popular culture. He is author of *Modern Occult Rhetoric: Mass Media and the Drama of Secrecy in the Twentieth Century*. His work in the humanities is so exciting that he is routinely invited to submit articles to "open access" journals as varied as *Advances in Linear Algebra and Matrix Theory*, *Criminology*, and the *Journal of Scientific Theory and Methods*.

MIRKO M. HALL is associate professor of German studies and chair of the Department of Languages, Cultures, and Literatures at Converse College, a liberal arts college for women in South Carolina. He has published articles on the nexus of music, philosophy, and politics in journals such as *Communication and Critical/Cultural Studies*, *Eighteenth-Century Studies*, and *Telos*. He is currently finalizing his book manuscript, *Musicking against the Grain: German Musical Discourses, 1800–1980*.

LISA HORTON is an assistant professor in the Department of Writing Studies at the University of Minnesota Duluth. She holds a doctorate from Western Michigan University in English with an emphasis on medieval literature. Her current research examines how the literatures of earlier periods are transformed by cultures of later periods, particularly the similarities between the medievalism of Victorian culture and the neo-Victorianism of twenty-first-century culture. A lifelong aficionado of Sherlock Holmes, she has belonged to the Sherlockian society the Norwegian Explorers of Minnesota since 1995.

ANDREW MARA is an associate professor of rhetoric and writing and director of upper-division writing in the Department of English at North Dakota State University. He edited a special issue in *Technical Communications Quarterly* and has published articles in *Technical Communications Quarterly*, the *Journal of Business and Technical Communication*, *IEEE Transactions in Professional Communication*, *Kairos*, the *Journal on Excellence in College Teaching*, *Academe*, and *Innovative Higher Education*, as well as several essays for collections.

JOHN M. MCKENZIE is an assistant professor of communication at Lakeland College in Plymouth, Wisconsin. His research focuses on identifying and understanding ideology as it permeates popular culture and mass media. He has published his research in *KB Journal* and *POROI*, among other venues. He has also contributed chapters on communication ethics and professional communication to the textbook *Professional Communication Skills* (Pearson).

KRISTIN STIMPSON currently teaches at the University of San Francisco and San Francisco State University. She earned her B.A. in communication studies from Loyola Marymount University and her M.A. in communication studies from the University of Texas at Austin, where she is finishing her Ph.D. in rhetoric and language. Her research focuses on the intersection between style and space, and her dissertation examines gentrification in Austin, Texas.

MARY ANNE TAYLOR is a doctoral candidate and assistant instructor at the University of Texas at Austin. She has published in *Women and Language*, and her most recent publication, found in *Venomous Speech*, explored gendered journalism in the 2008 presidential election. Her research, at the intersection of feminist rhetorical theory and political rhetoric, investigates how gender and discourses surrounding gender are played out in public life.

JOHN R. THOMPSON is adjunct professor of business communications at Saint Edward's University School of Management and Business in Austin, Texas. He is a Ph.D. candidate in communications studies at the University of Texas at Austin. He is a contributor to works such as *The Rhetoric of Food* and *Food as Communication: Communication as Food*.

DR. JAIME WRIGHT is an associate professor of rhetoric and the assistant director of the Saint John's Debate Society at Saint John's University in Queens, New York. She studies the intersections between argumentation theory and performance of culture. Currently, her research focuses on the acquisition and dissemination of ethos—in other words, the mechanics behind and beneath different claims to believability. Her recent publications focus on the dangerous casuistic devices of argumentation in Holocaust denial, the cultural politics of zombies, and the sociopolitical implications of former president Clinton's globalization rhetoric.

INDEX

CPSIA information can be obtained
at www.ICGtesting.com
Printed in the USA
FFOW04n1507280217
32956FF